Montana's Indians
YESTERDAY AND TODAY

NUMBER ELEVEN

BY WILLIAM L. BRYAN, JR.
WITH PHOTOGRAPHY BY MICHAEL CRUMMETT

PUBLISHED BY

Montana Magazine, Inc.

HELENA, MONTANA 59604

RICK GRAETZ, PUBLISHER
MARK THOMPSON, DIRECTOR OF PUBLICATIONS
CAROLYN CUNNINGHAM,
EDITOR — MONTANA MAGAZINE

D1441798

This series intends to fill the need for in-depth information about Montana subjects. The geographic concept explores the historical color, the huge landscape and the resilient people of a single Montana subject area. Design by Len Visual Design, Helena, Montana. All camera prep work and layout production completed in Helena, Montana. Typesetting by Thurber Printing, Helena, Montana. Printed in Japan by DNP America, San Francisco.

ACKNOWLEDGMENTS

So many people have contributed to this book that there is no way to mention them all in an appropriate manner. First of all, I want to thank all the members of Montana Indian tribes who participated in interviews and data gathering for this book. Marjane Ambler, Roger Clawson, Jeanne Eder, Carling Malouf, Barney Old Coyote, Arti Clarke, Richard Whitesell, Bob Staffanson and Bill Yellowtail all shared invaluable insights on a variety of subjects. Bob Bailey and Alvin Josephy offered helpful guidance so many years ago. Ted Swem gave both his support and a continued flow of information while I was working on this book.

Renee Cook deserves special thanks for helping with most of the initial transcript and I also want to particularly thank Mark Thompson and Rick Graetz for their encouragement and patience in seeing that this book became a reality. This book would not exist if not for Rick Graetz's enduring commitment to see that it happened.

And finally I want to give special thanks to Michael Crummett, who went beyond the call of duty to provide most of the photography for the book. His enthusiasm and high professional standards made what the reader sees here possible.

William L. Bryan, Jr.

To this photographer's way of looking at things, making an image of another human being is one of the greatest challenges and joys of the art. And when the peoples are from other cultures and reside in different "countries" in one state, amassing a collective portrayal is, at best, incomplete.

To the scores of Montana Indians who permitted me to enter your lives, your tipis and your traditions with my camera, I'm forever indebted. As much as for the photographs we created together, I thank you for sharing with me the way you see things. It is my earnest hope that these images reflect those visions.

Michael Crummett

Montana Magazine, Inc.
Box 5630, Helena, Montana 59604

ISBN: 0-938314-21-1

CONTENTS

Montana's Indians

YESTERDAY AND TODAY

7 reservations

10 tribes + 1 additional group (Little Shell)

p. iii

a. View south to Blackfeet Reservation from Chief Mountain. Bruce Selyem

b. Tidying the braids, Milk River Indian Days. Michael Crummett

c. Inside tipi, Crow Fair. Michael Crummett

d. Officers of Native American Church on Rocky Boy's Reservation. Michael Crummett

e. Heart Butte Mountains from Palookaville Road, Blackfeet Reservation. Bruce Selyem

INTRODUCTION

The Indian Flag during celebration at Fort Belknap. Michael Crummett

Having been raised in Maine, my only exposure to Indian people in my formative years was to those who would come from Indian Island in the Penobscot River near Old Town, Maine, to sell deerskin moccasins and various items made out of birchbark. I recall a family friend by the name of "Big Chief" Stanwood, who was part Indian and was treated by most of our family as something of a novelty. He was a good storyteller, and taught us from his store-house of common sense about the woods and fishing. I still carry memorable impressions from sitting around the potbellied stove with "Big Chief" and waiting eagerly for every tale.

It wasn't until 1972, on moving to Montana, that I encountered members of western tribes. I was working with citizen organizations to develop political strategies for energy issues when an attorney from Bozeman called to ask if I would like to do some work on the Northern Cheyenne Reservation. A few days later I was sitting across a table from Marie Sanchez, a Northern Cheyenne, who asked bluntly: "Who are you and what do you think you can do for us?"

Straight talk followed and Marie invited me to the reservation where I became immersed in the tribe's coal-lease cancellation efforts. Over the next several years with the Northern Rockies Action Group, I worked with the Northern Cheyenne, mostly in relation to pending coal development. I soon found myself doing similar work on the Crow Reservation and related environmental work on the Blackfeet Reservation as well. From there, the Northern Rockies Action Group became involved in a variety of Indian-related projects, including their nationally recognized Indian, Environmentalist and Agriculturalist Conference in Billings in 1975. After striking out on my own in 1982, I expressed an interest to the publisher of *Montana Magazine* about working with Indian people once again. This book is the result.

I am neither a historian nor a specialist in Indian affairs. Rather, what I've tried to do here is to outline the history of tribes in Montana to bring the reader to the present situation and, based on my experience with them, to elaborate on the conditions they face and their future prospects. I started work on this book by going to the seven Montana reservations and conducting interviews before I settled down to research in libraries or to talk with experts on Indian affairs because I wanted the book to reflect the views of Montana Indians rather than add to the extensive literature on their history. As a result, readers may find historical omissions or technical inaccuracies about current tribal information, but that is perhaps to be expected because accurate current information about Montana Indians is hard to come by.

This book leaves out much information about Indian people, for it is not a comprehensive description or assessment of Montana tribes. For example, there is an emphasis on the seven reservations and those who live on them. Unfortunately, there is little information available on the some 10,000 Indians who reside in Montana but who live off the reservations.

There is a natural-resource bias, partly because of the uniqueness of an ethnic minority having a land base, but also because the environment is the basis of Indian culture, religion and way of life.

The reader also will notice an effort to portray present-day Indian people and leaders. Much has been said about Plenty Coups, Dull Knife, Sitting Bull, Charlo, Heavy Runner and other historical leaders of Montana tribes; but one also needs to include Earl Old Person, John Windy Boy, Allen Rowland and Norman Hollow, the contemporary elder statesmen of Montana Indians. Furthermore, the Dan Deckers, Bill Yellowtails, Windy Shoulderblades, Gail Smalls, Peg Nagels and Joe McKays have to be portrayed if one wants a suggestion of where the tribes of Montana are headed.

I also tried to dispel stereotyped concepts and misconceptions about Indian people, as well as to provide certain insights to the Indian way of thinking and living. The book doesn't try to do justice to Indian culture and spirituality; those subjects are too extensive and intricate to describe in a review. The bibliography can lead readers to the works of experts.

This is a book about more than 48,000 people of Montana, many of whose ancestors called this country their home well before Lewis and Clark reached the mouth of the Yellowstone on the Missouri River. Their forefathers were, in a sense, the first modern-day settlers of Montana. They had different cultures, customs, languages and governments than those Americans of European descent. These people are the Indians of the Northern Plains and Columbia Plateau, who now happen to live primarily on the seven Indian reservations in the state of Montana.

Slightly more than a hundred years ago, they hunted the buffalo in the Big Sky country. Today, through executive order and treaty, many live on reservations that have semi-sovereign legal status in relationship with the state of Montana and the United States government.

The subject of this book is not so much "the Indians of Montana," but rather tribes of people native to Montana who like to be thought of as Assiniboine, Sioux, Gros Ventre, Kootenai, Salish, Blackfeet, Cree, Northern Cheyenne, Crow and Chippewa. George Snell, an Assiniboine tribal leader, put it quite simply, "The non-

Indian has a way of lumping us all together, and I don't like it. Blacks don't like to be lumped with the Spanish, and Irish don't like to be lumped with the English, so why does everybody have to call us Indian?" He has a point: The differences between the Blackfeet and the Salish, the Cheyenne and the Crow, are enormous.

It is true, though, that Indians do work together in this country on a variety of issues of common concern, just as do other American ethnic minorities on issues like employment and civil rights.

As tribal elders told me time and again, one can't begin to understand the present status of the Indian without beginning to comprehend his past, as the past so dictates the present and heavily influences the future. That is why this book includes not only a general history of Montana Indian peoples, but also specific histories of each tribe.

While I was creating this text, so many white colleagues, who seemed well-intentioned, asked, "What is so special about an Indian and an Indian tribe?" "Why can't we treat the Indian just like we do anyone else?" It became clear that many believe the reservation is an anachronism to be phased out. So many of us in this country cling to the concept of assimilation, and truly wish to believe that the United States is a melting pot in which all its citizens want the same government, have the same aspirations and share the same perception of the American dream. Applying this stereotypical thinking to Indians can only lead to confusion.

Many non-Indians also believe that the Battle of Wounded Knee in 1892 was the last gruesome battle between the U.S. government and Indian people. Since that was the end of an admittedly abominable era almost 100 years ago, many believe we should put it behind us and get on with social progress.

It is hard for many to understand the different historical perspective and culture that Indians have, and that most don't necessarily want to join the mainstream of American culture. To most Indians, Wounded Knee was only one of countless battles that are still being fought around the basic issues of cultural, economic and even physical survival.

So, why are Indians so special? Perhaps the best way to look at this is to examine first the concept of Indian preference. Preferential treatment is the official policy of the Bureau of Indian Affairs, a federal agency. As recently as 1974, the U.S. Supreme Court reaffirmed unanimously the principle of Indian preference. However, if this were to be applied to whites or other cultural groups in this country, preferential thinking immediately would be branded as racist. However, Indian preference is a political, not a racial, concept. It assumes that a tribe is a cultural entity, and that it also has a political right to self-government. It also presumes that there is a government-to-government relationship between each tribe and the federal government. In other words, tribes are quasi-sovereign, have been treated as such in law starting with the U.S. Constitution, and each of the 488 federally recognized tribes in this country (including the many different tribes of Alaska) has a unique relationship to the United States as a result of various Congressional laws that apply to all tribes as well as to the acts and treaties that apply to specific tribes.

Treaties have not been signed between the U.S. government and any other ethnic minority in this country, and treaties are, by definition, between two sovereign entities.

Therefore, when the United States government signed treaties with various Indian tribes, there was an assumption of sovereignty. However, this concept of sovereignty is limited by the recognition that the United States has a trustee relationship with federally recognized tribes. This means that the tribes don't have external sovereignty, but have limited internal sovereignty, with self-government powers being the most obvious example. Tribes can make and enforce many laws over themselves and their own reservations. Thus, tribes have legislative, executive and judicial powers as well as constitutions. There are certain limits to this, such as the 14 major crimes catalogued by the United States, on which Indians must defer to the federal government. Furthermore, tribal laws are prohibited from conflicting with acts of Congress.

Over the years the semi-sovereign rights of tribes have eroded in federal law and policy. Such erosion was most evident during the assimilation era of federal policy, between 1913 and 1934, and during the termination era of the late 1940s and 1950s.

Today, the federal government recognizes that tribes will never consent to being completely governed by this country, and that the nation cannot legislate tribes out of existence without tribal consent, through brutal acts of force or by making changes in the Constitution. Perhaps the best summary about preference is to say that the concept is still evolving and most tribes are working to further define Indian sovereignty.

Plains Indian Names

Yellow Robe, Red Dog, Chilling Blackbones, Mountain Chief, Curly Bear, Tall Bull, Knows Gun, Old Coyote, Yellow Kidney — are all glorious Indian names that remain a curiosity to the non-Indian culture. "What's their origin? What do they mean?" The answers vary.

When Europeans first encountered Indians, they frequently gave them simple European names to make communication and identity easier. Later, when midwestern tribes began to be placed on newly established Indian reservations, federal agents rejected Indian names for English names such as Smith, Shields, Adams or Russell. This also occurred when missionaries converted Indian people to Christianity.

With the Allotment Act in 1887, came an additional motive for Indian agents to tinker with names. Many thought giving allottees English names made the tribal rolls "look good" to their superiors in Washington, showing that Indians were being quickly assimilated into white culture.

Another aspect of Indian names is the traditional practice of name-giving, which is still very prevalent among Montana tribes. Given names are in addition to Indian family names. This second name is assigned during a special ceremony and comes from a relative of the father, or from an important traditional person within the tribe. Such names are derived from either a specific action or past event in the life of the person giving the name, or from a vision or a wish.

For example, Patricia Old Coyote, a member of the Crow tribe, describes her own name, Many Good Days or Many Good Fortunes, this way: "It was given to me by my clan uncle, Joseph Medicine Crow. He tells the story behind my name:

'When I was a warrior in World War II, I was fortunate enough to have followed a good and safe path ... the weapons of the enemy showered me for 90 days and nights. I was never scathed. I was never sick. I was never afraid. I consider myself very fortunate that the Great Spirit had given me a good trail to follow. Thus I give my clan niece the name "Many Good Days" or "Many Good Fortunes" — wishing for her that she, too, in her lifetime would enjoy good days and good fortune'."

Patricia now is the proud bearer of this name and will keep it through the remainder of her life unless she is having bad luck, is ill, or if somebody else within the tribe would like to rename her as an honor. When a person dies, his or her name is generally no longer used because it is felt that both the person and the name have returned to the Great Maker.

An important aspect of name-giving is that all names have to be true. Indians believe that when a child is born, it is a gift of God, and that person has the potential to be great at anything. The Indian name given the person is supposed to be the truth about that person, which has been envisioned by the name giver. The name can't be conjured up or embellished, according to belief, because the child would suffer for it later.

Native American or Indian?

In the '60s and '70s, when many ethnic groups were seeking clearer identities, they often sought to be called by new, more accurate, and more dignified names: Blacks instead of Negroes, or Hispanics instead of Mexicans. The term Native American became widespread in certain circles. However, among most Indians in Montana today, one rarely hears the term Native American, but rather, Indian.

In most interviews for this book, I made a point to ask, "Do you prefer to be called an Indian or a Native American?" The answers were not unanimous. These are some of them: "First, I'm a citizen of my tribe, and then I'm a citizen of the United States." "Call me a Gros Ventre, that's who I am." "If you need to refer to several tribes, then call us Indians."

Indians believe that it is mainly the academic world that refers to them as Native Americans. As one person put it, "If you've got to call me something other than Indian, call us Natives, because we were here before you were." But the inevitable conclusion was that Indian people want to be called by a name that is tribal; then in a collective sense, to be known as Indian.

Traditional Indian Values

(from *New Realities, the Tarrytown Letter,* No. 32, October 1983)

1. Reverence for the Earth and Nature
2. Government by Consensus
3. Team Sports and Competition
4. Respect for the Feminine
5. Holistic Healing
6. A Belief in Dreams and Visions
7. Generosity
8. Belief in Transformation
9. A Sense of Heroism
10. An Inclusive Value System

The Reservation

The reservation system evolved from the belief of the United States government that Indian tribes were essentially foreign nations who owned land and resources and should be dealt with differently than other ethnic and racial minorities. As a result, by the end of the treaty era in the 1870s, large tracts of land in Montana, through various treaty rights and executive orders, were formally reserved for Indian tribes.

Despite the continued efforts by the government and others to change the status of the reservation in this country, it is still the cornerstone of Indian life and policy. Montana's seven reservations include approximately 8,292,289 acres of land within their boundaries, or 9 percent of Montana's land base.

The major problem concerning the integrity of Montana's reservations occurs where there are large, non-Indian land holdings within reservation boundaries, as on Flathead, Fort Peck, Crow, and to a lesser extent on the Blackfeet reservation. In spite of this, most Montana reservations are recognized as such by Montanans and are governed primarily by tribal and federal law.

The reservation is far more than a political entity. To Indian people, land is an integral part of religious beliefs. That's why reservations symbolize so much of what the American Indian is all about. Former BIA Commissioner Philleo Nash said, in a paper presented at the Indian Self Rule Conference in 1983, that "The reservation system, with all its faults, is an integral part of Indian continuity, for it is the reservation that gives the tribes territoriality in the modern world."

For Indian people the reservation is a proud link to their past. It's a place where the Indian can live his or her own way, follow customs and traditions and not be judged by the standards of American culture that often conflict with communal, non-materialistic Indian values. Although the image of the reservation in the non-Indian world can often be extremely negative, it's definitely home to Indians. It is the last retreat of Indian people and the foundation of tribal identity and traditional ways.

Ideally the reservation also would be an economic resource that can guarantee a viable economic future for a tribe, in addition to protecting its culture and traditions.

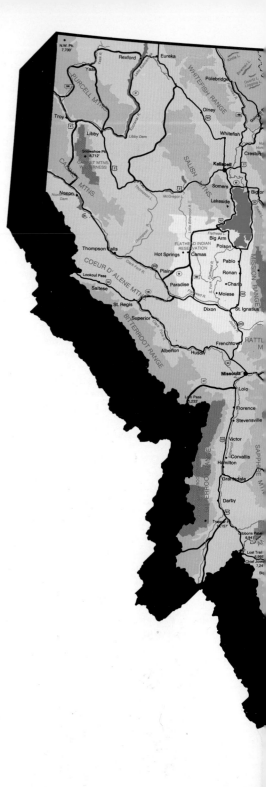

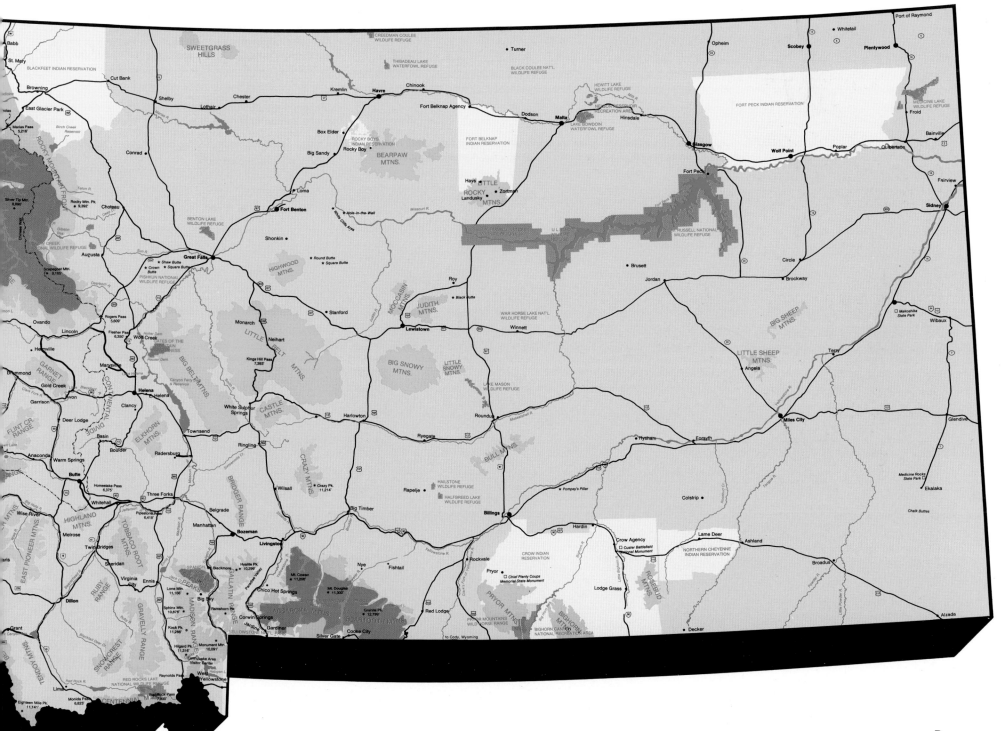

7

MONTANA'S INDIANS IN THE PAST

It is easy to make the assumption that present-day Montana Indian tribes were in Montana long before the first white explorers and fur traders came into the region. But surprisingly, most came shortly before Lewis and Clark ventured into what is now Montana in 1805. Some, like the Northern Cheyenne, Sioux, Cree and Chippewa, came into the state well after that famous journey. This section briefly traces Indian history in Montana up through the "Treaty Era," which ended in the 1870s. It then describes the history of federal Indian policy and how it has affected Montana Indians in general.

Sioux at ghost dance, 1890. The ghost dance was part of a messianic religious movement that held that white men would disappear from the land and the ghosts of Indian people would descend to live again. Courtesy, Montana Historical Society.

Early History

Archaeologists believe that prehistoric populations of aboriginal man came into North America some 12,000 to 30,000 years ago from Asia. These people wandered from the north on what is called the Great North Trail, which is thought to have dipped into Montana along the Rocky Mountain Front and continued through east-central Montana. These early hunters are referred to as Paleo Indians or Clovis man, the latter term being the name of a stone projectile with a distinctive fluted base characteristic of this culture. Some of these projectiles have been found near Townsend, at the McHaffie site near Clancy and at the Anzick site near Wilsall. The oldest of these Clovis artifacts were found near Townsend and thought to be 12,000 to 13,000 years old with others found near Clancy being estimated at 10,000 years. In August 1985, archaeologists found the remains of a prehistoric buffalo near Pipestone that is thought to have been ambushed by Indian hunters some 11,000 years ago. Beginning about 5000 to 4000 B.C., a major climatic change brought much drier conditions to the Northern Rockies region. Very few, if any, animals survived in this area and the Clovis people probably disappeared. Later, prehistoric or Meso-Indians ventured back into Montana, probably from the Southwest. They were foragers and small-game hunters who occupied some western Montana valleys.

About 2,000 years ago a new prehistoric people appeared from the south and west in the area now defined as Montana. These are called the Late Hunters and in many ways were direct ancestors of contemporary Indians. It is believed that these people thrived on an expanded bison population that had re-established on the plains and in river valleys.

Because Europeans did not appear in the West until the 1700s, written records date only from then. However, it is widely believed that the first "Montana" Indians who lived here were the Kootenai, who came into northwestern Montana from the north, and the Flathead (Salish) and Pend d'Oreille, who came from the north and the northwest. Although the Kootenai stayed mostly in northwestern Montana around Flathead Lake, the Salish and the Pend d'Oreille ventured east of the Divide into the Three Forks country and as far east as the Bighorn Mountains. These people are known as Plateau Indians because of their Columbian Plateau origin. Before 1600, no permanent resident Plains Indians inhabited what is now Montana except for the Shoshone, a Great Basin Indian tribe, which had started to appear by that time in southwestern Montana.

During the early 1600s, major changes in Montana Indian populations began to occur. The Crow appeared from the east, coming up the Missouri River in approximately 1620. Also the Shoshone began to appear from the south and ventured onto the Great Plains in far greater numbers than before. As a result, the Salish and the Pend d'Oreille retreated from the eastern plains into the mountains west of the Continental Divide.

Before long the Shoshones had become the dominant tribe of the Montana plains, primarily because of the horse, introduced by the Spanish far to the south. Soon thereafter, the Blackfeet arrived in Montana from the northeast. Having been one of the western-most eastern plains tribes, they already had felt the domino effect created by the arrival of the early European settlers on the east coast.

The appearance of the Blackfeet, who shortly thereafter also acquired the horse, drastically changed the arrangement of Indian tribes in Montana. The Kootenai, who at times traveled from western Montana or from the north to hunt the bison on the plains, were quickly pushed into northwestern Montana by the aggressive Blackfeet. The Salish also retreated to the western Montana mountain valleys and would venture into the Great Plains only with their allies, the Nez Perce, for annual buffalo hunts. Never again would they consider the plains to be part of their home.

By the mid-1700s, the Blackfeet were the dominant Indian force in Montana. Although the Crows would be found in southeastern Montana, northeastern, northcentral and central Montana became Blackfeet country. By the late 1700s, the Blackfeet, now some 15,000 strong, had pushed the Shoshone back into the Great Basin country, and had become the rulers of Montana's plains by force of their large population, excellent horsemanship and acquisition of firearms.

Although the Blackfeet would dominate the Indian tribes of Montana throughout the 1800s, this did not stop other tribes from coming into the territory. It is believed that the Gros Ventre first appeared in Montana around 1750 as allies of the Blackfeet. Around 1770, the Assiniboine also appeared and also became aligned with the Blackfeet Nation.

When Lewis and Clark traveled up the Montana portion of the Missouri River in 1805, the Gros Ventre, Assiniboine and Blackfeet all were viewed by the explorers as essentially one people — the Blackfeet. The Crow were to the south in the upper Yellowstone River country, and the Salish, Pend d'Oreille and Kootenai were met by the explorers only after they had crossed the Continental Divide into western Montana.

Therefore the Montana Indians that Lewis and Clark met were people who recently had gone through major changes. Not only were they new to the territory, but also they recently had experienced rapid cultural changes as a result of the introduction of horses and guns.

When Lewis and Clark were in extreme southwestern Montana, they also encountered representatives of the Great Basin Indians: Shoshones, Bannocks and Sheepeaters, all of whom were from Shoshonian linguistic stock. These tribes were not residents of any part of present-day Montana and came here only to hunt the buffalo, always on the alert for the dominant Blackfeet.

In the early 1800s, the Yanktonai Sioux expanded their territory into the eastern edge of Montana. Around 1830 they were joined by the Northern Cheyennes from the Black Hills country, the last major tribe to arrive in Montana.

It wasn't until the 1870s that the Rocky Boy and Little Bear bands of Chippewa and Cree came into Montana along with the Chippewa/Metis band led by Chief Little Shell. The Montana Cree were a small sub-group of the Canadian Cree. The Chippewa were small bands from the Ojibwa who had been living mostly in North Dakota and the prairie provinces.

Thus, many of the Montana Indian tribes arrived later than many of the state's earliest European settlers.

Approximate Dates When Resident Tribes First Appeared in Montana

1500 - Flathead (Salish), Pend d'Oreille, Kootenai
1620 - Crow
1730 - Blackfeet
1760-1770 - Assiniboine, Gros Ventre
1800 - Yanktonai Sioux
1830 - Northern Cheyenne
1870-1875 - The Montana Chippewa & Cree Bands

It should be noted that during the 1800s, the plains culture dominated among Montana Indians. The plains tribes were not farmers, but nomadic hunters whose lives depended upon the buffalo. These tribes divided into small bands of extended families to follow the buffalo across the plains taking with them little besides their tipis, horses and travois. Extremely spiritual, the plains peoples integrated their religion closely with the natural world. Unfortunately, their nomadic life and much of their culture came to an abrupt end in the early 1880s when the buffalo became almost extinct.

Finding Signs of Ancient Life in Montana

The prehistory of Indian people in Montana has been reconstructed mostly by historical archaeologists. Few archaeological digs took place in Montana until the 1930s. Then, because of a variety of public works projects, several occurred, with perhaps the most famous one being at Pictograph Cave near Billings. Other digs were made at the Hagen site south of Glendive, and near Red Lodge.

Not until after World War II did archaeological activity begin in earnest in the state. This was partly the result of the Pick-Sloan Act, which identified 589 potential water projects in the United States, with 105 proposed for the Missouri River basin alone. The law required archaeological surveys of sites that would be inundated by dammed water. Digs were completed in areas now covered by Medicine Lake and Tiber and Canyon Ferry Reservoirs.

The success of the river basin's surveys influenced the government to implement digs by other agencies responsible for highway and pipeline construction, and oil and gas drilling. Prominent Montana anthropologist Carling Malouf, professor at the University of Montana, has called this type of archaeological research "salvage archaeology." It probably has played the dominant role in piecing together the prehistory of Montana's Indian people.

The list below, prepared by Dr. Malouf, identifies the main types of sites that archaeologists look for in Montana when they are trying to find signs of ancient Indian life. They are:

Occupation Sites — many found around Flathead Lake

Dwelling Depressions — Potlodges or dwellings found in some places in the upper Missouri River basin

Rock Shelters and Caves — Pictograph Cave near Billings is a good example

Campsites — found all over the state

Tipi Rings — very common east of the Continental Divide but not so on the west side

Root Roast Pits — found west of the Divide

Sweathouse Remains — found near lakes and rivers

Pictograph Panels — there are at least 45 sites in western Montana alone

Vision Quest Sites — usually found on the highest mountains or hilltops

Stone Piles — piles of rock used for location markers or as offerings to guardian spirits who would protect the traveler, found in western Montana

Stone Quarries — like the Obsidian Quarry in northwestern Yellowstone Park

Above: *Tipi rings along Madison River.* Courtesy, Montana State University Archives
Right: *Tipi ring south of Sun River.* Courtesy, Montana Historical Society

Burials — found throughout the state

Eagle-Catching and Wolf-Catching Pits — the eagle-catching pits are often found on tops of hills

Hot Springs — most hot springs in Montana have some evidence of prehistoric Indian life nearby

Dance Grounds — usually found along with other evidence of a major campsite

a.

b.

e.

c.

d.

f.

a. Battle scene on buffalo hide at Buffalo Bill Museum, Cody, Wyoming. Tim Church
b. Archaeological crew at Cameron Buffalo Jump, Harlowton. Michelle Church
c. Petroglyph near Decker. Tim Church
d. Stone Artifact found at Decker. Tim Church
e. Medicine Wheel. Tim Church
f. Ghost cave pictograph, Ghost Cave State Monument near Billings. Tim Church

11

Federal Indian Policy and the Montana Indian

The cornerstone of federal policy toward the American Indian is found in the Constitution of the United States. It states that "Congress has the power to regulate commerce with Indian tribes," and it explicitly withholds from the states the power to regulate this commerce. From the time of the Constitution forward, state judicial systems have had to yield to federal courts on almost all matters involving Indian people. Therefore Indians have had Constitutional standing from the time that the Republic was created.

Felix Cohen describes tribal Constitutional standing in his 1982 *Handbook of Federal Indian Law* this way, "Perhaps the most basic principle of all Indian law, supported by a host of decisions, is the principle that those powers which are lawfully vested in an Indian tribe are not, in general, delegated powers granted by express acts of Congress; but rather, inherent powers of a limited sovereignty, which have never been extinguished." So, with the U.S. Constitution, and the concept of limited sovereignty firmly in place, the era between 1789 and 1871 has become known as the Treaty Policy Period of federal-Indian relations, because during this time, Indian tribes were treated much like foreign nations, and approximately 400 treaties were negotiated, 371 of which were ratified by the United States Senate.

Since the approval of the Constitution, federal Indian policy as a practical matter has been based on some form of assimilation. Thomas Jefferson played a key role in developing early Indian policies that primarily were aimed at forcing Indians to give up their communal hunting grounds. In return they were given ground to till to encourage them to become farmers. Jefferson and others after him believed that besides encouraging agriculture to support Indians, various annuities could be made to them in the form of services (such as health care and education) as well as money, to help ease their transition into American culture.

Despite such early assimilation thinking and actions, the government still dealt formally with the tribes as foreign nations. Not only were tribes addressed by treaty to settle issues, but also most dealings with Indians were channeled through the War Department. In 1824, when the Bureau of Indian Affairs was created, it too operated within the military.

Federal Indian policy was refined further in the 1830s by the Supreme Court and Congress. Perhaps most important was Chief Justice John Marshall's decision in 1831 that defined for the first time the federal government's trust responsibility with Indian peoples. He used the term "domestic dependent nation," which he explained as being subject to the U.S. Congress, not to state laws. Congress in 1834 followed up this thinking by passing the Indian Trade and Intercourse act. This further refined federal policy by suggesting that "paternalism" was the nature of the relationship of the federal government with tribes. This act also legitimized the removal of most eastern Indian tribes from their ancestral lands east of the Mississippi. However, the government still continued to deal formally with western tribes as if they were sovereign nations. U.S. treaties in the mid-1850s with the Flathead, Blackfeet, Assiniboine, Crow, Northern Cheyenne and Sioux all illustrate this concept.

In 1859 the Bureau of Indian Affairs was transferred from the War Department to the Department of Interior to more appropriately reflect Chief Justice Marshall's trust responsibility interpretation, which had taken precedence over the foreign-nation relationship concept. Nevertheless, when the 14th Amendment to the Constitution was ratified in 1868, extending citizenship to all those who were born in this country, it did not include Indians.

The 1870s brought major changes in government thinking with regard to Indian nations. During this decade the few last significant conflicts between the government and the Indians were waged. In Montana, the Baker Massacre of Piegan (Blackfeet) on January 23, 1870, was one. The U.S. Cavalry fought the Sioux and Cheyenne at the Battle of the Rosebud, on June 17, 1876. Eight days later came the Battle of the Little Bighorn. However, by then, most Indian tribes were on federal reservations, and the federal government decided that treaties with Indian people were no longer necessary.

After abandoning the treaty approach, the federal government renewed its efforts to assimilate Indian people into the mainstream of white society. Federal leaders had accepted the belief best expressed in 1862 by Colonel John Mullan, the Montana road builder, that "The Indian is destined to disappear before the white man, and the only question is, how it may best be done and his disappearance from our midst tempered with those elements calculated to produce to himself the least amount of suffering and to us the least amount of cost."

Federal policy, in the form of the Dawes Act of 1887, embodied that widely held sentiment. Better known as the General Allotment Act, this law hid behind the romantic notion of assimilation espoused by Thomas Jefferson. Promoting an agricultural way of life for Indians, it was a blatant attempt to dissolve the reservation system and to make the Indian "disappear" into American life. The act was designed to force Indians to cease their communal ways and to become individual farmers on small plots of allotted land. Once parcels of land were allotted to Indians, the rest of the reservation could be and was opened up for non-Indian use. The purpose was clear: break up the reservation, destroy tribal culture and incorporate Indian people into American life as individual citizens.

For the next 47 years, the Allotment Act took a tragic toll on Indian people. Some tribes such as the Blackfeet pleaded with the government not to allot their land. Fortunately, allotment could not take place unless the tribe voted in favor of it. Many did, including the tribes on the Flathead, Fort Belknap, Fort Peck, Crow Reservations and eventually even the Blackfeet and Northern Cheyenne.

Nationally, the Allotment Act was devastating. When it was passed in 1887, Indians held title to 137 million acres of land in this country. When the Allotment Act was rescinded in 1934, only 52 million acres remained in tribal ownership, with the government having appropriated 38 million acres and having declared another 22 million acres as surplus and thus open to homesteading. And to make matters worse, 25 million acres that originally were allotted to individual tribal members eventually were allowed to be sold to non-Indian people. There is no question that at the turn of the century the federal government, with its Allotment Act leading the way, was doing everything in its power to end the reservation system and force Indians to give up their tribal identities.

Each reservation was run by an Indian Agent within the Bureau of Indian Affairs. These people were in a sense, local dictators. Many took on the title "Major," even though they had no official military standing. Their arbitrary manner of governing reservations resulted in great abuses of human rights and dignity. For example, they would issue passes and then demand their use for visiting Indians, for those wanting to briefly leave the reservation, or for those that might be out after a designated hour during the day. Such agents, following government policy, severely punished young people when they heard them utter a single word in their native tongue, and they made sure that religious rituals such as the sun dance and ghost dance were abolished.

Economic development was a total disaster, and misappropriation of funds was the rule. Reservation Indians lived in unbelievable poverty, their only food coming from daily rations supplied arbitrarily by the local agent. It was indeed a time of incredible mistreatment of human beings — all in the name of assimilation.

Indian tribes somehow survived into the 1920s. And the abuse continued. For example, despite the fact that the allotment system by then had taken 90 million acres out of Indian ownership, there still was a strong clamor by non-

Left: *A sun dance encampment at Browning in July 1900.* Courtesy, University of Montana Archives
Below: *Contemporary encampment on Fort Belknap.* Bruce Selyem

Indian interests for the rest of Indian land. This was promoted by timber, cattle and corporate interests, which began to see the remaining Indian natural resources as their own, regardless of treaty and executive order.

Somehow during this incessant destruction of the Indian's way of life, voices for change began to be heard. In 1911, the Society of American Indians was formed by a group of non-Indians interested in reforming government policy as it related to Indian people. The Society, the Women's Clubs of America, a social reformist by the name of John Collier, and many others came together in 1922 to defeat the anti-Indian Bursum Bill. This bill would have allowed old Spanish land grants to be taken away from the Taos Pueblos in New Mexico and to be given to Anglo and Spanish settlers. Although specific to one tribe, it became a national focal point for those seeking major Indian reforms. When the bill was rejected in Congress, it gave Indians and Indian reformers a new sense of power and identity and promoted passage of the Indian Voting Rights act in 1924, which granted Indians citizenship and the right to vote.

Indian reformers then concentrated their efforts on documenting and publicizing the plight of the reservation Indian. In 1928 the Merriam Report was released by the Brookings Institute exposing the gross inadequacies of federal Indian administration and policy. The Brookings staff, along with many U.S. Senators, among them Montana's Burton Wheeler, had visited Indian reservations including several in Montana during the fact-finding phase. They returned to Washington with stories of destitute poverty and massive fraud that were sobering. The report revealed woefully inadequate federal personnel on reservations, little if any health care, no economic planning, totally inadequate education in government boarding schools and great confusion over a host of legal and jurisdictional issues involving Indians, the states and the federal government. The report also severely indicted the Allotment Act and concluded that it was causing social genocide on reservations.

The Merriam Report created a public outrage and, fortunately for Indians, they were included in the tide of social reforms that swept across the nation during and after the depression. Remembering the Merriam Report and insisting on major changes in Indian policy, President Franklin D. Roosevelt named John Collier, the Indian reform advocate, to be his Commissioner of Indian Affairs in 1933. Collier wasted little time in revamping federal Indian policy and the Bureau of Indian Affairs.

On June 18, 1934, the Wheeler-Howard Act or Indian Reorganization Act (IRA) was passed. Senator Wheeler was one of two Senators who took the lead in this bill's passage. This became the administration's and John Collier's "New Deal" for the American Indian. From the outset controversy surrounded the IRA because it was conceived and written by people from the academic world, with little help by those who had practical experience with Indian policy and Indian people. Even more tragically, Indians were not involved in generating and writing the act. Upon consultation with Indian tribes during the political fight for passage, it was found that many didn't like or understand what was being proposed. Therefore the act was amended to give tribes the right to accept or reject the reorganization proposals on their own terms. It also made it very clear that the act did not replace treaty rights unless the tribes agreed.

Once the Indian Reorganization act was passed, the government began a determined effort to get Indian tribes to agree to its terms. In Montana, the Northern Cheyenne, Blackfeet, Flathead, Rocky Boy's and Fort Belknap reservations quickly agreed to reorganization terms. By 1938, 189 tribes had accepted IRA with 77 tribes rejecting it. In a sense Collier had succeeded in gaining Indian acceptance. But there are many stories of Collier's staff acting arbitrarily with certain tribes, pressuring them to accept the act and to then develop and adopt a constitution and charter.

IRA went a long way in returning to Indians their right to make their own decisions. It gave Indian tribes the authority to form businesses and establish credit systems and it outlined a variety of rights for home rule. It also encouraged tribes to develop their own constitutions and governments after decades of federal policy had destroyed their original ways of governing themselves. The act provided clear criteria for tribal membership. It also promoted the conservation and development of Indian lands and resources by Indians. Perhaps, most importantly, it abolished the infamous Allotment Act of 1887.

IRA was clear in defining how the federal government would exercise its trust responsibilities. Although it clarified self-determination rights, it also put the Bureau of Indian Affairs in a supervisory role. The agency had the power of approval over almost everything that tribes did, right down to ratifying council meeting agendas and policies and actions passed by the tribal councils. Again, the Department of Interior through its Indian agent, the BIA, became paternal trustee overseeing the semi-sovereign nations of Indian people. The Indian Reorganization Act would have to be called the most important change in federal policy of the 20th century regarding Indian people. Even though John Collier aggressively pursued Indian approval of the Reorganization Bill, Indians were not involved in its drafting and many did not understand it, so opposition was inevitable. Nevertheless, most social reformers of the 1930s supported the act, and believed that it was of great social benefit for Indian people. It represented another push by the federal government toward assimilation of Indian people into the dominant society.

Although it stopped allotment, greatly improved conservation practices on Indian lands, and provided far better educational and economic development than any previous federal program, it failed to bring permanent economic programs for self-determination onto reservations. Another major criticism of the act was that it applied one Indian policy to approximately 250 culturally diverse tribes in, at that time, 48 states. It was programmed to work for some, but not for others.

The IRA demonstrated little faith in Indian people by placing the BIA in a position of approval of tribal acts and put too much faith in limited self-government. In other words, Indian governments with illusory self-governing powers were not governments of, by and for Indian people. Even today tribes can't sign contracts, pass ordinances or amend their constitutions without BIA approval. Therefore, tribes have the illusion of governing themselves, but in reality the Bureau of Indian Affairs, acting in the trustee capacity, is ever present. What makes such paternalism even more difficult is that to Indians the actions of the BIA often seem to be capricious and arbitrary exercises of its trust responsibilities, adding a sense of uncertainty to governance on Indian reservations.

On top of this uneasy governance by the BIA, the IRA gave the Secretary of Interior power to revoke tribal constitutions and by-laws, even for tribes not organized under the act. Indeed the BIA revoked the 1927 constitution of the Fort Peck Reservation in 1961, because the bureau staff believed that it was not operating in the best interests of the tribe. Many Indians believed those tribes that reorganized under the act have fewer powers than so-called treaty tribes, because reorganizing limited the tribe to its constitution, and to the federal trustee policy under which a tribe operates with the bureau's permission. This is a major reason why Montana's Crow tribe elected not to reorganize under IRA and why it has the general council form of government today.

During World War II, Indian relationships with the federal government were put on the back burner. John Collier stayed on as head of the Bureau of Indian Affairs until 1945. But by the time he left, he had become a very controversial figure. His self-determination and cultural rights advocacy had worn thin with the American public, who along with Congress, had begun to swing toward a new Indian policy concept called termination.

Termination began to appear in Congressional debates after the war as many conservative interests were focusing on the perils of big government. Many Congressional leaders began to push for the end of total government intervention on Indian reservations. Their idea was to

Left: *Two Medicine Lake, Mount Sinopah, center, on the boundary of the Blackfeet Reservation and Glacier National Park.* Bruce Selyem

Above: *The Bear Paw Mountains on Rocky Boy's Reservation in the distance from Snake Butte on Fort Belknap Reservation.* Michael Crummett

15

"liberate" Indians from reservations and from the Bureau of Indian Affairs and to force them to become participants in the "better" arrangements of the dominant society. Senator Arthur Watkins from Utah was a leader in the termination thrust. According to Dr. Gary Orfield at the Indian Self Rule Conference in 1983, Watkins often compared his role to that of Lincoln in emancipating the slaves. The Senator believed that termination would stimulate Indians to behave like the "freedmen" and they would "get out and work, so that they could take care of themselves."

Although the concept of terminating reservations first appeared with the Allotment Act of 1887, the effort of the late 1940s and early 1950s was far more blatant. Some thought that termination was a way to save money and help Indians, but it also gained the favor of those interested in eliminating the special relationship between the United States government and Indian tribes, because that relationship stood in the way of cheap land, grass, water, timber and minerals on Indian reservations. Termination efforts reached a peak in 1953, with the passage of Public Law 280. This federal act transferred to certain states jurisdiction over civil and criminal law, and authorized all other states containing Indian reservations to assume similar jurisdiction. Since state laws had not applied in the past to Indian reservations this meant a direct change in Indian-state relations that infuriated many Indian tribes.

That same year, Congress adopted the infamous Concurrent Resolution 108, that declared that Indians should be free from federal supervision and control as soon as possible. This resolution directed the Secretary of Interior to review existing laws and make recommendations about reservations that could be and should be terminated. In 1954 Congress, on the recommendation of the BIA and with the approval from the two tribes, ended its trust responsibility with the Menominee in Wisconsin and the Klamath in Oregon. Both had huge forest reserves that were in great demand by timber companies. In rapid order other termination proposals were made for as many as 13 Indian tribes despite the fact that some tribes were so poor, they were not even able to have representation at federal termination hearings.

Fortunately none of the Montana tribes was among these, although serious attempts to instigate termination proceedings on the Flathead Reservation were made. Also in 1954, the Secretary of Interior lifted John Collier's restrictions on Indian allotment lands, an action that allowed 1.8 million acres of Indian-owned land to pass into non-Indian ownership in a short time. Finally, in 1958 Senator James Murray of Montana urged the Department of Interior to halt termination until its effects upon the Indian economy and future could be studied, but the secretary did not halt termination until late 1959.

Although Montana tribes were not directly affected by termination proceedings, Montana tribal members in the 1950s were influenced by another more subtle form of termination, called relocation. This was another attempt to get reservation people into the mainstream of American life. The Bureau of Indian Affairs encouraged Indians to move off the reservation; the bureau paid the expenses for an Indian family to move, helped obtain housing and jobs and provided living expenses until the family could become economically self-sufficient in the city. Over a thousand Montana Indians relocated to Los Angeles, San Francisco and other cities.

Thousands of Indian relocatees experienced great difficulty adjusting to life in large cities and the types of jobs offered to them in factories were completely foreign to their experience on rural reservations. Although the bureau eventually set up field offices to help provide counseling services to the new urban Indian, the flow of relocatees back to the reservations continued at a high rate. Furthermore, complaints were made that those participating in the relocation program tended to be potential tribal leaders, leaving behind on the reservation a leadership void and an even greater proportion of tribal members who couldn't qualify for any kind of employment.

By the mid 1950s, the bureau dropped the term relocation in favor of "Employment Assistance Program" and began to work more carefully to help people adjust to city life and their urban jobs. Employment Assistance offices were established on reservations and also in the cities to help newly relocated families. In 1956, an adult vocational training program was begun as a part of the program as well. This emphasized specific job training followed by job placement. By 1965 the government was spending as much as $15 million per year on vocational training in this program.

These new relocation efforts and strategies helped many Indians adjust to urban life and to develop skills for urban jobs. By the mid-1960s those Indians who sought to take advantage of these programs were much better screened as to whether they had the ability to adapt to an urban environment. The intensive Indian group sessions, organized by the bureau in urban communities, seemed to be more effective in keeping Indians in their new urban environment. By 1970 relocation had resulted in approximately 125,000 Indians living in urban areas.

Even though the government had turned away from termination policies by 1960, the termination era has had a serious, negative and lingering effect on most Indian people. If there had ever been any trust between the federal government and Indian people, termination negated it. Most Indians today look back at termination as a blatant form of genocide. Even though every president after Eisenhower has renounced the termination policy of the 1950s, it was not until the Menominee Restoration Act of 1973, which restored the Menominee tribe's charter, some of its land, and its federal recognition, that Indian people began to think that they had finally beaten back the government's attempts to eliminate Indian reservations. However, most Indian leaders today will say termination is still waiting in the wings. As a matter of tribal procedure, any new initiative that comes from the federal government is scrutinized for traces of termination. As Blackfeet Tribal Council member Leonard Mountain Chief says, "The issue is still there and will never go away."

In a sense, Mountain Chief is right. Certainly, Secretary of Interior James Watt's comments on Indian affairs in 1983 showed that termination thinking still can exist at the highest levels of government. The state of Montana in 1984 had a candidate for U.S. Senator (Republican Chuck Cozzens) who said that "Termination may be a long range alternative for Indian reservations."

Even though termination ceased as a blatant government policy, its effect has promoted a certain survival mode among Indian tribes. Many observers of Indian affairs believe that the threat of termination may have been a major impetus behind the recent push for tribal sovereignty, but it also has made Indians retreat from society, be more defensive, and view the rest of the world more suspiciously than ever before. Those who share this perspective think the erosion of good will between Indians and American society is a long-term liability for the health of Indian nations.

As the government officially turned away from termination policies in the 1960s, President John F. Kennedy ushered in a new federal policy toward Indians, that of self-determination. Its basic tenet is that Indians should determine their own future, and that the role of the federal government should be to facilitate self-determination as efficiently as possible.

Self-determination took on an even greater meaning with the passage of the Indian Self-Determination and Education Act of 1975 (Public Law 93-638), which allowed Indian tribes to provide some of their own services by contract with the Bureau of Indian Affairs. For example, contract schools can be governed by tribally elected school boards and operated with money provided by the federal government. Busby School on Northern Cheyenne, Two Eagle River School on Flathead, and Rocky Boy's High School on Rocky Boy's Reservation are examples of contract schools in Montana.

Public Law 638 also allows Montana tribes to manage their housing programs, tribal courts, law and order agencies, career development programs and others and the BIA has authority to provide technical assistance to tribes in contract areas. Unfortunately, this substantial development in government-to-government relations is being eroded seriously by federal funding cutbacks, and many tribes confront the possibility of giving back contracts because of a lack of money to run them.

In the mid-1970s, a variety of programs and assistance was made available to tribes by other agencies to promote self-determination. These include housing programs from the Department of Housing and Urban Development, job training and technical assistance and training programs in the Department of Labor, energy conservation programs through the Department of Energy and the Office of Native American Programs in the Department of Health and Human Services.

Such a sudden abundance of federal attention epitomized the Great Society impact on Indian reservations. It was inevitable that these programs overwhelmed the capability of many Indian tribes to plan, set priorities, seek and then effectively administer the opportunities suddenly available to them. It all led to a warped priority where it became important to tribes to have programs because of the dollars involved regardless of whether the programs were needed. Therefore grantsmanship began to take priority over administrative management and employment, and having a federally funded job became more important than articulating and identifying tribal goals.

In the heyday of the Great Society, Indians traveled to and from Washington as they wanted. If they wanted to initiate a new program, all they had to do was to write a grant. That was fine for short-term needs, but did little for long-term tribal planning around the hard issues of economic self-sufficiency and determination. Although the Office of Economic Opportunity came onto the reservations like an express train, it since has been criticized for not having solved any serious problems. One could say that it employed people and gave Indians some administrative experience that helped create a small managerial class. Some Indian policy analysts believe this has led to a new entrepreneurial perspective on reservations.

By the end of the 1970s, new hope was found almost everywhere on Indian reservations. More people were employed, more were returning with college educations, and tribes began to believe that termination had been put firmly into the background. Besides, the themes of sovereignty, self-determination and self-sufficiency were being promoted in almost all levels of tribal and federal government.

However, in 1980 government programs began to decrease and a sense of worry about tribal futures pervaded Montana reservations because tribes still depend greatly on their government-to-government and trust responsibility relationships with the federal government. As of now, they are still mostly dependent on the federal government economically and for basic social services, even though great strides have been made.

Top: *On Crow Reservation*
Above left: *On Crow Reservation*
Above right: *On Fort Belknap Reservation*
Michael Crummett photos

17

The Buffalo

The Plains Indian culture from the 1600s through the mid-1800s was entirely built on the American bison, or buffalo. Even the plateau tribes —the Kootenai and the Flathead — were heavily influenced by the vast buffalo herds east of the Contintental Divide.

At one time bison ranged over 40 percent of North America. Historic evidence shows that they once were found as far south as the Mississippi Delta and northern New Mexico, as far east as Pennsylvania, as far north as the Great Slave Lake. However, they were rarely found west of the Continental Divide. The buffalo was enormous, weighing up to 2,000 pounds, a migratory animal that moved in herds numbering from 20 into the millions of animals.

It is estimated that as many as 13 million buffalo once could be found in Montana, probably in two distinct populations. One was the northern migratory herd from the northern provinces of Alberta, Manitoba and Saskatchewan that wintered in Montana. The other migratory herd moved into Montana in the summer from Colorado, Nebraska and Wyoming.

Although the buffalo could be found grazing almost anywhere in Montana east of the Divide, the best buffalo country was from the Rocky Mountain Front east along the Hi-line, across the Missouri River, into the grass-rich river valleys of the Musselshell and the Yellowstone.

The plains Indians had first encountered the buffalo before the horse entered their culture. Even so these tenacious hunters were able to herd the enormous animals and to stampede them off cliffs or buffalo jumps. Found throughout Montana, the largest concentration of buffalo jumps is in the Two Medicine, Sun and Milk River countries.

Archaeologists have described five parts of a buffalo jump. The first part is the grazing area where the buffalo would be encountered. The second identifiable areas were rock lines five to ten yards apart and from a hundred yards to a mile or more in length. Only a foot or so in height, these lines defined paths that led to the brink and sufficed only get the buffalo moving in the direction of the cliff. The cliff or jump itself could be as much as several hundred feet above the fourth area, usually a talus slope where the buffalo would have either been killed outright or wounded in its fall and where the Indian would finish the kill. The fifth part of a buffalo jump was the occupation site where the Indians stayed while they harvested the buffalo.

Often scores of buffalo would be run off these jumps at one time and then the Indian party would spend days gutting the carcasses, drying the meat and hides. Buffalo meat was the mainstay of the plains Indian's diet. Hides were used in clothing as well as in covering lodges. The

Left: *The American bison: The entire plains Indian culture depended on it for existence.* Tom Ulrich
Top: *Cameron buffalo jump site near Harlowton.* Tim Church
Above: *Bone layers from Cameron site.* Tim Church

Artist's conception of buffalo jump showing the drive lines, the jump itself, the kill site at its bottom and the occupation site in the distance. Courtesy, Museum of the Rockies.

bones would be used in making a variety of implements and sinews were used in sewing.

Although the buffalo jump was extremely popular as a hunting technique with most Indian tribes, all tribes had their own methods of stalking buffalo and getting them to move toward the jump. Furthermore, many tribes, like the Blackfeet and the Sioux, became adept at splitting out small groups of buffalo, surrounding them and killing them with bows and arrows or, later, rifles.

In the 1840s when the beaver was no longer plentiful in the west, the white fur traders and trappers turned to hunting buffalo and trading with Indians for buffalo hides. By the time of the Civil War, the great western buffalo hunt was in full swing. For example, from 1874 to 1877 between 80,000 and 100,000 buffalo robes were shipped from Fort Benton annually. Obviously the herd size began to decrease dramatically.

White buffalo-hunters, along with Indians, now swift with horses and the new repeating rifles, took a devastating toll. By 1881 there were very few buffalo left, yet in 1882 as many as 5,000 white buffalo-hunters and skinners, plus Indian hunters, were in search of remnant populations of the buffalo. One story, in Douglas Branch's book *The Hunting of the Buffalo,* tells of a buffalo army coming upon 5,000 animals and killing all of them in two days. Another story tells of 75,000 buffalo being found in the Musselshell River country in December 1882. A few weeks later all were gone.

For all intents and purposes the buffalo had disappeared from Montana by 1883. The last recorded Indian buffalo hunt was by the Piegan in October 1884 near the Sweet Grass Hills, and the last shipment of buffalo hides went out of Dickinson, North Dakota, in one boxcar on the Northern Pacific in that year.

Suddenly the buffalo was gone. A few stray animals survived in Yellowstone National Park and a small semi-domestic herd was maintained in the Flathead Valley. The latter were sold to Canadians north of the border and it wasn't until 1908 that the U.S. government, through executive order, created the National Bison Range on the Flathead Indian Reservation. This range was stocked with buffalo bought from Canada, which established herds that are now found in various parks and recreation areas throughout the country.

When the buffalo became extinct on the northern plains in the 1880s, it meant the end of a culture and the end of a way of life for the Great Plains Indian. With the loss of the buffalo they also lost their land and their source of food and shelter. And it happened so suddenly, that the tribes of the plains had no means of support besides the federal government and its Bureau of Indian Affairs. The Bureau became the "new buffalo." It was the Indian's sole source of food and shelter. Today every Montana Indian reservation, except for the Flathead, has an enclosure with a buffalo herd. These herds are all used by the tribe for ceremonial purposes. Usually a few buffalo are harvested each year for tribal celebrations. A few tribes have expressed the hope that they will be able to have herds large enough to sell buffalo meat commercially, but that has yet to come to pass.

Nez Perce Flight Through Montana

Chief Joseph in May 1903. Courtesy, Montana Historical Society

During the mid-1800s, bands of the Nez Perce tribe regularly traveled over the Bitterroots from Idaho to join with their Salish friends to hunt buffalo on the Great Plains. However, the small band of Nez Perce who spent five months fleeing through Montana in 1877 made the most historic Nez Perce visit to the state. It is second only to the Custer battle of the previous year as the most famous Indian episode in Montana history.

To understand the flight of the Nez Perce through Montana in 1877, one should know something of their history. The Nez Perces' home originally was what is now central Idaho, as well as some of southeastern Washington and northeastern Oregon. They were mainly mountain-dwelling people who led a gathering and hunting existence. As do all Indian peoples, they had very strong religious beliefs which eventually played a pivotal role in a part of the tribe's flight through Montana. As Harrison Lane in his paper *The Long Flight* stated, a religious movement called the Dreamer Movement evolved within the Nez Perce in the mid-1800s. It repudiated Christianity and argued that the earth, a living being, could not be disturbed by plowing or mining, that forms in nature had spiritual and mystical powers and that Indian leaders would be followed by dead ancestors and defeat non-Indians. Such beliefs gave some Nez Perce strong feelings of self-confidence and superiority over non-Indians.

While this was happening, the first treaties with the Nez Perce were signed in 1855 and 1863. Their contents promoted an agricultural way of life for the tribe and also took some of the Nez Perces' original lands for gold mining and railroad rights-of-way. Some of the Dreamer Movement followers refused to accept the treaties for spiritual reasons. These non-treaty Nez Perce, numbering between 600 and 800, lived in the Wallowa Valley under the leadership of Old Joseph, father of Chief Joseph, who became a leader when his father died in 1871. These Nez Perce were more or less left alone until the spring of 1877 when they were ordered onto the reservation in Idaho. They resisted, and the so-called Nez Perce war began.

The non-treaty Nez Perce retreated eastward across Idaho, over Lolo Pass, where they met Captain Charles Rawn with 230 volunteers and regulars and some 50 Flathead Indians. The Nez Perce negotiated with Rawn for permission to pass through Montana peacefully to Canada. Rawn balked, but the Nez Perce moved around him, down Cole Creek and up the Bitterroot Valley. Lean Elk and Looking Glass were their military chieftains and Joseph was their spiritual leader.

The Nez Perce decided to take a circuitous route to Canada through the Yellowstone Valley, because Looking Glass knew that country and hoped that the Crows would help them. After going up the Bitterroot into the Big Hole, the Nez Perce rested at a site about 10 miles west of Wisdom. It was here on August 9 that Colonel John Gibbon, with troops and volunteers, attacked. The Battle of the Big Hole ensued, ending when the Nez Perce slipped away and retreated quickly toward Yellowstone Park. Once in the park, they encountered tourists, kidnapping some, and as a result of a skirmish killed two people. They feigned leaving the park via the Shoshone River, but instead went up the Clark's Fork of the Yellowstone River canyon. The army caught up with the Nez Perce at Canyon Creek near present-day Laurel. Once again, they slipped away, this time toward Judith Gap.

On September 23rd, the small Nez Perce band crossed the Missouri River at Cow Island, where they were able to replenish their supplies and weapons. They proceeded through the divide between the Bear's Paw and the Little Rocky Mountains. Looking Glass, seeing that his group was near exhaustion and thinking that the army was way behind, decided to rest. He didn't realize that Colonel Nelson Miles was coming up from the Tongue River country. On a bitter cold September 29, Miles attacked. The Nez Perce fought under desperate conditions, with Lean Elk, Looking Glass and several other chieftains being killed in the fight. The remaining chieftain, White Bird, escaped into Canada.

On October 5 Joseph surrendered with some 418 other Nez Perce. It is estimated that 150 escaped to Canada and that the total Indian losses over the 1,500-mile flight were 151 killed and 88 wounded. These were estimates, as was the official Army report that 127 soldiers and 57 civilians were killed, with 147 soldiers wounded.

Following the surrender, the Nez Perce band was moved to Kansas and then to Indian territory in Oklahoma. In 1885 some returned to the Lapway Reservation in Idaho and others to Fort Colville in Washington. Joseph went to Colville and died there in September 1904.

Even though Colonel Miles had sought Joseph out at the Bear Paw battle presuming he was the "Napoleon of the West" and had led the Nez Perce on the flight through Montana, historians now agree that Joseph was only a band leader and not the war chief. He did not make any of the tactical or strategic decisions throughout the flight. Rather he was known as a wise and level-headed person highly respected within the non-treaty Nez Perce. His famous surrender speech with the words, "Hear me my chiefs," was made to his people, not to Colonel Miles. In the years after the surrender, Joseph's sincerity and dignity continued to impress the whites who met him.

Left: *Battle Mountain, Big Hole National Battlefield.* Jeff Gnass
Below: *Sketch of the Big Hole Battlefield.* Courtesy, Montana State University Archives

The Bureau of Indian Affairs

"The mission of the Bureau of Indian Affairs is to act as the principal agent of the United States in carrying on the government-to-government relationship that exists between the United States and federally-recognized Indian tribes; and, to act as principal agent of the United States in carrying out the responsibilities that the United States has as a trustee for property it holds in trust for federally-recognized tribes and individual Indians." *(Department of the Interior, 1984)*

More often than not, people concerned with the plight of the American Indian today cast the Bureau of Indian Affairs in a negative light, particularly Indians who refer to a job it should be doing but isn't. And yet if the BIA suddenly disappeared, such an event would practically guarantee termination of reservations and the unique status of tribal governments. So, despite Indian people's criticisms of the bureau, it is a resource essential to the future of Indian tribes. Besides, as one Indian put it, "We are owed the BIA."

Congress removed Indian affairs from the Secretary of War and gave official recognition to a Bureau of Indian Affairs in 1834, although still housing it in the Department of War. The bureau operated in the 1800s through superintendents, who were usually responsible for a large geographical area with several Indian tribes, and through Indian agents who lived on reservations and oversaw the residents' day-to-day affairs.

It wasn't until 1849 that the BIA was moved to the Department of Interior. In the 1860s the bureau began to undertake the responsibility of educating Indian people, and for all practical purposes fed, clothed and housed Indians. By the early 1900s the bureau engaged in developments like irrigation, forestry, employment projects for self-sufficiency purposes and social services, including law enforcement and health. Indian health programs were established in 1911 and stayed within the bureau through 1954, when they were transferred to the Department of Health and Human Services.

After the buffalo became extinct, the Bureau of Indian Affairs was virtually the sole provider of food and everything else that Indian people needed.

In 1949 the bureau was reorganized into three tiers. The first is the headquarters in Washington, headed by the Assistant Secretary of Indian Affairs, who is directly under the Secretary of Interior. The second level comprises 12

Top: *Reaching for entrails at the Blackfeet Agency slaughterhouse, 1887.* Courtesy, University of Montana Archives
Bottom: *Indian camp, possibly Crow, near Billings circa 1910.* Courtesy, Museum of the Rockies

area offices. All Montana tribes, except those on the Flathead Reservation, are under the Billings area office, which also oversees the Wind River Reservation in Wyoming. The Flathead Reservation is under the administration of the Portland-area office. The third bureau tier is the agency or field office on each reservation. Montana's are located at Moiese (Flathead), Browning (Blackfeet), Rocky Boy Agency (Rocky Boy's), Fort Belknap Agency (Fort Belknap), Poplar (Fort Peck), Crow Agency (Crow), and Lame Deer (Northern Cheyenne).

The Bureau of Indian Affairs has two guiding roles: to maintain the government-to-government relationship with tribes and to be the trustee in the federal trust relationship. Also the bureau actively promotes the concept of self-determination, and acts more as advisor than as protector. Its main functions are (1) to act as trustee for Indian lands and for funds held in trust, and to assist Indians in making the most effective use of their land; (2) to provide public services directly or through contracts in areas such as education, welfare, law and order, when these services aren't available to Indians from other federal agencies; (3) to furnish guidance and assistance to those Indians who wish to leave the reservation; (4) to collaborate with Indians in the development of programs leading toward self-determination and self-sufficiency; and (5) to help Indians develop programs to attract economic development to reservation areas.

The Bureau of Indian Affairs also continues to provide directly a wide variety of services to the tribes. Thanks to Public Law 638, passed in 1976, many of these services are under contract with the tribes. Contracted services can include fire protection, agricultural extension, tribal enrollment, employment assistance, housing, law enforcement, social services (including foster home care, child welfare, senior citizens, etc.), forest fire suppression, forest management, credit and financing, natural resource programs, agricultural programs, road maintenance, wildlife and parks programs, irrigation and power operation programs, and many others. The bureau's national budget was $929 million for fiscal year '85, with $932 million proposed for fiscal year 1986. Just under 30 percent of the total budget is for education. It is estimated that the bureau employs approximately one of every 54 Indians who live on reservations.

Despite the bureau's essential role in Indian affairs, it continues to be much maligned. One reason is that it has the next-to-impossible mission of taking care of Indians while, at the same time, helping them move toward self-determination. In spite of this inherent contradiction and the confusion it can cause, it is primarily a bureaucracy of Indians helping Indians, and it is still an essential part of Indian life today.

The Indian Agent

The Indian agent was the federal government's supervisor of Indian reservations. At a time when the government was trying to get Indians to live on reservations with no buffalo to hunt, the Indian agent became the most important white person in everyday Indian life. Most agents obtained their jobs through the patronage system, which meant that they had no training nor familiarity with Indian affairs. Two contrasting examples of Indian agents, one good and the other bad, are given here.

Peter Ronan, an Indian agent on the Jocko (Flathead) Reservation from 1877 to 1893, was a respected agent deeply concerned about the welfare of Indians. He arrived at the Jocko reservation when Chief Charlo still was resisting government demands to move from the Bitterroot Valley to the Flathead and in the midst of escalating pressure by non-Indians to have the Jocko Reservation opened to homesteading. Unlike so many others, Peter Ronan showed patience, administrative ability and exceptional sensitivity about the plight of the Salish-Kootenai. His longevity on the Jocko was unusual. Over his 15-year tenure he oversaw the slow transition of the Pend d'Oreille and Kootenai from nomadic hunters to agriculturalists. When the Northern Pacific Railroad began to build its track along the reservation's southern boundaries, he realized that the tribes didn't want the railroad and agreed with them that it would bring more whites and conflict to the reservation. In 1883 he helped to mitigate the railroad's impact by limiting the amount of timber it could use and he strongly enforced timber trespass laws. Ronan was furious when the railroad proceeded to disregard their tribal contracts and went ahead and made cuts on their own.

Ronan attempted to restrict white settlement on the reservation not only by limiting the impact of the railroad, but more importantly by preventing the allotment of tribal lands despite intense pressure from would-be homesteaders. He welcomed Chief Charlo and his small band when they finally came to live on the reservation in 1891 and eased their relocation. Still, many of the promises made to Charlo did not come about. Charlo supported Ronan's policies of restricting non-Indians on the reservation, so when Peter Ronan died in 1893, Chief Charlo tried to fill the void and argued long and hard against tribal allotment.

Unfortunately most Indian agents were incompetent and ill-suited for their patronage agent job. On particularly bad

Arthur McFatridge, Superintendent, Blackfeet Agency 1910-1915. Courtesy, Helen Chase and Keith Purtell

agent was Arthur McFatridge, assigned to the Blackfeet Reservation from 1910 to 1915. His four-and-a-half years of supervision of some 2,600 Blackfeet was fraught with mismanagement, dishonesty, nepotism and disaster. McFatridge looked the other way when there were substantial trespasses by outside cattle ranchers. He promoted the development of reservation irrigation projects, but most were not for Indians. He was friendly with the half-breeds who did not share as strongly the cultural beliefs of their tribe and were more interested in making "a quick dollar" at the expense of long-term tribal interests. But he could have cared less about the full-blood Blackfeet who remained hostile to white culture and government Indian policy. As a result there was actually starvation and extreme poverty among full-bloods at Heart Butte in late 1914.

Another charge against McFatridge was nepotism. Both his son and wife worked for him, earning the family the titles of "The Father, the Son and the Holy Terror." The "Holy Terror" was retained as financial clerk and she controlled the finances of the reservation.

Ultimately stories about McFatridge spread beyond the Blackfeet Reservation and on four different occasions, officials of the Department of the Interior and various private citizens reported to McFatridge's superiors about conditions on the reservation and the agent's incompetence. In February 1915 BIA Commissioner Cato Sells relieved Major McFatridge of his post, but in his last week of service he embezzled $1,200 of tribal revenues from grazing permits and fled to Canada.

Today the Indian agent has been replaced by a far more competent individual with the title Superintendent. All agency superintendents in Montana are Indians and some, like the superintendent on Flathead, have Ph.Ds. All have accomplished skills in management, which is a far cry from their predecessors around the turn of the century.

The Forts of Montana

Dozens of forts built in Montana in the 1800s had two purposes, to protect white settlers and to serve as trading centers with Indian tribes. The first significant fort was Fort Benton, constructed in 1844 some 50 miles north of Great Falls. The end of the line for steamboats ascending the Missouri River, this was originally a staging and trading center for the fur trade. Later it housed the first Blackfeet Agency in 1855.

However, the golden age of Montana forts began after the Civil War, in 1866, and extended to 1893. It was at this time that the U.S. Army turned its attention to controlling the hostile Indian population of the west. Fort C.F. Smith (1866-70) on the Big Horn River, Fort Shaw (1867-91) on the Sun River, Fort Ellis (1867-86) on the East Gallatin, Fort Custer (1877-98) on the mouth of the Bighorn and Fort Logan (1869-81) on the headwaters of the Smith River were

constructed mostly because civilians in Montana were afraid of Indian hostilities, and were able to exert enough pressure in Washington for the army to build such garrisons.

Before the Battle of the Little Bighorn, approximately 700 military people were stationed in Montana. Soon after the battle there were more than 2,000, and by 1877 there were 3,300 U.S. Cavalry and Army personnel. Most of these troops

Above: *Fort Parker on Mission Creek at the Yellowstone River was the first Crow Mission.* Courtesy, Montana Historical Society
Below: *Fort Assiniboine, morning guard mount.* Courtesy, Montana Historical Society

were experienced veterans of the Civil War. Many saw living in the Montana wilds and going on Indian patrol as much easier duty than they had survived.

After the Custer Battle a new generation of forts was built, including Fort Keogh at the mouth of the Tongue River on the Yellowstone, Fort Missoula on the Bitterroot River, just south of Missoula, and Fort Assiniboine, 12 miles south of Havre. These served a dubious value because there were no more large hostile Indian forces. Fort Assiniboine was built to insure that Sitting Bull would stay in Canada and the Yanktonai Sioux would remain at the Fort Peck Agency. It was a good place for border patrol work, and this is where Lieutenant John Pershing, who became this country's most famous general in World War I, received his first field training at the head of the 10th Cavalry in 1896. As a matter of fact he received his nickname Black Jack because the 10th Cavalry was an all black unit.

Most Montana forts were abandoned by 1900 and some were used for other purposes. Fort Assiniboine, for example, has been used as an agricultural experiment station. The rest either were burned or rotted away, marked only by a colorful spot on a highway map.

Indian Leaders of Yesterday

Chief Charlo. A Bitterroot Salish Chief, Charlo is known for refusing to leave the Bitterroot Valley with his band, in spite of an executive order to do so in 1871 from President Ulysses S. Grant. Charlo stayed in the Bitterroot until 1891, when he and his band of 200 people left for the Flathead Reservation. There he fought against the allotment of Indian land until his death at the age of 76 in 1912.

Stone Child. Stone Child was the leader of a wandering band of Chippewas who desperately looked for a home in Montana around the turn of the century. His band frequently came together with Little Bear's Cree band. When the time came to negotiate for a reservation, the U.S. government found Stone Child more acceptable because he had been born in the United States and was less aggressive than Little Bear. Stone Child became known in the non-Indian world as Rocky Boy and was thus honored by the naming of Rocky Boy's Reservation. Stone Child died on April 18, 1916, only months before his dream of a reservation for his people came true on September 17, 1916.

Little Bear. Little Bear, or Imasses, was the son of Big Bear, a renowned Cree Chief who aligned his tribe with the Metis in the 1885 Riel Rebellion in Canada. Big Bear was jailed for his part in the rebellion, but Little Bear escaped to the United States with 100 to 200 Crees. Little Bear spent the next 20 years looking for a home for his people and wandered from reservation to reservation throughout Montana.

During negotiations that would establish Rocky Boy's Reservation, Little Bear remained in the background. But when Stone Child died, Little Bear became the leader of the 451 Chippewa-Cree. He was thus the first tribal leader on Rocky Boy's Reservation.

Little Wolf. One of the greatest of the Old Man Chiefs in the Northern Cheyenne tribe and a member of the Elk Society, which was widely respected for war strategy and scouting, Little Wolf built a reputation as a bold warrior in intertribal conflicts of the 1830s.

In the mid-1800s, Little Wolf promoted peace between the Cheyennes and the federal government. He is perhaps

Stone Child

Little Bear, 1895

Right: *Sitting Bull*

Courtesy, Montana Historical Society

best known within his tribe as the bearer of the Sacred Chief Bundle, which carries with it the highest responsibility for the preservation of the Northern Cheyenne people.

In keeping with this tribal responsibility, Little Wolf, along with Dull Knife, decided to return their tribe from the reservation in Oklahoma to the Yellowstone River country of Montana. Although Dull Knife and his band surrendered in Red Cloud, Little Wolf managed to make it to the Yellowstone country and shortly thereafter surrendered at Fort Keogh. He spent the rest of his life in the Fort Keogh area and was on the Cheyenne reservation when he died in 1904.

Dull Knife. The Morning Star of the Northern Cheyennes, Dull Knife was perhaps the tribe's most famous chief. He was an Old Man Chief and a member of the Dog Soldiers Society, which helped to carry out the orders of the Cheyenne Council of Chiefs. The Dog Soldiers had the duty to look after people whenever the tribe broke camp and therefore became renowned for their rear-guard exploits against invading Indian or white soliders. Dull Knife was closely tied through marriage to Red Cloud of the Sioux nation. Dull Knife was one of the Cheyenne leaders at the Battle of the Greasy Grass (Little Big Horn).

After many attempts to get an agency for the Northern Cheyennes, Dull Knife finally led his people, with Little Wolf, back to the Yellowstone country. Although Dull Knife surrendered at Red Cloud, he was later allowed to settle on the Northern Cheyenne Reservation when it was established. He died in 1883.

Sitting Bull. Perhaps the most famous Indian warrior of all time, Sitting Bull, a Hunkpapa Sioux, was a soldier, diplomat, statesman, prophet, and the general leader of the Sioux nation. On June 14, 1876, at a sun dance on Rosebud Creek near what is now Lame Deer, Sitting Bull had a vision of Custer's defeat. A few days later, Sitting Bull was involved in the Battle of the Rosebud where the Sioux soundly defeated the cavalry under General Crook. Sitting Bull believed this battle was not the one of his vision and that the larger battle was still coming —indeed it was! Sitting Bull was acknowledged the major leader of the Indian people at the Battle of the Greasy Grass (Little Bighorn) on June 25, 1876. In July 1881 Sitting Bull returned from Canada, where he had stayed since the Battle of the Greasy Grass, and surrendered at Fort Buford in North Dakota. He then went to live at Fort Yates on the Standing Rock Reservation in South Dakota. In 1890 he was killed during a government attempt to arrest him.

The Battle of the Greasy Grass (Little Bighorn)

The mythology and intrigue surrounding Custer's Last Stand makes it the most famous Indian battle in Montana and in the west. Volumes have been written speculating about exactly what happened on that fateful day of June 25, 1876, when this country was in the midst of celebrating its centennial. Not all the details will ever be known because no one from Custer's group survived.

We do know that 36-year-old Lieutenant Colonel George Armstrong Custer was pursuing the Sioux and Northern Cheyenne because they had resisted placement on Indian reservations. Custer wanted to teach these tribes a lesson and, in the process, gain personal glory that might help him become a United States President.

We also know that on the 25th of June, Custer divided his 700-man Seventh Cavalry into 11 companies. He kept five under his control, Captain Frederick Benteen took three, and Major Marcus Reno commanded the other three companies. They separated after designing a battle strategy. Custer found himself confronting 10,000 to 12,000 Indians, including as many as 4,000 warriors. Reno and Benteen tried to carry out their part of the strategy but had to fortify themselves against an onslaught of Indian warriors. They never arrived to reinforce Custer. No one did; by sundown no one remained alive from Custer's five companies. His Arikara (Crow) scouts also had disappeared. Reno and Benteen had joined and were dug in several miles away. But for whatever reason, the Indians, under Sitting Bull, decided not to annihilate these companies as well. Thus ended the Battle of the Greasy Grass, as it is called by the Sioux and Cheyenne.

Why were there so many Indians in one place? As far as is known there was no specific military purpose in this gathering. Instead, the Indians were exercising their age-old custom of following buffalo herds on their annual migration north. The encampment consisted primarily of Northern Cheyenne and various Sioux bands, including the Ogalala, Brule, Sansarc, Minnneconjou, Blackfeet, Yanktonai and Hunkpapa. There were some Arapaho, Gros Ventre and a few from other Indian tribes as well. They had joined Sitting Bull, the leader and medicine man of the Hunkpapa Sioux, to hunt buffalo as they had for centuries. Besides, they wanted no part of reservation life and intended to continue their nomadic hunting and gathering ways.

When they decided the battle was over, the tribes dispersed, successfully eluding the U.S. Army throughout the remainder of the summer. Some Ogalalas and Brule surrendered in a battle near Slim Buttes in the Black Hills country in September. Dull Knife, of the Northern Cheyenne, surrendered in November and the rest of the Greasy Grass participants either slipped back onto

Left: *Crazy Head, the third-ranking Cheyenne chief at the Battle of the Greasy Grass.*
Right: *Gall (shown here), Sitting Bull's military leader, and Crazy Horse, leading mostly Cheyenne, are generally credited with attacking Custer's last position on June 25, 1876. Courtesy, Montana Historical Society.*

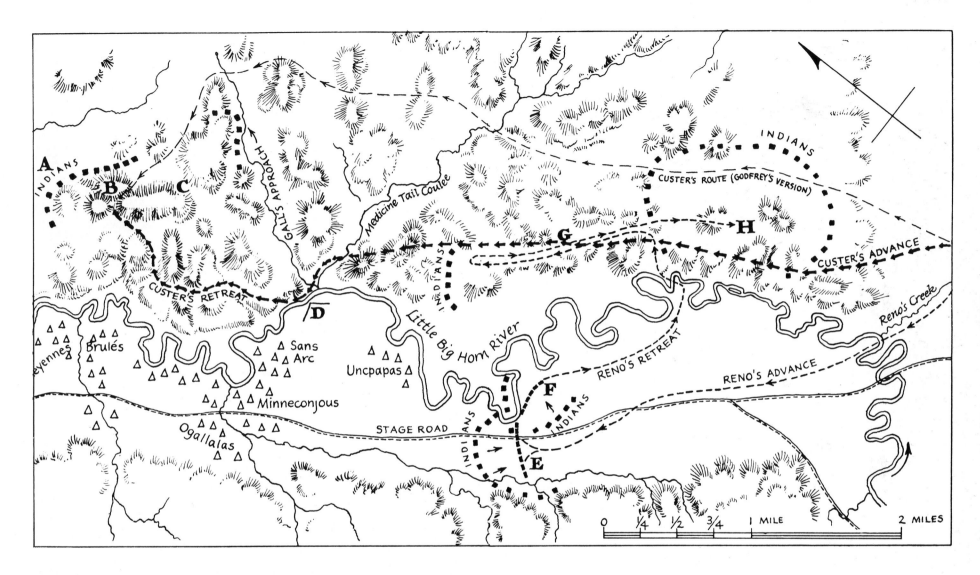

The map contains the following labels:

INDIANS · CUSTER'S ROUTE (GODFREY'S VERSION) · CUSTER'S ADVANCE

A · B · C · GALL'S APPROACH · Medicine Tail Coulee · G · H · INDIANS

CUSTER'S RETREAT · D · Little Big Horn River · Reno's Creek

Cheyennes · Brulés · Sans Arc · Uncpapas · RENO'S RETREAT · RENO'S ADVANCE

Minneconjous · INDIANS · F · INDIANS

Ogallalas · STAGE ROAD · E

0 1/4 1/2 3/4 1 MILE 2 MILES

reservations that winter or went north with Sitting Bull to Canada.

The victory dance at the Battle of the Greasy Grass was the last hurrah for the free-roaming plains Indian. They won the battle, but the war already was over. Few buffalo were left, treaties were no longer being made, and the reservation life was their only choice. The national monument and battlefield is not only a symbol of an intriguing and mystifying military encounter but more importantly, a symbol or the end of the plains Indian's old way of life.

A   *Crazy Horse's attack*
B   *Final positions on Custer Ridge of Capt. Tom Custer, Capt. G.W. Yates, Lt. Algernon F. Smith, and Lt.-Col. George A. Custer*
C   *Near-by positions of Capt. Miles Keogh and Lt. James Calhoun*
D   *Minneconjou Ford*
E & F   *Major Marcus A. Reno's first and second positions*
G   *Capt. Thomas Weir's reconnaissance attempt to locate Custer*

H   *Bluff to which Reno retreated and where he, Capt. Fred Benteen, and the rest of the command spent the night of June 25.*

With permission, from *Custer's Luck,* by Edgar I. Stewart. Copyright 1955 by the University of Oklahoma Press.

The Custer Battlefield was operated by the United States Army as a national cemetery until 1940, when it was taken over by the Department of Interior, and it is now a national monument. It encompasses 800 acres with two parts. One is the hill where Custer died, and the other is the hill where Reno and Benteen managed to hold off the Indians. A national cemetery remains, along with a visitor's center and museum and self-guided interpretive trail. More than 250,000 people a year visit the monument.

In 1983 a prairie fire engulfed the monument and revealed intriguing sites for archaeological work. As a result of the fire and increased archaeological digs in the springs of 1984 and 1985, many artifacts and bones have been uncovered, giving new insights and further confirmation of what actually happened on June 26, 1876. The superintendent of the battlefield is coordinating a major effort to develop an archaeological base map and master plan for the monument. A private non-profit preservation committee has also launched a fund-raising drive to add 5,200 acres to the national monument so that it will be one contiguous site.

Above: *Two Moons, a Cheyenne chief, with interpreters 25 years after the Battle of the Rosebud, in which Cheyenne warriors pinned down General George Crook's column from Wyoming about a week before the Custer battle.*
Right: *Two Moons on Custer Battlefield*
Courtesy, Montana Historical Society.

At the Custer battle site today. Michael Crummett

John Collier, the Champion of Indian Policy Reform

Most Indian historians believe understanding Indian affairs in the 20th century requires a full understanding of John Collier and his influence on American Indian policy. Collier was born in Atlanta, Georgia in 1884. His parents died at an early age, which greatly influenced him for the rest of his life. He went to Columbia University and worked in New York City as a social worker for a dozen years and in 1915 established a training school for social workers and organizers.

Collier moved his family to the west coast, and in 1920 they took an extended trip into New Mexico. There he learned about the Taos Pueblo near Santa Fe. He became awed with the tribe's communal and environmental values and thought they offered an excellent alternative to American society, which seemed so dominated by materialism.

This experience launched Collier into a career that earned him a place in history as possibly the best white advocate of Indian reforms that this country has ever known.

John Collier thrust himself into the national Indian controversy by lobbying hard against the Bursum Bill that threatened the Taos Pueblo's Spanish land grants. This bill appeared to be another attempt at taking away land from Indian people. After the bill's demise, Collier became very much involved in completing and publicizing the Merriam Report of 1928. He did all of this during his 10 years as a board leader of the American Indian Defense Association.

Franklin D. Roosevelt, when elected president in 1932, appointed Collier Commissioner of Indian Affairs, and Collier wasted no time in revolutionizing federal Indian policy. Less than a year after he had become commissioner, the Indian Reorganization Act had been drafted and was being debated in Congress. When it was passed in June of 1934, Collier set out to make sure that it was implemented. At times Collier was insensitive and even ruthless in trying to impose Indian reorganization on Indian tribes. The act had faults, and Collier's implementation strategy was often

wrong, but it was a huge step forward for Indian people.

Collier championed self respect and personal dignity among Indians, which was why he saw the Indian Reorganization Act as being so important. Collier is noteworthy for his combination of moral passion and scientific expertise in a 12-year tenure as commissioner. He worked to protect the religious freedom of Indian people, and cut through bureaucracy to make sure that a whole variety of the government's social reform and relief programs came to reservations, including the massive Depression-era programs of the Civilian Conservation Corps and the Works Progress Administration. He set up an Arts and Crafts Board to promote Indian culture and ordered the codification of Indian laws. Collier promoted Pan-Indianism, which he thought was important in promoting self-esteem to indigenous people throughout the western hemisphere.

Despite the fact that Collier was white and had a sophisticated paternalistic view toward Indian people, he may have been just what Indian people needed at the time to bring self-esteem and hope for the future.

ASSINIBOINE & GROS VENTRE

The first Fort Belknap tribal delegation to Washington, D.C., circa 1870s. Courtesy, Museum of the Rockies.

Tribal Histories

The Fort Belknap Reservation is home for both the Assiniboine and the Gros Ventre tribes, which have different historical backgrounds. The Assiniboine were the northernmost group of the seven divisions of Yanktonai Sioux that resided in the region between the Mississippi River and Lake Superior. It is believed that they split from the other divisions into a separate tribe in the late 1500s or early 1600s and went to live in Lake of the Woods and Lake Nipigon country of Canada. From there, they allied with the Cree and, like most of the other plains tribes, began to move slowly westward, displacing the Blackfeet in the Lake Winnipeg country of the northern prairies. The tribe then temporarily divided, with one group going to northern Canada to trap fur-bearing animals and the other staying farther south on the prairies to hunt bison with the Cree.

Before 1774, the Assiniboine divided again, with some staying in the area west of Lake Manitoba and others going south and west up the Missouri River. This second division was much more settled than the first, and it was helped by the establishment of the U.S. boundary in 1818. By 1820, the Assiniboine were firmly established in northwestern North Dakota and northeastern Montana where the Yellowstone River met the Missouri. The deadly smallpox first ravaged the Assiniboine in 1780, and in 1838 the tribe was reduced again, from 1200 lodges (or families) to 400 lodges. It was a much smaller tribe of Assiniboine who in later years stayed north of the Montana portion of the Missouri River.

But their small population encouraged them to become allies with the Cree because of their common enemy, the Blackfeet, who had been joined by the Gros Ventre. By the mid-1800s, the Assiniboine had established themselves as small, adaptable band of plains people who were excellent buffalo hunters and horsemen. Their small numbers, though, did not permit them to be a powerful tribe on the northern plains. They quickly agreed to the Fort Laramie Treaty of 1851, which gave them standing with the federal government and provided territory in which to hunt buffalo.

The Gros Ventre are one of the least known tribes of the northern plains. An offshoot of the Algonquian-speaking Arapaho, they were believed to be the northernmost group of five related Arapaho tribes. They were also known as the Atsina — the Gros Ventre of the Prairie. The term Gros Ventre means the "belly" or "gut" people. The Blackfeet and the Shoshone also had similar names for the Gros Ventre, but there is no evidence anywhere to explain why their name is derived from the word belly.

In the late 1600s, the Gros Ventre split from the Arapaho tribes. They were first found as a separate entity in the upper reaches of the Saskatchewan River in the Eagle Hills country of the northern prairies. No one is certain what happened with the Gros Ventre for the next hundred years, but by the late 1700s they were found with the Blackfeet on the northern plains. Many whites, including Lewis and Clark, actually thought that they were Blackfeet because most by then spoke Blackfeet as well as their own language.

Like so many plains tribes, the Gros Ventre were decimated by smallpox, having first contracted it in 1780. Shortly thereafter, following a major confrontation with the Cree and Assiniboine, the small tribe was forced from its extensive northern plains territory to a region that included the south fork of the Milk River and nearby portions of the Missouri. To claim their new home, the Gros Ventre had to displace the Shoshone, Kootenai, Flathead and Pend d'Oreille.

By the 1820s the Gros Ventre split, with one group remaining in the Milk River basin and the other traveling far south to join their Arapaho relatives in the Southwest. But only five years later, the southern splinter group returned.

On their return in 1832, they participated in a major skirmish with fur traders in Pierre's Hole on the west side of the Tetons, in which three Gros Ventre chiefs were killed.

Smallpox again devastated the Milk River Gros Ventre in 1829. But when so many tribes on the northern plains contracted smallpox again in 1838, the Gros Ventre weren't affected because they had built up an immunity. By 1833 the two Gros Ventre divisions were united again. And by 1840, because so many plains tribes were incapacitated by smallpox, the Gros Ventre found themselves with the Blackfeet in control of the plains in eastern Montana, their only enemy being the Crow, a tribe to the south. They roamed almost at will across the plains in the 1840s and 1850s, with the buffalo as their primary source of food and the center of their culture.

In 1855 the Gros Ventre signed, as part of the Blackfeet nation, the Treaty of Friendship with Isaac Stevens, the territorial governor of Washington. This was the beginning of a totally new life for the Gros Ventre. The treaty called for annuities to be distributed to the tribe at Fort Benton, and the agency there became their focal point. After 1859, when the first steamboat arrived bringing trade goods and whiskey, their subsistence culture on the plains began to wane quickly. Alcohol soon ravaged the tribe and warfare ensued between the Piegans (Blackfeet) and the Gros Ventre. By 1861 the Gros Ventre and Blackfeet were well on their way to becoming bitter enemies, and in 1867 the two tribes fought a major battle which the Gros Ventre lost. The Gros Ventre were on their own from then on and they began to form new alliances with the River Crow and Assiniboine. By 1870, the Gros Ventre and Assiniboine had become close allies and were found living together primarily in the Milk River country.

After 1867 the Gros Ventre never did return to the Fort Benton area because of the Blackfeet. Their annuities were distributed downstream on the Milk River at the newly created Fort Belknap Agency, which had been named after President Grant's Secretary of War. A few years later the federal government tried to move the Gros Ventre to Fort Peck, but the tribe refused. By 1878 the Gros Ventre had settled near the Fort Belknap Agency and south in the Little Rockies, relying almost entirely on federal rations and distributions since the buffalo had almost completely disappeared.

The Fort Belknap Agency, having come into existence in order to protect the Gros Ventre and the Assiniboine from more powerful tribes, soon served a huge geographic area, and was embroiled in many intertribal issues. Since the Agency was unable to protect the assigned tribes, Congress in 1886 authorized the Northwest Indian Commission to negotiate with the Sioux, Assiniboine, Gros Ventre and Blackfeet to persuade them to give up their lands, which

Gros Ventre returning from hunting trip. (No date given.) Courtesy, Montana Historical Society.

stretched from the Continental Divide to the eastern border of Montana Territory, south to the Missouri and north to the Canadian border. With no buffalo, the federal government wanted the tribes to lead a farming life and to make their domain available for homesteading. A treaty was ratified in May 1888, from which the Gros Ventre and the Assiniboine received $1.15 million and the "opportunity" to live on the same reservation encompassing 840,000 acres of prairie and foothills. A new agency was established down river at Fort Belknap Agency's present location. At the time there were approximately 1,100-1,200 Gros Ventre, and between 800-1,100 Assiniboine.

The next major assault on the Gros Ventre and Assiniboine land base began in 1884, when gold prospectors explored the Little Rockies on the southern end of the reservation. A succession of Fort Belknap Indian agents in the 1880s realized that there was no way to keep these trespassers out. At the same time, these Indian agents saw their farming programs on the reservation failing. No one seemed much interested in planting crops, and the weather was abominable. Besides, whiskey had completely altered the lives of both tribes.

By 1895, with the federal program completely failing for the tribes, the government appointed a three-man commission, headed by George Bird Grinnell, to negotiate with the Assiniboine and Gros Ventre for a small piece of

land seven miles long and four miles wide in the Little Rockies. This was land the commission believed the Indians couldn't use anyway, because they didn't have the capability to mine the gold that had been found there. Although the commission met initial resistance, the tribes eventually gave in and sold the parcel of land for $360,000. This agreement was ratified in June 1896.

An important footnote to this agreement was that the Grinnell Commission asked if the tribes wanted the reservation allotted and the resounding response was "no." The answer delayed allotment on the reservation until 1924.

The 1895 land sales monies didn't go directly to the tribes, but, instead, to the Bureau of Indian Affairs to help make reservation improvements. Over the next seven years, notorious Indian agents, who dominated tribal affairs through the spoils system, did nothing to help the tribes of Fort Belknap.

In 1904, things began to take a turn for the better, partly as a result of a new Indian agent, Major William R. Logan, who convinced the combined tribes to develop a government. A few years alter, the Supreme Court handed down the Winters Doctrine decision, which focused on the Fort Belknap tribes' jurisdiction of water rights in the Milk River. The Winters Doctrine clearly stated that the federal government owned the land and water on Indian reservations

Above: *Indian encampment on Fort Belknap. The Little Rocky Mountains in the background.* Bruce Selyem
Right: *Eagle nest atop Snake Butte, Fort Belknap Reservation.* Michael Crummett

and therefore was responsible for Indians and for helping them make good use of their water. This doctrine established an Indian water rights precedent that is still followed throughout the country.

Acculturation through agriculture continued to be the government policy toward Indians and toward the Gros Ventre and Assiniboine in particular. Finally, in March 1921 an allotment plan for the reservation was put forth by the tribe and the local BIA agent, but it wasn't approved by the Washington office of the BIA until 1924. When it was passed, each Indian allottee received 40 acres of irrigable land and 320 acres of non-irrigable land. Timber land as well as some recreational sites on the edges of the Little Rockies remained tribal property. The latter included the headwaters of Big Warm Creek, Mission Canyon, and the Snake Butte spring country in the middle of the reservation. No surplus lands were put up for sale to non-Indians.

The same year that the Merriam Report was published, Montana Senator Burton Wheeler visited the reservation in 1928. He was appalled at the poverty, malnutrition and disease he saw and it is reported the this visit motivated him to co-sponsor the Indian Reorganization Act of 1934. Meanwhile attempts were being made to retrieve some of the Jefferson National Forest that had been given away in both 1888 and 1895 agreements with the U.S. government. However, the Regional Forester of the U.S. Forest Service

objected on the grounds that gold mining could best continue under Forest Service ownership and not under the ownership of the tribe.

The Fort Belknap tribes drifted into the Depression years. The St. Paul's Mission School in Hays burned in 1931 and the only educational facility that remained was the agency boarding school at Fort Belknap. Depression relief programs did help people improve the range and forest conditions, but huge fires in 1936 destroyed much of the timber reserve and burned over most of the grazing lands.

Two Indian livestock associations were established in the 1930s, and the government purchased cattle to build the herds. The range fires and drought then decreased the herds by 60 percent, with only 2,400 animals remaining in 1938. In spite of these hardships, the federal relief programs and the 1934 Indian Reorganization Act brought relative prosperity to Fort Belknap. Conditions certainly were better than in the previous decades.

From 1940 to 1960, some tribal lands were irrigated, but with little long-term success. Emphasis was also put into ranching, but still most of the allotted tribal lands continued to be leased to non-Indians, a situation which continues to this day. The Termination Era didn't affect Fort Belknap. There were approximately 729 Assiniboine and 1013 Gros Ventre in 1947, and practically all of them were on some form of relief. Certainly, Blaine and Phillips Counties didn't want any form of termination; officials

feared it would bankrupt them. Further, Fort Belknap lands were not seen as significantly incoming-producing.

Throughout the '60s and '70s, tribal leadership at Fort Belknap was preoccupied with the problems of unemployment and the lack of a major natural resource. There was hope for oil and gas, or large coal deposits, but nothing significant was found. Great Society programs provided an infusion of funds for new social service programs and economic development projects such as Fort Belknap Builders, Inc., a small shopping center and an industrial building and park. But lack of management skill, a coherent and unified direction and other factors severely hampered these projects and others. Therefore, Fort Belknap has continued to drift economically, relying almost solely on government assistance and the Bureau of Indian Affairs. Both tribes still get along relatively well together although some factionalism surfaces occasionally. Most Gros Ventre live in the Hays-Lodgepole area on the southern part of the reservation and the Assiniboine are concentrated along the Milk River near Fort Belknap Agency.

Fort Belknap Today

As of January 1985, there were 4,215 tribal enrolled members, 1,853 Assiniboine and 2,362 Gros Ventre. Approximately 2,200 or 50 percent of the enrolled members live on the Reservation.

Tribal enrollment is governed by the tribe's constitution, which stipulates that a member must have relatives who were on the tribal roles in 1921 when land allotments took place. In 1959 the tribes passed a constitutional amendment requiring tribal members to have a total of one-quarter Indian blood in order to be enrolled. This means that one could be one-eighth Assiniboine and one-eighth Gros Ventre and still be a tribal member. It also is interpreted to mean that one could be one-eighth Assiniboine or Gros Ventre and one-eighth Blackfeet or other tribal origin and still qualify. A restricted enrollment policy is important to the tribes because of the reservation's small resource base.

Reservation Lands

Fort Belknap Reservation contains 645,576 acres, of which 210,954 acres are tribally controlled, and 406,533 are allotted and are held by tribal members. Almost all of the land within the tribal boundaries is controlled by the tribe or by the state, which has about 19,000 acres within reservation boundaries. Only some 9,000 acres are owned by non-tribal members.

Approximately 80 percent of the reservation is in Blaine County, and 20 percent is in Phillips County. Its topographical extremes range from 2,300 feet on the Milk River to 5,700 feet at Antoine Butte on the southern edge of the reservation. The reservation climate is semi-arid, having an average annual rainfall of 9-10" with the highest precipitation being 17" on the southern boundary in Little Rockies.

Tribal Government

Although the Fort Belknap tribes had developed a constitutional form of tribal government as early as 1894, they reorganized again under the Indian Reorganization Act in 1935. Today 12 members of a community council are elected from districts on the reservation, six Assiniboine and six Gros Ventre. Council terms are four years in length and are staggered. Officers of the tribe are not elected at large but are selected from within the council to two-year terms. The tribal president has changed five times in the past ten years, which has caused leadership continuity problems.

The Milk River forms the northern boundary of Fort Belknap Reservation. Michael Crummett

Tribal Budget

Fort Belknap tribes have one of the smallest operating budgets of any tribe in Montana. Their general fund of $110,000 of tribal revenues is increased to $300,000 through a surcharge on federal grants that come to the tribes. Federal program expenditures on the reservation in 1985 will be approximately $7 million. Ninety percent of the general fund income is from various uses of tribal lands such as agricultural leasing in the form of grazing and dry-land farming permits.

Natural Resources

Unlike those on some reservations in Montana, the Fort Belknap tribes have a sparse natural resource inventory. Thus leaders within Fort Belknap have an unwritten policy of seeking the best education possible for tribal members so that they can obtain jobs elsewhere.

Agriculture

Until the 1930s one attempt after another to make farmers of the Gros Ventre and Assiniboine failed. Then a renewed effort was made to get the tribes' members to become ranchers. A range-management program was initiated in 1930 through the forestry branch of the Bureau of Indian Affairs. The program encompassed 533,000 acres, almost the entire reservation. Farming and several irrigation projects continued to be emphasized in the 1960s despite traditional religious beliefs of the Assiniboine and Gros Ventre that it is a sin to tear up the sod because the earth is a living creature.

Today farmland occupies approximately 123,500 acres. The primary crops are wheat and barley, yielding an average of 30 to 45 bushels an acre. About 25 tribal members are in farming. Even though agricultural lands within the reservation gross $15.4 million, the tribes and their members realize only about 0.5 percent because most of the land is leased to non-Indian people.

Digging fire line on a 1984 fire on Fort Belknap Reservation. Michael Crummett

There are 460,000 acres in range and pasture land, of which almost half is leased to non-Indians. The current cattle population is approximately 12,000. With pristine native grasses covering a good portion of the range, the rangeland on Fort Belknap is as good as any in Montana.

Forest Resources

There are approximately 34,000 timbered acres of lodgepole, ponderosa and Douglas fir on the reservation. Around the turn of the century, this relatively small forest was in great demand for the timber needs of the mining towns just south of the reservation in the Little Rockies, but by 1912 the tribes' 90 million board feet was of little value because it was so far away from commercial markets. In 1936, a forest fire burned almost the whole forest in the Little Rockies and even today reforestation work needs to be completed on some 4,500 acres. Some post and pole cutting takes place, and two part-time sawmills are operated by tribal members. Otherwise, the reservation has no commercial forest activity nor is any expected since the present 10-year forest management plan calls for only half a million board feet of ponderosa to be cut — hardly enough for a successful forest enterprise. Furthermore, in the summer of 1984, yet another substantial forest fire in the Little Rockies burned some of the mature ponderosa. Fortunately the tribes have an excellent fire-fighting crew that controlled the fire before it wiped out what little commercial timber is on the reservation.

Wildlife

Unlike many reservations, Fort Belknap has a fairly comprehensive hunting ordinance that has been used as a tool in wildlife management. Even though there are no wardens, tribal members have by and large, respected the ordinance which sets an ungulate hunting season from September through December. As a result, the antelope population has increased from approximately 110 to 600 in the past three years. The whitetail deer population on the northern part of the reservation is in excellent condition and some of the largest whitetails in the northern plains inhabit the Milk River valley bottom. They receive far less hunting pressure on the reservation side of the boundary than they do just off the reservation to the north. A small herd of bighorn sheep, as well as some elk, periodically occupy the reservation in the Little Rockies region.

Fort Belknap is one of the best places in Montana to hunt sagegrouse, sharptails and pheasants. The birds have excellent habitat, and tribal members rarely hunt them, a fact that contributes to above-normal bird populations. Bird hunting is open to non-tribal members who have a special tribal license. With 12,000 acres of prairie dogs, one might expect to find the black-footed ferret, and, like most areas with extensive prairie dog populations, rumors abound that this endangered species exists on Fort Belknap. Fox, coyote, bobcat, mink, muskrat, and beaver are all found in appropriate habitats on Fort Belknap.

Mineral Resources

The Assiniboine and Gros Ventre still resent the fact that more than $25 million worth of gold and silver is mined annually at the Zortman-Landusky mine from land the tribes sold to the government in 1895. The tribes have an exploration team working on their side of the Little Rockies boundary line. The reservation has bentonite reserves, which remain undeveloped because of the lack of a market. Some low-quality lignite deposits have been found, but not of the quality and quantity found in the coal fields in other parts of Eastern Montana. No oil and gas have been discovered to date, despite extensive exploration. Montana Power Company has a gas pipeline near the reservation and there has been hope that MPC will sign an exploratory lease with the tribes that would cover the whole reservation. Although negotiations are proceeding, they do not look promising.

Snake Butte in the west-central part of the reservation has some potential for geothermal activity. However, there are no plans to accurately assess the potential or develop this resource.

The tribes are trying to consolidate the irrigable and dry-land farmlands that they own on the reservation. They are also trying to buy key allottee farmlands that may come up for sale and could pass into non-Indian fee status. The tribes are now trying to buy an 8,000-acre farm and ranch for tribal farming purposes.

Mission Canyon. Michael Crummett

Another major land-acquisition program is the consolidation of 25,000 acres of so-called "submarginal" lands west of the reservation, so that they can be managed in a more unified manner. Submarginal lands came from bankrupt and abandoned homesteads of the 1930s that were deeded to the Bureau of Indian Affairs. The Fort Belknap tribes have always had use of most of them and the BIA formally gave the tribes title to them in 1975. At present they are leased to non-Indian ranchers.

Perhaps the most important natural-resource issue facing the Fort Belknap tribes concerns water rights. The 1908 Winters Doctrine, which decided a water issue on the Milk River, made it clear that the government is supposed to make sure that water is available to the tribes to irrigate their lands. However, the state of Montana's present adjudication program, which has been supported by the U.S. Supreme Court, puts the rights to water from the Milk River in some doubt. A negotiating team headed by tribal president Randy Perez has entered into preliminary talks with the Montana Water Compact Commission. The tribes hope to resolve their adjudication issues and stay out of court. They also realize that it is essential to have an agreement that will adequately supply their irrigation and domestic needs.

Celebrations

"Fort Belknap Indian Days" are held each year in late July at Fort Belknap Agency. They feature dancing, giveaways and a variety of games. During the first week of October the tribes hold the "Chief Joseph Memorial Dance" and a "Winter Fair" is held in February featuring dancing and boxing.

Above left: *Fort Belknap Community College*
Above: *New Town, Fort Belknap Agency.* Michael Crummett photos

The Future of Economic Development on Fort Belknap

The economic situation on Fort Belknap is not in good shape. More than 78 percent of tribal members are unemployed and the median family income is $4,892, compared to a Montana average of $18,418. Just under 700 families are on general assistance. There are an average of 43 applicants for every unskilled position opening, nine applicants for every professional opening, and 27 applicants for every skilled laborer opening. It's no wonder that a community-needs survey in the fall of 1984 ranked creating employment opportunities and long-term jobs as the number-one issue facing the tribe. The need to develop the reservation's natural resources was ranked second, followed by the need to develop the capacity to generate venture capital for tribal investments and operations. The fourth priority was the need to raise the educational level of all members.

The tribes' economic-development program set a goal of reducing the unemployment rate by 15 percent by 1990, and expanding tribal farming operations by 3,000 acres by 1990.

It is interesting that the tribal leadership returns to agricultural development on the reservation, despite the tribes' poor success with agriculture. However, with irrigation, tribal leaders believe that could change and that is why the adjudication of the tribes' water rights is so

critical. Another question that lingers over any major push for irrigation is the Gros Ventre and Assiniboine's feelings toward the land. Both tribes historically have resisted full-scale irrigation since the reservation was established in 1888 because of traditional spiritual beliefs about land and Mother Earth. These beliefs are a major reason why as many as six irrigation districts on the reservation are not now functioning despite major efforts on the part of the Bureau of Indian Affairs to make each a successful operation in past years. So despite the potential for large-scale irrigated farming, tribal traditions may well prevent its success. Still, the tribes have set up an independent corporate entity called Milk River Farms to develop the agricultural potential of the reservation; there are few other economic-development choices at this time.

Industrial development has not fared well either. In 1969, the tribes set up a semi-independent construction corporation called Fort Belknap Builders to build houses on and off the reservation. The Builders soon had a debt that exceeded $3 million as a result of ineffective management. Its financial record has kept the tribes from securing any loans for quite some time.

Another failed activity was the establishment in 1970 of an industrial park and a 38,000-square-foot factory building. It has never been used. Recently a security electronics firm from Sacramento has been interested in

using the facility. They are tempted by not having to pay a state corporate tax, the use of "free" land and a free building as well as an eager labor force. But tribal leaders over the past 15 years have seen people interested before, and the dream of having an industry like A&S Industries on Fort Peck remains a fantasy.

The tribes are attempting a small step toward economic self-sufficiency by trying to get a community post office at Fort Belknap Agency by 1989. Without a post office, most of the tribal members must travel five miles into Harlem every day, where they may also patronize a cafe, gas station or other basic businesses that can't succeed on Fort Belknap as a result. It is possible that irrigated farming will be economically successful and it is also possible that the small industrial park and factory building will be utilized, but in the meantime, a bleak economic future motivates the tribal leadership to promote the best possible education so tribal members can seek livelihoods off the reservation. It is painfully obvious that the reservation has a very limited resource base and limited economic-development opportunities. Perhaps this reservation can be viewed as a place where most tribal members can live while seeking adequate employment elsewhere. The role of the reservation for tribal members may need to be rethought. At present, the Assiniboine and Gros Ventre of Fort Belknap face survival day by day.

The Great Gold Robbery of 1895

In the late 1880s and early 1890s, prospectors roaming the hills of the Little Rockies found gold, and they paid little attention to the fact that their strike was within the boundaries of the Fort Belknap Reservation. In 1894, the acting Indian agent on Fort Belknap admitted in an annual report to the BIA commissioner that illegal mining was taking place and that he didn't know how to stop it. He estimated that in 1894 alone, $75,000 worth of gold had been taken out of the hills by white prospectors.

In 1895, President Cleveland appointed three commissioners to negotiate with the Fort Belknap tribes for the gold mining country. They were W.C. Pollock, W.M. Clements and George Bird Grinnell, the famous naturalist, originator of the idea for Glacier National Park and later a well-known author of several books on the Northern Cheyenne and Blackfeet.

When the Assiniboine and Gros Ventres sat down with Grinnell, Clements and Pollock, many of them were not in favor of another land sale. In the last ten years, they had already seen their reservation shrink substantially. Therefore, in spite of the destitute condition of their people, the chiefs made many statements that they didn't want to trade more of their precious land for money. Pollock and Grinnell insisted that the Indians were going to starve if they didn't sell the land.

An example of the kind of hard-nosed bargaining that took place is George Bird Grinnell's initial negotiating statement:

"I see that some of you people are pretty blind, you can't see far. You see the things that are close to your face, but the things that are further off you can't see at all. You are like people looking through a fog, you see things nearby, but the things far off are hidden. You think that because for seven or eight years, you have had plenty to eat and have lived well, for the next year or two you are going to have plenty to eat, that it will always go on like that. That is not true; it is not going to last. I go about among different people and see them, how they are fixed, how many cattle that they've got, how they farm; I don't see anybody as poor as you people."

"Two years from now, if you don't make any agreement with the government, you will just have to kill your cattle and then you will have to starve. It makes me feel badly to think of this. If you sell some of this land and get money

The old gold-mine mill and Pegasus Gold Company's current mine operation in the Little Rocky Mountains. Michael Crummett

enough to keep going for some years longer and then work, and take care of your cattle, after that, you will be like white people and be able to take care of yourselves."

"When a white man wants money, he takes something and goes to the stores and the trader gives him money that he can put in his pocket; that supports him, that buys food for him and his wife and children. The only thing you have to sell is this little piece of land that you do not use. I should like to see you sell that, because if you don't, I cannot tell how after two years have gone by you are going to live."*

Over a two-day period, Grinnell and Pollock were able to convince the Indians to sell a strip of land seven miles long and four miles wide, for $350,000. This small "bite" out of the Reservation was a steal for the U.S. government. The Zortman-Landusky mines quickly became the largest gold mines and industry in the state of Montana from 1900 to 1904, and they are still going today.

*Proceedings of the commission appointed to negotiate with the Fort Belknap Indians, from the Records of Bureau of Indian Affairs. This document comes from file 25450-1922-051-General Service.

Today the Zortman-Landusky mine is the largest low-grade heap leach gold mine in production in the Western world. It is owned by Pegasus Gold in Spokane, Washington. It operates from late March to early December. Over the last two years, the gross value of the gold and silver taken from the mines ranged between $20 to $25 million. The mine employs approximately 100 people, of whom 40 are seasonal. The annual payroll is about $5 million, and the mine pays taxes to the county, the state and the U.S. government that exceeded $1 million in 1984. This is hard for the Fort Belknap tribes to take, when the entire reservation generates only $100,000 in annual income.

To add insult to injury, over the years that the mine has been in operation, some of the ground water in the southern part of the reservation has been polluted by cyanide used in the leaching process, and at times, Peoples Creek has been contaminated. Fortunately that is not as big a pollution issue now as it used to be. Bob Marshall, the man after whom the Bob Marshall Wilderness was named and who was Chief Forester for the BIA at the time, supported an attempt between 1915 and 1920 to return the

The Little Rockies. Even before the Fort Belknap reservation was formed, the GrosVentre revered the Little Rockies. It was a place with abundant game and wood for campfires, and one that carried important religious meanings as well. Mission Peak and Eagle Child Peak are sacred mountains of the Gros Ventre. Gros Ventre medicine men went to the summit of Eagle Peak to fast and to meditate for four days and four nights to gain supernatural powers. According to legend, no medicine men ever completed a four-night pilgrimage on top of Eagle Child, because terrifying scenes and visions would force them to abort their vision quests and return home.

Today these mountains still are looked upon as sacred by the Gros Ventre. They are also a source of abundant rains in a primarily semi-arid area where there are still a good wood supply and some wildlife resources. Mark Thompson

lands to the tribes for timber and grazing purposes. The tribes also believed that the original 1895 agreement was flawed and should be revoked. However, the regional supervisor of the U.S. Forest Service objected because he didn't believe that the Indians had the capital or the management expertise to mine in the Little Rockies. The last attempts to rectify the situation took place under the auspices of the late Montana Senator Lee Metcalf. Nothing resulted, and the Fort Belknap tribes have more or less resigned themselves to the fact that their land had been nearly stolen by Pollock and Grinnell, acting with the support of the U.S. government.

The Modern-Day Warrior: The Indian Veteran

We all know the stereotype of the Indian warrior on horseback fighting against the U.S. Cavalry, but we are not as aware that the modern-day Indian warrior also has served valorously in the United States military.

Although definitive statistics may not even exist, most Indian military observers believe that, proportionately, more Indians than other minorities were killed in World War II, the Korean War and the Vietnam War. This is ascribed to their bravery and willingness to volunteer for highly dangerous missions.

Indian veterans of World War II live throughout Montana. An Assiniboine on Fort Belknap survived the Bataan death march. Another Fort Belknap Assiniboine was one of three Indians from Montana who were members of Merrell's Marauders. A Yanktonai Sioux served as a scout in the Buna-Gona campaign. Another Fort Peck tribal member was one of the most-decorated Vietnam War veterans as a Green Beret. It's well known that one of the GIs who raised the flag on Iwo Jima was Ira Hayes, a Pima. Actually, the first flag-raising at Iwo Jima involved Louis Charlo, a Flathead. When this flag was thought to be too small, another was raised for the famous picture.

One contemporary Montana Indian warrior even upheld the age-old tradition of counting coups in World War II. Joe Medicine Crow of the Crow tribe sneaked behind German lines to steal a horse to "count coups" as in the old days when stealing an enemy's horse was given high regard.

Indian veterans, their families and friends, are proud of their military experiences and military service carries weight in tribal leadership. Many Northern Cheyenne on the reservation mentioned Windy Shoulderblade's military career during the Vietnam era as an important qualification for leading the tribe. Windy, like so many other Indian leaders throughout the state, is very active in the VFW and still participates in paratrooper exercises with the National Guard.

Top: *The Little Rockies near Zortman.* Mark Thompson
Above: *Indian patriot, Blackfeet Reservation.*
Michael Crummett

37

b.

a.

c.

d.

a. Milk River Indian Days, Harlem.
b. The Mosquito Run south of Harlem.
c. Running Child Singers, Milk River Indian
Days.
d. Personalized, Indianized Forest Service shirts.
Michael Crummett photos

a.

c.

d.

b.

a. *Doug Johnson, at Milk River Indian Days*
b. *Miss Chief Joseph attending Milk River Indian Days*
c. *Stairsteps to Heaven and the wages of sin, Mission Canyon.*
d. *The Mission on Fort Belknap Reservation.* Bruce Selyem
e. *Catholic cemetery.*
All photos except (d), Michael Crummett

e.

Wrangling horses near Hays. Michael Crummett   Right: *Delmar Bigbee.* Michael Crummett

Delmar "Poncho" Bigbee

An Assiniboine, Poncho is a classic example of an Indian in his mid-40s who has led somewhat of a rollercoaster life. Bigbee grew up in a log house in the northern part of the reservation. He graduated from Harlem High School in 1960. Bigbee immediately went into the service at the age of 17. Discharged in 1965, he did odd jobs and became a victim of alcohol.

As for his Indian past, Poncho said bluntly, "I have no Indian name. I also knew nothing about the reservation while I was growing up. I guess I'm a product of the assimilation era."

He went to Los Angeles through the Bureau of Indian Affairs relocation program but didn't last long. He came home and found work with a Choteau-area rancher. He worked for a while, drank for a while, continuing this dismal cycle for several years.

In 1970 he was married, and came back to the reservaton and began working for the Bureau of Indian Affairs. In 1976, after he held several Bureau jobs, the BIA loaned him to the tribe as Tribal Realty Officer. He then played musical chairs with the Bureau and the tribe, going back and forth several times in the areas of realty and land-planning.

In 1978 Poncho faced a tough decision about his drinking. Following an abusive New Year's Eve celebration, he made the choice, and he has not taken a drink since. It wasn't easy, because so many of his friends drank and he had to go friendless for a while, but he knew that he had to get off the bottle and "do it for himself."

Today Bigbee is one of the tribe's up-and-coming bright leaders. He is involved in the water-rights negotiations, lobbies for the tribe in the state legislature when necessary,

Franklin Perez. Michael Crummett

Franklin "Randy" Perez

Born in 1949, Randy is an Assiniboine with a proud family heritage. His great-grandfather was Frank Buck, a famous Assiniboine chieftain. Perez grew up in the Milk River area and was graduated from Harlem High School in 1968. After one year at Montana State University he entered the service and served in Vietnam. He returned to the reservation in '72 and in 1975 ran successfully for the tribal council. He has been secretary/treasurer, vice president, and became tribal president at the age of 34 in January 1984.

Perez wants to serve several terms as tribal president to maintain leadership continuity, which has been severely lacking on Fort Belknap in recent years. The most important issues facing the tribe, according to Perez, are the retention of its land base and water rights. Although the tribe and its members own almost the entire reservation, there is constant concern that some of this land could revert to fee title.

Perez leads the tribes' committee negotiating with Montana's Water Compact Commission, for he knows that water is as critical to the future of Fort Belknap tribes as the land base. Since the Winters Doctrine, which spells out U.S. policy toward Indian water rights, was developed with Fort Belknap as its subject more than 80 years ago, it's clear that these are tough, long-standing issues.

and is without doubt one of the Assiniboines' most eloquent spokesmen. He has been the tribe's water and natural resource specialist, but once again had to return to the BIA's payroll as the irrigation specialist because of the extremely tight tribal budget. Fortunately for Poncho and the tribes, the BIA has an extremely close working relationship with the tribes.

Jack Plumage

Born in 1946, Jack is a full-blooded Assiniboine and Gros Ventre. A graduate of Harlem High School, he attended the University of Montana, before serving in Vietnam for more than a year. Upon returning to the Reservation he ran the tribe's Manpower Program campaigned for the tribal council in one of the Assiniboine positions. He was elected by his fellow council members as tribal president in 1976. At the time, he was 27 years old and the youngest tribal president in the United States. He served in that position for two terms.

Jack's major accomplishment as a tribal leader was starting the tribal education department. During a three-year period, the two tribes on the reservation saw an increase from 40 people with high school or graduate-equivalency diplomas to more than 120. Jack also brought Fort Belknap tribes into the Council of Energy Resource Tribes because of the reservation's potential oil, gas and coal reserves. He set up the land department and began to develop a land-use plan for the reservation. Perhaps one of Jack's biggest disappointments as an elected tribal leader was that there was never any breakthrough in the serious unemployment problem.

Today Jack is the administrative officer of the Bureau of Indian Affairs, which means he supervises all BIA programs. Since the tribe is so dependent on the bureau for employment, this is perhaps the most significant position a tribal member can hold on the reservation.

Despite the ups and downs, Jack says, "I'm where a lot of people are trying to get back to." A lot of tribal members, he points out, wish to work on the reservation but can't and he feels lucky to be able to. Jack's major project now is to get a better educational program for students at Harlem High School. Although more than 70 percent of the school's students are members of the Fort Belknap tribes, no school board members are tribal members and Jack believes this must be changed.

Elmer Main

Elmer Main's mission in life is getting as many Indian kids as possible to school. In his 60s, Main is three-quarter Gros Ventre and is one of the few people left who speak Gros Ventre fluently. He went to a one-room school in Hays and then to St. Paul's Mission High School near the southern part of the reservation. Main grew up on a small farm where he rode as much as he could during his youth.

After attending Gonzaga University, Elmer went into the Army for four years and was in the Pacific campaign for the Solomon Islands, the Phillipines and Japan. Upon returning from the war and being recognized by tribal elders for his military service, Main was strongly urged by his parents to return to college. In 1950 he graduated from the University of Montana and he taught and coached in various schools before earning a masters degree in School Administration. Main spent 17 years as a school administrator in schools along the Hi-Line as well as in Lodge Grass on the Crow Reservation.

In 1967 Main returned to the reservation and worked in the higher education program at the Bureau of Indian Affairs. He spent 11 years in this program and was pleased to see how many tribal members went on to higher education during his tenure. In his first year on the job, 13 students went on to higher education; in 1974 there were 206 tribal members in higher education programs around the country.

"Education is the most important thing we can give tribal members," Elmer says. "I don't care whether they only go for two years of school and they then get out and get a job. I would consider it a success. It's essential that people from the tribe get some kind of higher education since there are essentially no jobs back here. People from here need to go out and compete in the world," because, as he says, "if you want to obtain a comfortable living, one needs to get away from here."

Main was the BIA superintendent for Fort Belknap agency until 1983, when he became the elementary principal at Hays. Now he is the superintendent and sees his immediate task as one of trying to upgrade the academic climate at the high school. This includes standardizing the curriculum and providing a supportive environment to encourage tribal students to complete high school and go on to advanced training. Main has a difficult objective, though, in that only 60 percent of the high-school-age students in the southern part of the reservation currently attend school and very few are going on to college.

As Elmer blesses his office daily in the traditional method of burning sweetgrass, he prays for the future of the young people on the reservation, expressing hope that they will get as much education as possible. "We can't be afraid to leave the reservation and afraid to face the world. If we are afraid, we're going to have a very sad future."

As for Main's immediate future, Hays-Lodgepole offers a huge challenge. After that he may even get involved in politics. "I refuse to give up in helping my people better themselves," he says.

Jack Plumage. Michael Crummett

Elmer Main. Michael Crummett

ASSINIBOINE & SIOUX

For decades Indian assimilation meant agriculture, as symbolized here by a Fort Peck homestead. Michael Crummett

Tribal Histories

Fort Peck, the second largest reservation in the state of Montana, is the home of two different tribes: the Assiniboine tribe, Yanktonai and Sisseton Wahpeton Sioux. Both have been allies for centuries and coexist on the reservation today.

Assiniboine history is covered somewhat in the Fort Belknap section, as both Assiniboine groups are bands of the same tribe. Most historians believe that the Assiniboine originally were an offshoot of the Yanktonai Sioux, having broken away sometime in the 1600s and returning as a distinct tribe on the Fort Peck Reservation in the 1860s. The Assiniboine originally were found by whites in the 1600s in northern Canada near the Lake of the Woods and Lake Nipigon and as far west as the Saskatchewan River. Their name, Assiniboine, reflects their original Siouan ancestry; the word *ass-ni-pwan* means "stone Sioux," apparently referring to the Assiniboine method of cooking food with hot stones and boiling water.

As mentioned in the Fort Belknap section, the Assiniboine divided in the 17th century, one group staying in the northern woods of Canada and one going to hunt the buffalo on the Great Plains. Sometime before 1744 the southern group divided again. One group went into the Missouri Valley region and others moved west and north into the valleys of the Assiniboine and Saskatchewan Rivers. When the U.S.-Canada boundary was established in 1818, the two divisions were even further separated. Those who stayed south of the border were primarily plains hunters and, by and large, were quite friendly with the fur traders who were traveling through the country, providing them with buffalo, jerky and pemmican. In 1838 smallpox reduced the Assiniboine by approximately two-thirds of their original numbers, making them vulnerable to other plains Indian tribes. In 1851 the Assiniboine gladly accepted the terms of the Fort Laramie Treaty as their weak position limited the area they could defend for hunting. In 1855 they were included in the friendship treaty that Isaac Stevens made with the Blackfeet because Stevens saw the Assiniboine as part of that larger tribe.

For the next ten years, the Assiniboine spent most of their time in northern Montana hunting buffalo. When not hunting they were usually found at Fort Benton, Blackfeet Agency and Fort Belknap trading buffalo robes and accepting annuities due from treaties and settlements with the federal government. Increasingly, along with the River Crow and Gros Ventre, they frequented the Fort Belknap Agency and tried to distance themselves as much as possible from the Blackfeet. In 1869, another smallpox epidemic debilitated the Gros Ventre and the Upper Assiniboine band. The so-called Lower Assiniboine — a name coming from the fact that they frequented the lower portions of the Missouri River in Montana — were not affected. They stayed away from the Upper Assiniboine and went with their chief, Red Stone, to live with the Yantonai Sioux, who had come into northeastern Montana to hunt buffalo on their traditional hunting grounds.

The Fort Peck Agency was established in 1871, mainly because the Sioux couldn't seem to get along with anyone except their newly found allies, the Lower Band of the Assiniboine. This alliance has remained in effect ever since.

The history of the Yanktonai Sioux is far more complicated than that of the Assiniboine. The Sioux traditionally have been a very large and powerful nation. Historically there are seven bands or council fires of the Sioux tribe, all of whom speak a language of Siouan descent. These seven divisions have evolved into three distinct language groups: the Dakotas, the Nakotas and the Lakotas. The Dakotas are the Santee people. The Lakotas are the Teton Sioux and the Nakotas are both the Yankton and the Yanktonai Sioux.

There is not enough space available here to describe the development of the Sioux tribes other than to say that those who are on Fort Peck are part of the middle band of Sioux or the Nakotas. Like so many other Indian tribes, the Sioux originally came from Canada. They began their migration west soon after the Europeans began displacing Indians on the east coast, and they lived in central Minnesota by the late 1600s. At about that time, the Nakotas split into two bands. One was the Yankton Band which moved south across the northern plains. The other, the Yanktonai Band, stayed to the north. Today parts of the Yanktonai Band are found not only on Fort Peck but also on reservations in North Dakota, South Dakota and in Canada.

In the Mendota Treaty of 1851, the Dakota or Santee Sioux ceded much of their original homelands in the Minnesota area to the federal government. This controversial treaty forced them to move west, a very bitter people. By 1862 they were openly hostile toward whites over the loss of their lands. Several battles ensued, causing as many as 1,500 Sioux to be imprisoned and the rest scattered westward across the Great Plains. This led to a continuing battle between the various Sioux tribes and non-Indian people moving into the current-day Dakotas, eastern Montana, eastern Wyoming and Nebraska. It didn't change until the Battle of the Little Bighorn, fought by the Ogalala, Brule, Sansarc, Minneconjou, Yanktonai, Hunkpapa and Blackfeet Sioux bands.

The United States sent a peace commission in 1868 to negotiate with the Sioux chief Red Cloud. An agreement was drawn up to close the Bozeman Trail and to abandon all forts along it. This Fort Laramie Treaty also stated that the Indians could have the Powder River Country extending east to include the Black Hills of South Dakota. In return the Sioux gave the government permission to let the Northern Pacific Railroad pass south of these recognized northern plains hunting grounds. No sooner was the ink dry than gold was found in the Black Hills. Lt. Colonel George Armstrong Custer reported this find to the government and the rush was on, with the Fort Laramie Treaty of 1868 being cast to the wind. This infuriated the Sioux because they knew that they could not prevent a non-Indian invasion of the Black Hills. The government

Sioux dancing. Courtesy, Montana State University Archives.

responded to this predicament by desperately trying to buy the Black Hills from the Indians, but found that impossible. Instead, a few years later (in 1875), the government decided to order all Indians onto reservations by January of 1876. Most of the Sioux refused and the Battle of the Little Bighorn in June 1876 was a direct result.

Although the Custer battle was a great victory for the Sioux and their allies, it signified the end of their way of life. Shortly thereafter, under relentless pressure by the United States Army, several Sioux bands went to their designated reservations, signing away the Black Hills and their traditional hunting grounds in Nebraska, Wyoming and Montana. In return they received some annuities and many promises from the government regarding rations, which quickly became their sole source of support now that the buffalo had disappeared.

In the late 1870s and early 1880s, the area around the Fort Peck Agency was filled with tension. Most of the Sioux there were descendants of participants in the unrest in Minnesota after the Mendota Treaty, or had themselves

participated in the Battle of Little Bighorn. Teton Sioux chief Sitting Bull had even stopped temporarily at Fort Peck before going into Canada. Many of his followers stayed on the reservation or returned a year or two later. By 1879 an estimated 1,116 members of Sitting Bull's band lived near the Fort Peck Agency. In 1881 Gall, the Hunkpapa Sioux chief, surrendered at Fort Peck with 300 members of his band.

In the early 1880s, Fort Peck was one of three agencies serving the huge Indian reservation that extended from the eastern border of Montana Territory west to the Continental Divide and north from the Missouri River. With the disappearance of the buffalo came an increase in intertribal skirmishes, making living in northern and northeastern Montana in the mid-1880s very difficult. In 1886 the federal government approached the Sioux, along with the Assiniboine, Gros Ventre and Blackfeet, to make another land agreement. The Sweetgrass Hills Treaty of 1888 negotiated the establishment of the Fort Peck Reservation for the Yanktonai Sioux and the Band of the Lower

Top: *The Missouri River Valley — Fort Peck's southern boundary is the Missouri River just east of where it issues from Fort Peck dam.*
Bottom: *The "Hi-Line Hauler" into Wolf Point.*
Michael Crummett photos

One reason the government wanted to establish a clear reservation boundary at Fort Peck was that the Great Northern Railroad had constructed its transcontinental northern line to within a few miles of the Fort Peck Agency on the Poplar River. The railroad could go no farther until clear agreements had been made with the various Indian tribes north of the Missouri River and south of the Canadian border. The Sweet Grass Hills Treaty, and those made with the Blackfeet and the tribes at Fort Belknap, paved the way not only for the Great Northern Railroad, but also for the establishment of Montana statehood a year later.

With its newly-established boundaries, Fort Peck (named after a successful white supplier of military posts and Indian agencies) was populated in 1890 with 1,891 Indians. Out of these, 1,178 were Yanktonai and other bands of Sioux, and 713 were members of the Lower Band of Assiniboine. Disease and malnutrition prevented these small bands from growing over the next decade or two. In fact, their numbers decreased, so that in 1904 Fort Peck population was 1,651. With such a small group of Indians and more than two million acres of land on the reservation, the pressure to allot tribal lands became insurmountable.

Thousands of non-Indians who had arrived via the Great Northern Railroad wanted to homestead the reservation. As a result, the first Fort Peck Allotment Act was passed in May 1908. Once the land had been surveyed and allotments made, the reservation was opened to homesteading and the sale of surplus land in July of 1913. At the time each eligible Indian received 320 acres of grazing land, plus some irrigable land and timbered (cottonwood) lands. After allotment some 40,229 people had registered for the "surplus" lands and about 1.3 million acres were opened up to settlement by the 12,000 applicants who drew land shares. Fortunately for contemporary tribal members, not all of this land was taken in the prescribed five years. Nevertheless, most of the best agricultural land is out of Indian hands, having been lost in the surplus-land sales.

Over the next 50 years, the tribes at Fort Peck tried to make a living from agriculture. As with most of the Great Plains tribes, the government tried to turn the Assiniboine and Sioux into agriculturalists. Irrigation projects were proposed and implemented but did not do especially well. Since the reservation land has sizeable lignite deposits, the government promoted their development as well, with little success.

Starting in the early 1900s, attempts were made to settle the Assiniboine claim to lands taken away from them before 1876. This land claim didn't reach the courts until 1927 and wasn't settled until 1984, when $11 million was awarded to the Lower Band of Assiniboines on Fort Peck.

Assiniboine. After Congress ratified this treaty, the Ogalala and Hunkpapa Sioux living near Fort Peck were told to return to their respective reservations in the Dakotas. They refused, and since the government seemed unable or unwilling to force them out and since they were no longer a hostile threat, the government allowed them to stay. They have done so ever since.

Fort Peck Today

Population

As of April 1983, 5,022 enrolled members live on the reservation and approximately 4,170 members live off the reservation. Most living on the reservation live along its southern boundary. Although Fort Peck tribal members have been a minority within their reservation for some time, the 1980 U.S. census shows that this is changing. According to the census, 9,898 people live on the reservation, 4,273 of whom are Indian people. This was an increase of Indian people by 34 percent since 1970. At the same time, the non-Indian population decreased by 16 percent so some people predict that tribal members will become a majority.

Enrollment at Fort Peck is controlled by the Tribal Enrollment Ordinance of 1960, which states that people who were members before 1960 must be on the basic roll, be a descendant of a person on the basic roll, or have been adopted by the Council prior to 1960 and approved by the Secretary of the Interior. Those members enrolled since 1960 who do not qualify under the basic-roll rule must have one-quarter or more Assiniboine or Sioux blood.

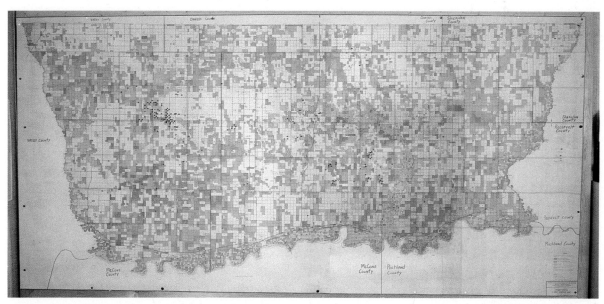

A map of subsurface mineral ownership on Fort Peck Reservation shows how much of the resources are controlled by non-Indians. Yellow indicates allotted Indian oil and gas; pink is tribally owned; white is non-Indian owned. Michael Crummett

Reservation Lands

Of the 2,093,318 acres within the Fort Peck Reservation, more than 54 percent is owned by non-Indians. The tribe has under its control approximately 950,000 acres, of which 627,800 acres are owned by allottees or individual tribal members and the remaining 322,200 acres are directly owned by the tribe. Approximately 816,900 acres are classified as agricultural land, 11,700 acres as irrigated crop land and more than 630,000 acres classified as grazing land.

The reservation is approximately 110 miles long and 40 miles wide. Except for its northern border, it has natural boundaries, with Big Muddy Creek on the east, the Missouri River on the south and Porcupine Creek to the west. Most of the reservation is in Roosevelt County, but there are parts of it in Daniels, Valley and Sheridan Counties. The city of Poplar is the center of tribal activities.

The reservation is a flat and rather austere place with gently rolling hills. Except for the cottonwoods that are found along the creek bottoms, there are no forests. Winters are severe and summers are hot and dry. Precipitation averages between 11½ and 14 inches and the elevation is between 1,900 and 3,100 feet.

Tribal Government

Fort Peck tribes were not organized under the Reorganization Act of 1934, but retained the tribal constitution that was adopted in 1927. It was first amended in 1952, and again in 1960.

The constitution provides for an elected tribal executive board of 12 members, plus a tribal chairman, a vice chairman and a sergeant-at-arms. The tribal chairman has no vote on the executive board, but has general supervision over all tribal employees. All tribal council members are on the seven committees for safety, finance, development, land and minerals, oil and gas, health, education and welfare, and legislature. Any development plans or changes in tribal policies go through these committees, which handle almost all tribal business. Tribal council members usually attend two committee meetings a day, with the whole council or executive board meeting twice a month. A council member can serve on three committees, but can chair only one.

Council members have two-year, non-staggered terms so, like the Blackfeet, Fort Peck's tribes are susceptible to major changes in tribal leadership every two years. As one council member said, "We don't want to go to four-year terms, as we could elect one bad council member and not be able to get him out in four years." On the other hand, another council member said that the problem with two-year terms is that "You spend six months getting to learn how the council works, then you spend twelve months being a council member, and the remaining six months working hard for re-election." However, it is important to say that Fort Peck has been blessed with leadership continuity over the last several decades. This is particularly true at the tribal-chairman level.

Tribal Budget

The tribal budget for fiscal year 1985 at Fort Peck was just under $5.5 million. Approximately 51.6 percent of the budget goes toward social and human resource delivery programs and activities. The remaining 48.4 percent is for governmental operations, capital improvement, natural resources development and economic development.

Natural Resources

The Assiniboine and Sioux tribes have been fortunate to have a rather diverse and fairly abundant natural resource base on the reservation. This is demonstrated by the fact that 85 to 90 percent of tribal revenues comes from the natural resources. Most of this is from oil production.

Even though less than half of the reservation is controlled by the tribes and tribal members, it has an abundance of good grassland, oil and gas, coal deposits and a substantial water supply under tribal control, but many of these resources have yet to be developed.

Agriculture

Earlier attempts to make the Assiniboine and Sioux into farmers have had mixed results because so much of the high-quality farmland on Fort Peck had been sold to homesteaders in the first two decades of this century. Nevertheless, agriculture today is a significant part of the tribes' way of life.

Most farming is on non-irrigated land. In 1975 only 600 acres of Indian land were under irrigation. Today, this amount has increased to almost 12,000 acres and the tribes hope to add another 8,000 acres by the year 2000. Most of the water used in irrigation comes from the Missouri River, but there are plans to develop two reservoirs on the West and East Forks of the Poplar River. Wheat, barley and cereal grains are the reservation's primary crops. Yields of winter wheat are as much as 25 to 30 bushels per acre and barley at times yields as much as 40 bushels an acre.

There is extensive hay production and some cattle ranching. Normally, approximately 8,000 head of cattle are under tribal allottee ownership, but the number is much less now because of current market prices. The tribes and allottees control 500,000 to 600,000 acres of grazing land.

Forest Resources

Fort Peck Reservation has no commercial forests. The total forested land is approximately 12,000 acres, and is almost all cottonwood. The BIA believes 2,700 forest acres have commercial potential, but there is no market now other than for firewood and other domestic needs.

Wildlife

As on most reservations, the potential exists for significant wildlife populations, but the lack of tribal management and law enforcement have kept these populations small. Wildlife on Fort Peck includes mule and whitetail deer, antelope, a good population of upland game birds and waterfowl. The tribes have established goals to provide the maximum amount of wildlife habitat development and land acquisition, to develop and sustain maximum game populations compatible with present dryland uses, and to allow wildlife populations to reach a level where both subsistence and recreational opportunities are available for enrolled tribal members.

While goals are in place and codes are being developed, the question is whether the tribes will be able to implement an enforcement policy that will allow wildlife populations to increase so that the goals of the tribes' Fish and Game Commission can be attained.

Water Resources

For a semi-arid area, Fort Peck Reservation has relatively abundant water, primarily because the Missouri River flows at approximately 8 million acre-feet per year through the reservation. The Poplar River's flow averages about 92,000 acre-feet per year and Muddy Creek and Porcupine Creek average about 21,000 acre-feet per year and the Milk River averaging around 521,000 acre-feet. Now that there is a signed agreement with the state as to how much water belongs to the tribes, they face planning water use for agriculture and other development.

Mineral Resources

Coal. Substantial reserves of lignite in the Fort Union coal formation are found on the reservation, but there is no interest at this time in developing this resource. Any future development would require mine-mouth conversion facilities, because large quantities of lignite, which has a relatively low heat value, would be needed in order to produce electricity or synthetic gas. It is estimated that between one-half and two-thirds of the reservation is underlain by lignite, most of it between the Poplar River and Big Muddy Creek.

Oil & Gas. In the late 1940s, oil was discovered on tribal lands. From the outset the tribes relied a great deal on the U.S. Geological Survey to determine the extent of the resource and how best to use it. Early leases paid out 12 percent in royalties and $1.25 per acre in land leases.

In the late 1970s, when interest in developing oil resources escalated, the tribes began to realize that they should be getting higher royalties, since they owned the land and the minerals. With companies such as ARCO, Sun Oil, Exxon, Hess and others vying for contracts on the reservation, the tribes decided to establish a minerals research office to look into how best to negotiate contracts. With help from the Council of Energy Resource Tribes (CERT) and other outside consultants, royalties from the newly-negotiated contracts went from 12 percent to 16.5 to 25 and even to 55 percent after the payout period (or, after drilling and related costs are recouped).

New stop sign showing lower speed limit than set by Montana near Poplar elementary school attended mostly by Indian students. Michael Crummett

These increases in royalty percentages tell the story of the Fort Peck tribes learning about the oil and gas business. They believe that the BIA and the U.S.G.S. didn't review bids as carefully as they could have, nor did the agencies reject any leases offered them. Tougher, more thorough and more equitable negotiations demanded that the tribes educate themselves about oil exploration, drilling and production. The tribes began to evaluate producing wells, production data and existing leases. They obtained well logs and hired their own consulting engineer to educate the tribes about them.

This new-found knowledge encouraged the tribes to drill their own well and in March 1984, at the Wenona Well hole, they struck oil.

After the euphoria over their success, the tribes realized that they had been lucky and that in spite of their success, contracts with non-Indian corporations for leasing and drilling could be better financial arrangements, because the tribes have no tax write-offs in case of a dry hole. Such write-offs apply only to private corporations and not to tax-exempt entities such as an Indian tribe. To avoid carrying 100 percent of the risk, the tribes have developed a royalty arrangement with U.S. Energy, which is drilling in the new Lustre Field, and pays a 25 percent royalty to the tribes during the payout period and 55 percent after payout.

U.S. Energy already has drilled seven wells with five producing under this contract. Like most wells on the reservation, these vary from 6,000 to 11,000 feet in depth. Some of the oil produced on the reservation goes to Tesoro Petroleum Corporation's refinery between Wolf Point and Poplar to make jet fuel, diesel and gasoline.

No commercial gas is produced at this time on the reservation, but gas flare-offs occur at some oil wells. The tribes' future in oil is an important one. In 1984 up to 24 seismic crews were exploring on the reservation, all working through the tribes' Minerals Office. The Bureau of Indian Affairs has played only a minor role in present exploration and development activities. The tribes independently have identified tracts of land for lease and have developed a new five-year leasing plan for the reservation.

The tribal Minerals Office estimates that approximately 200 people work in some oil-related capacity on the reservation. The office has a budget of approximately $200,000, of which 70 percent comes from tribal income. The Minerals Office is controlled by the Oil and Gas Committee of the Tribal Executive Council.

Economic Development

The Fort Peck tribes have been the Montana tribal leaders in economic development programs. From Tribal Executive Board policy through day-to-day operation, it is impressive how much the Assiniboine and Sioux have accomplished. The tribes have sought a balanced economy based on agriculture, natural resources and manufacturing, and currently 85 to 90 percent of tribal revenues come from land-related activities.

Where Fort Peck tribes have been particularly innovative is in developing a manufacturing industry on the reservation. In 1968, the tribes were selected by the Economic Development Administration as one of 14 planning groups to pursue manufacturing. A tribally-owned industry started up with a defense contract to refurbish M-1 rifles; however, by 1972 it had ceased production because of lack of additional contracts.

A year later Tribal Chairman Norman Hollow was able to convince Department of Defense contractors to look again at the Assiniboine and Sioux. Slowly but surely A&S Tribal Industries flourished. To date A&S Tribal Industries has received over $40 million in contracts, employs approximately 420 people, 75 percent of whom are members of the tribes.

The Executive Board has established two other manufacturing programs, A&S Products Company and West Electronics Company. Although not as successful as A&S

47

Tribal Industries, both have operated at break-even financial levels until recently. A&S Products Industry, operated with a labor force of 10 to 12 making small plastic valves and washers. Its future depended greatly on whether the tribes could build a new manufacturing facility and succeed in obtaining further contracts. However, its building burned in spring 1985 and the company's future is in doubt.

As for West Electronics Inc., it also has operated with a workforce of about eight employees. In 1984 it produced approximately $750,000 worth of printed circuit cards. The tribes are constructing a 15,000-square-foot building to house the company.

Perhaps one of the best ways to measure the success of Fort Peck economic development is by examining its unemployment statistics. In the early 1960s, unemployment on the reservation was between 60 and 70 percent, and today, it averages between 23 percent in the summer and 40 percent in the winter. Although this is still at an unacceptably high level, it is far better than any other Montana reservation except for Flathead. The credit for this lies in many areas. The reservation has a good natural resource base, but the tribes are to be credited for diversifying their economy through the development and maintenance of a substantial manufacturing business. Much can be attributed to clear economic goals and continuity of tribal leadership. Furthermore, tribal politics have not played a negative role in business development.

Major Environmental Issues

Until May 15, 1985 the issue of water rights had been a very important matter for the future of the tribes. Water rights were finally adjudicated and on that date the tribal chairman and the governor of Montana signed the Fort Peck Water Rights Compact. Of course, it remains to be seen how the implementation of the water compact will proceed, but the decision can only enhance the tribes' plans for increasing agricultural production through irrigation.

The Poplar River Generating Station in Coronach, Canada, continues to provide an ominous threat to the tribes' environment. Reduced flow in the Poplar River is occurring and the quality of the water is threatened. Furthermore, the air quality on the reservation will greatly decrease if the generating station is allowed to double again with no sulfur dioxide control equipment.

A tribal member, trained in the Environmental Studies program at the University of Montana, is employed with Environmental Protection Agency funds to monitor air quality and the tribes are developing an air-quality ordinance. Operation of 19 reservation oil fields creates a

Top: *Before the Missouri freezes.*
Left: *Poplar Elementary School. About 75 percent of students in Poplar schools are Indian.*
Right: *Cooling off at Iron Ring celebration.*
Michael Crummett photos

48

concern about their effect on ground water. Plugging abandoned holes and the burn-off of gas emitted from oil wells are environmental issues stemming from oil production. If gas flaring continues to increase on the reservation, it could conflict with the tribes' Class I Air Quality classification. There are land-use issues as well. The tribes would like to consolidate their holdings so that land can be managed more effectively in systematic units, and there is a small land-purchasing program on the reservation.

The traditional cultures of the Assiniboine and Sioux dictate that environmental protection be a high priority at Fort Peck. The tribes have their own Office of Environmental Protection, they have obtained Class I air quality status and most monies used in the tribes' environmental quality endeavors come directly from tribal revenues.

Education

There are no contract or BIA boarding schools on Fort Peck. All school systems are public. Brockton has 140 Indian students (97 percent of the total student population), Frazier has 165 Indian students (100 percent of the school population). Wolf Point enrolls 451 Indian students (44 percent of the the total school population) and Poplar has 685 Indian students (76 percent of the total number of students). Some tribal members attend Nashua and Culbertson public schools and a few go to BIA boarding schools. The tribes are also strongly supportive of the Fort Peck Community College, which is affilitated with Dawson Community College, and NAES College has a strong program in Poplar as well.

In school year 1982-83, 48 tribal members entered college as freshmen. This number increased to 56 a year later. Although the dropout rate is high, the tribes have an incentive awards program funded with oil revenues. These awards amount to approximately $200 per year for those in vocational training or college. The fund also has helped to increase the number of Fort Peck tribal members in the Job Corps. This money is part of an overall assistance program that includes help from the Bureau of Indian Affairs and the national Pell grant program. In 1984-85, 95 awards were made.

Celebrations

The Fort Peck tribes have more celebrations or powwows than any other reservation in the state. The first celebration is the Red Bottom Celebration held in Frazier in June. This is to commemorate the Lower Band of the Assiniboine. Their second celebration is the Badlands

Above: *Sun dance lodges on Fort Peck Reservation.*
Left: *Cloth gifts to the sun dance ceremony.*
Michael Crummett photos

Celebration held later in June at Brockton. The third celebration is the Fort Kipp celebration at Fort Kipp over the Fourth of July weekend. There is also the Wolf Point Wildhorse Stampede, which usually takes place during the second weekend in July. This is more of a rodeo than a powwow. Then during the third week of July the Iron Ring celebration is held in Poplar. This is to honor the last Sioux traditional chief at Fort Peck, whose name was Santee Iron Ring. And to highlight the end of the summer, the Oil Discovery Celebration takes place, which is a five-day festive occasion held north of Poplar during the last week of August. This helps celebrate the discovery of oil on the reservation and is the biggest celebration at Fort Peck Reservation.

a.   b.

a. *Dancing at the Iron Ring celebration.*
b. *Retiring the flags at Iron Ring.*
c. *Passing out food, a kind of giveaway, at the Iron Ring.*
d. *Couples dance.*
Michael Crummett photos

c.   d.

Left: *Sunset over Fort Peck Reservation.* Michael Crummett

The Poplar River Power Project

The Poplar River Generating Station or the Coronach Plant is a coal-fired electrical generating facility built by Saskatchewan Power Company 25 miles north of the Fort Peck Reservation, three miles north of the Canadian border. One 300-megawatt unit was constructed in 1981 and another of the same size went up in 1983; plans are to develop two more similar-sized units depending on demand.

Even though the generating station is almost 30 miles from the reservation, the Assiniboine and Sioux tribes have been worried about what the facility may do to the quality and quantity of water in the East Fork of the Poplar River, and what acid rain may do to air quality on the reservation. The International Joint Commission (Canada and the United States) has been actively monitoring the project.

In 1851 the U.S. government granted all the waters of the Poplar basin to the Assiniboine and the Sioux tribes as long as they could demonstrate past, present and future uses of such waters. The Winters Doctrine that delineated U.S. policy on Indian water rights in 1908 reaffirmed this right, but the Canadian government does not recognize U.S. tribal rights to trans-boundary waters, so the U.S.-Indian policy has no legality in Canada. Today the East Fork of the Poplar is dammed, creating a 30,000 acre-foot reservoir two

and one-half miles north of the border. As a result, the tribes are not at all sure how much irrigation water, if any, can be drawn from the East Fork of the Poplar River because flows have been severely reduced ever since the river was dammed in 1975. Their plans to develop a storage system for 10,000 irrigated acres from the East Fork are in limbo until some resolution occurs. Another consideration is that boron and other dissolved solids have increased dramatically in the East Fork of the Poplar River since the construction of the plant.

The power plant at Coronach uses only a minimal anti-pollution device known as a precipitator and there is no sulfur-dioxide control equipment. The facility emits 12 times as much sulfur dioxide as all three Montana Colstrip power plant units, which produce some 1,500 megawatts combined. As a result, the Fort Peck tribes in February of 1983 asked the Environmental Protection Agency to re-designate the status of air quality on their reservation to the pristine Class I, which was granted in February 1984. Consequently the federal government, through its trust responsibility, must assist in monitoring the air quality downwind of the generating station, and if that quality deteriorates significantly, the government must put pressure on the Canadian government to install pollution-control devices at the facility.

The tribes, along with the non-Indian citizen group, the Three Corners Boundary Association from Scobey, Montana, are limited as to remedies or preventive measures they can seek against Saskatchewan Power because it is an issue involving two countries, a reservation and a state.

Above: ***Quilting.*** *Florence King, who is one-half Yanktonai-Sioux, lives in Brockton on the Fort Peck Reservation. She has been a quilt maker for years and is known as one of the best in the state. The star quilt, an important part of Sioux culture, originally came to the Sioux from Presbyterian missionaries during early Christianizing days. The Sioux women particularly like the lone-star pattern which has become a tribal trademark, and have added a variety of bright colors. When Florence King and others make such quilts, several quilters help with the hardest part, the unique and intricate stitching.*

Quilts are made for a variety of occasions, such as for a newborn child, a person entering adulthood, a marriage, a person returning from the war, a star basketball player or tribal leader. This precious gift is presented at a traditional giveaway during one of the summertime celebrations. Michael Crummett

Brocton Community Center

Zion Lutheran Church on rural Fort Peck Reservation.

Bottom: *Burying a fallen warrior — George Thompson, Jr.'s, funeral. (Photo by family permission.)* Michael Crummett photos

A&S Tribal Industries, Inc.

Probably the most exciting economic development venture on Montana's Indian reservations is A&S Tribal Industries in Poplar. A&S (for Assiniboine and Sioux) is a manufacturing operation controlled by the Fort Peck tribes. It employs 390 people and plans to have employment of 460 by 1986. Of these, 75 percent are Indian people. Annual sales have gone from $13.4 million in 1983 to $21.8 million in 1985. A&S has projected sales of $26.8 million in 1989 in camouflage material and insulated metal food and medical storage boxes used by the Department of Defense.

How did this all happen, and why does it seem to be successful? The answers are found in tribal perseverence, entrepreneurship and strong leadership. In the late 1960s the Fort Peck tribes started an industry that worked on M-1 rifles for the Department of Defense, but because of mismanagement and insufficient contracts this industry closed down in 1973. At that time a manufacturing industry at Fort Peck was like many other Indian economic ventures — successful only in the short run. However, Fort Peck Tribal Chairman Norman Hollow decided that his reservation was going to be different and that in one way or another he was going to make a manufacturing venture on Fort Peck work. Hearing from defense contractors that tribes can't do defense contracting because they don't stick to work schedules, the quality of the work is shoddy, and contracts aren't done in time, Norman took all these allegations as a challenge and proceeded. He argued fiercely that if he got a contract the deadline would be met with a quality product. In 1974, A&S Tribal Industries was started. Extensive training of a work force took place, with Hollow meeting several times a week with the trainees to make sure they understood that this venture's success was in their hands.

A&S's Board of Directors, of which Hollow is a member, hired the Brunswick Corporation under a consulting agreement to do the financial, engineering and marketing management. The board also made sure that Brunswick was allowed to make critical financial decisions without interference from tribal politics.

What took place made history. Contracts were received, deadlines met and the job well done. Turnover has been a problem — it has been as much as 12 percent, but Norman Hollow gives each person who is terminated or leaves his or her job at A&S Tribal Industries a chance to meet

Gaynell Bear Cub, one of about 400 employees at the tribes' A & S Industries plant at Poplar. Michael Crummett

personally with him and discuss what went wrong. Norman is not interested in blaming the individual but in trying to find out ways the plant could treat its workers better and reduce turnover.

A&S received more than $40 million in contracts in 1984 alone. All of these were from the Department of Defense, but the A&S Board is considering developing camouflage material for hunters and photographers in the civilian market. Norman Hollow has the best vantage point to explain why A&S has been successful. Politics have stayed out of the business, he explains, and even though the company is run by the tribes, all profits are put back into the business. A&S is an employment venture, not an income-producing one, and the tribal leadership has respected that. Hollow said Brunswick Corporation has done an excellent

job of fiscal management, and he believes Brunswick has tried to understand the Assiniboine and Sioux and has been most sensitive to their culture. Hollow does not mention his own contribution of leadership, but his continuity of administration and ability to make A&S's success a tribal priority have been critical.

A witness to the value of A&S Industries is that other tribes are using it as a model for similar ventures on their reservations. Flathead, Blackfeet and Northern Cheyenne tribes have considered or have adopted similar ventures. A&S is a good example of industries that employ large numbers of Indian people on reservations and that are not directly related to the tribe's natural resource base.

The Fort Peck
Water Rights Compact

On May 15, 1985, the governor of Montana and the tribal chairman of the Fort Peck tribes, signed a historic treaty delineating water rights for the Assiniboine and Sioux tribes on the Fort Peck Reservation. This was the first such compact between the state and a tribe and it ended five years of sometimes bitter negotiations that threatened at any time to break down.

Because the U.S. Supreme Court upheld Montana's right to adjudicate all state waters, including Indian waters, the case of the Fort Peck tribes was viewed as a test of whether Montana and its Indian tribes could negotiate a water-rights settlement instead of having to go to court. It is now being used as a model in negotiations with other tribes. This historic treaty guarantees for all time the respective water rights of the Assiniboine and Sioux tribes and their nearby water users. It states that the tribes may divert 1.05 million acre-feet of water each year, or consume 525,236 acre-feet of water annually. An acre-foot is the amount of water needed to cover an acre of land to a depth of one foot.

The compact allows Fort Peck to use this water for any agricultural purpose they desire and to divert the water from any surface or ground water source except the Milk River, which is already over-appropriated. Most of the tribes' adjudicated water will come from the Missouri River, which forms the southern boundary of the reservation. Other sources of water will be Porcupine Creek, the western boundary of the reservation; Big Muddy Creek, the eastern boundary of the reservation; and Wolf Creek and the Poplar River. The tribe has agreed to honor existing water claims of non-Indian land owners within the reservation boundaries. It also has agreed to limit its industrial water use in the future, thus restricting major industrial development that uses a lot of water.

An important part of the agreement says that the Assiniboine and Sioux tribes have been entitled to the 1.05 million acre-feet of water since May 1, 1888, which coincides with the date of the Sweet Grass Hills Treaty. This is a priority date, preceding all non-Indian appropriated water rights claimed in the Fort Peck area, and preceding the establishment of the state of Montana, thus pre-empting existing state-appropriated water rights when the tribes actually put such water to use.

It's important also to realize that this compact deals with reserved water rights, a principle determined in the Winters Doctrine of 1906. In the Winters case the U.S. Supreme Supreme Court said "that in the act of establishing any Indian Reservation, one automatically reserves water to meet their future needs and that such water has reserve rights that have priority of all later water appropriations by non-Indians."

The Fort Peck Compact establishes separate state and tribal systems for administering water rights. The tribes will administer all uses of water by reservation agencies, Indian allottees and non-Indians within the reservation who claim a water right under federal law. The tribes also have agreed to adopt their own water code and resolve all disputes among parties under their jurisdiction. The state will administer all water rights established by state law, including those of non-Indians on the reservation. It also will resolve all disputes among state water users.

It is felt that these separate administrative systems will reduce the number of major disputes that might arise. However, to handle major cases, the compact has established a joint tribal-state board. This three-person board consists of a person chosen by the state, another chosen by the tribe, and a third agreed to by those appointees. This three-person board will arbitrate any disputes. The joint board was a provision critical to the tribes to prevent a situation where the state settled all disputes.

Norman Hollow

Perhaps the most important tribal leader in Montana today, Hollow has been on the Fort Peck council for 38 years. He was born in December 1919 on the far eastern portion of the reservation near what was called Fort Kipp. His mother was Assiniboine and his father was Sioux. He attended Fort Kipp Elementary School, then Culbertson High School. Hollow was good at sports, but his first love always has been ranching and riding horses. He raises quarter horses, and in the summer rides two to three hours every evening.

Like so many Indians, Hollow came from a very poor background. He started his ranching career with ten cows,

Norman Hollow. Michael Crummett

part of a cooperative tribal program with the Bureau of Indian Affairs. When he wasn't ranching, he was working with young people in sports and Scouting. In 1942 he was run over by a tractor, which left him with a limp, but he prides himself on being a spry, active person who is in excellent physical shape.

Tribal elders approached Hollow in 1947, urging him to run for tribal council. The tribal budget then was about seven to eight thousand dollars. Although he was reluctant, the elders said that they could see he worked well with young people and cared about the future of the Fort Peck tribes. He has been a councilman for nearly four decades and tribal chairman for 12 years. In 1982 Hollow received the national outstanding tribal leader award from Ken Smith, Assistant Secretary of Interior in charge of Indian Affairs.

Hollow attributes much of his success to learning from the tribal elders in his early years. As a young councilman, he talked with older people about how to approach reservation issues, and he realized early that employment must be the number-one priority for the tribe. Indian people, Hollow said, need to have jobs if they're going to feel good about themselves and raise good families. His commitment to employment and his leadership abilities have helped the tribe to tackle the economic situation in a very definitive way. And, Fort Peck Reservation has had one of the lowest unemployment rates of Indian reservations in the Northern Rockies.

Being on the Board of A&S Industries, a tribally owned enterprise, Hollow visits the plant at least once or twice a month for a first-hand inspection. He also insists on visiting with all tribal members who have been terminated by A&S Industries to learn about the job climate within A&S and how to make the business a good, sensitive employer of the Assiniboine and Sioux. In 1984 Hollow was named Minority Businessman of the Year by the Small Business Administration as a result of his plant operations.

While he was a member of the School Board at Brockton, funds were secured to construct a new elementary school. Although he was no longer a member of the Board in 1974, he was called upon to assist in planning for a new high school. Many believe he was the major reason Brockton was able to get a new high school building, which incidentally has a plaque that reads "Norman Hollow High School."

Despite his enthusiastic work schedule, Hollow's greatest pride rests in his two daughters and his four grandchildren. He is proud of his role in assisting one of his grandsons through high school and college. "And now," Hollow says with great satisfaction, "he is in the oil business on the reservation."

When Hollow finally steps down as tribal chairman, the Fort Peck tribes and the tribes of Montana will have a major leadership void to fill. His continuity of leadership, along with his personality and perserverence, have been essential factors in Fort Peck's economic successes.

Robert Dumont

Perhaps the toughest and brightest educational leader working on Indian reservations in Montana, Dumont was born in 1940 on Fort Peck. Of Assiniboine and Sioux ancestry, he graduated from Wolf Point High School in 1958, and went to the University of Montana for his bachelor's degree. He was one of four Indians at the University of Montana at the time, which had 40 percent of the total Indian enrollment in the state university system.

Dumont worked in the mid-'60s as an educational research assistant for Emory University, and then for Harvard University. Much of his field work was with the Ogalala Sioux in Pine Ridge, South Dakota. Before returning to school to get his master's degree, he also worked for the University of Kansas in educational research. In 1966 he became one of the few Montana tribal members to receive an advanced degree from Harvard University. He later taught at the University of Minnesota and Northeastern Illinois University.

In 1974 Dumont returned to the reservation as the tribal health director and set up the tribe's first health department. He worked in employment before serving briefly as acting president of the tribe's community college when it was started in 1978. Today he supervises and teaches the Native American Education Service (NAES) college program on Fort Peck. One of the founders, he is fiercely proud of NAES's accomplishment in educating key tribal leaders over the last few years, and of its influence on future leaders. He is quick to point out that it is a tough program: "You must be dedicated to get a degree from

Robert Dumont. Michael Crummett

NAES as you've got to hold down a full-time job at the same time."

In looking toward the reservation's future, Dumont believes that Fort Peck is in relatively good shape compared to the other Montana reservations. He strongly feels that the Assiniboine and Sioux of Fort Peck, not the federal government or the state of Montana, hold the key to their own future. Economic self-sufficiency issues are the biggest and toughest issues facing the tribe from his point of view but they won't be resolved, he believes, until there is capability within the Fort Peck tribes to manage businesses and programs. Management, particularly economic management, is the key to Fort Peck's future, and he is determined that NAES will assist the tribe in this area.

Caleb Shields

Caleb Shields recently has emerged as one of the most forceful and articulate tribal leaders in Montana. Of Sioux ancestry, he was born in April 1938 at Poplar. His early youth was spent in the Pacific Northwest and on the reservation. He began school in Poplar and then attended several Indian boarding schools including Pierre and Flandreau in the Dakotas, but still managed to graduate from Poplar High School in 1956. Shortly thereafter he enlisted in the Navy, and was a communications electrician with the Seabees in the early days of Vietnam. After his discharge in 1963, he attended a technical engineering school in Los Angeles and became an electronics specialist. He worked for Vanguard Electronics at several plants, including four years as an operations manager in Mexicali and Tepic, Mexico.

In 1974 Shields returned to the reservation and became the tribal planning director under the auspices of an Economic Development Administration planning grant. He has been very involved in Indian rights activism. He was a participant during the Indian takeover of Alcatraz and then followed the wagon train protest march from Fort Laramie to Valley Forge in 1976, a trip which became known as the Trail of Self-Determination. Shortly thereafter, he was arrested during the attempted occupation of the Bureau of Indian Affairs Interior building in Washington, D.C. He was also a participant in the 1978 "Longest Walk" to Washington, D.C., which was in opposition to anti-Indian legislation being considered at the time.

Shields was elected to the tribal council in 1975. He serves on three committees: safety, development and finance. He also has been the chairman of the Alcoholism Committee of the National Congress of American Indians

Caleb Shields. Michael Crummett

for the past six years. Moreover, he is the immediate past chairman of the Montana Intertribal Policy Board.

Perhaps the most forceful council member at Fort Peck today, Shields enjoys a huge following, and has worked very well with the tribe's chairman, Norman Hollow. Some say he will one day assume the chairmanship, but as he has said, "I want to continue to have a vote in tribal affairs, and a council position provides just that." At times he is controversial and still views himself as an Indian-rights activist and a "keeper of treaties." Shields represents a modern kind of leadership Indians throughout the country, and particularly in Montana, say they need if tribal agendas are to become a reality.

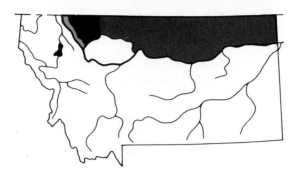

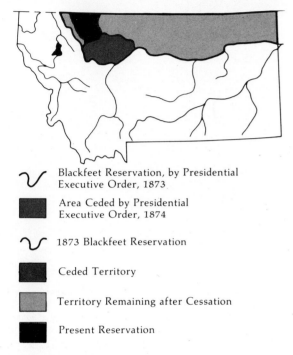

~ Blackfeet Reservation, by Presidential Executive Order, 1873

■ Area Ceded by Presidential Executive Order, 1874

~ 1873 Blackfeet Reservation

■ Ceded Territory

■ Territory Remaining after Cessation

■ Present Reservation

Source: H. G. Fagg and Assoc.: Browning-Blackfeet Comprehensive Plan, Jan. 1970; J. C. Ewers: The Blackfeet, University of Oklahoma Press, 1976.

■ Area Ceded by Agreement, 1888

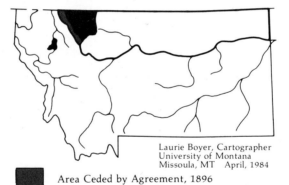

Laurie Boyer, Cartographer
University of Montana
Missoula, MT   April, 1984

■ Area Ceded by Agreement, 1896

BLACKFEET RESERVATION
BOUNDARY CHANGES, 1873 TO PRESENT
Map courtesy of William E. Farr, from *The Reservation Blackfeet, 1882-1945*

History

As the largest and most dominant Indian tribe in Montana, the Blackfeet have played a significant role in the state's history. Like so many of the Great Plains tribes, the Blackfeet originally lived far to the east in an area north of the Great Lakes. It is thought that they even ranged as far east as Labrador. Therefore, anthropologists sometimes classify them in prehistory as one of the eastern woodlands tribes. Like the Cheyenne, Gros Ventre and many others, the Blackfeet are of Algonquian linguistic stock.

After the arrival of Europeans along the eastern seashore in the 1600s, it is believed that the Blackfeet were probably one of the first tribes to begin moving west. Pushed westward initially by their traditional enemies, the Cree, the Blackfeet soon were roaming over a huge portion of the northern plains from northern Saskatchewan and central Alberta to the Rockies, the headwaters of the Missouri and as far south as today's Yellowstone National Park.

There is some controversy about the origins of the name Blackfeet or Siksika, which probably was derived from the blackened moccasins Blackfeet traditionally wore. The dark hue may have been painted purposely or the footwear may have been darkened by prairie fires.

It is thought that the Blackfeet Nation has always been a loose confederacy of three semi-independent tribes. The southern tribe was called the Piegan, the central group the Bloods and the northern division the North Blackfeet. Today, descendents of the Piegans live on the Blackfeet reservation in Montana, and the Bloods and North Blackfeet live on the Canadian reservations (reserves) in Alberta. Although there were some differences among the Blackfeet groups, all spoke a common language, had a common culture and more or less viewed the entire Blackfeet territory as their own.

When the three groups originally emerged onto the Great Plains, they quickly shed the life of woodland hunters and food gatherers and adopted the nomadic lifestyle of the plains Indian. Originally, the dog was their beast of burden, pulling travois in the Blackfeet's search for buffalo.

At the end of the 17th century, most Blackfeet were in what is now the Province of Saskatchewan. In those days before they had the horse, driving buffalo over the piskun, or buffalo jump, was the common way of harvesting buffalo. Long bows, lances and stone clubs were used to make the final kill.

Blackfeet typically traveled across the Northern Plains in bands of 20 to 30 people, which seemed to be the most effective number for hunting buffalo. However, the tribes would come together for various ceremonies and rituals like the sun dance or medicine lodge ceremony and to trade, separating again for the winter. Each band was led by a chief selected for his generosity, bravery and ability to speak well. Chiefs decided band movements and resolved internal disputes. In the early 1700s trading items such as light woven fabrics, pots and metal tools from French and Indian fur traders began to reach the Blackfeet. It is debated, though, who introduced horses to the Blackfeet. Some believe that the Blackfeet first got them from Shoshones to the south. But most historians believe their first horses came from the west through encounters with the Kootenai, Flathead and Nez Perce. Soon after the Blackfeet acquired horses, they also obtained guns by trading beaver pelts and buffalo hides with French fur traders.

All of these new items produced a technical and cultural revolution for the Blackfeet. Furthermore, they soon became perhaps the best horsemen of all the Great Plains Indian nations. They rapidly and aggressively expanded their territory by driving the Shoshone to the southwestern corner of Montana Territory and pushing the Flathead and Kootenai across the Continental Divide into the western

George Bird Grinnell with informants in front of the Sherburne Mercantile. Courtesy, University of Montana Archives

valleys of the territory. Historians speculate that in this advance west across the plains the Piegans were the vanguard, with the Bloods guarding both the northern and southern flanks, and that the North Blackfeet were the last to move west, protecting the rear guard against the Cree and Chippewa.

By 1780, there were as many as 15,000 members of the Blackfeet Nation. Their hunting grounds had shrunk somewhat, since other tribes also had obtained guns and horses, which made it difficult to maintain such large territorial borders. Nevertheless, the Blackfeet, the premier warfaring tribe of the northern plains, were battling almost everyone on the prairies by the 1800s. Their large numbers, horse skills and marksmanship enabled them to continue to be the dominant tribe on Montana's northern plains.

When Lewis and Clark moved through Montana in 1805 and 1806, Piegans controlled all of north-central Montana. In June of 1806 Captain Lewis caught a party of Gros Ventre, thought to be Blackfeet, near the mouth of the Milk River trying to steal some of the exploration party's guns. In the ensuing skirmish two Indians were killed, projecting in the minds of non-Indians the image of the Blackfeet as hard-nosed warriors and scoundrels unfriendly toward white people.

The Blackfeet didn't particularly like American fur trappers, as demonstrated by their hostility toward the Missouri Fur Company, which tried to open a trading post in Blackfeet country in 1810. It immediately had to close down and was reopened in 1821 only to close again. Finally, in 1832, the American Fur Company opened an outpost, called Fort Piegan, on the Missouri River near the mouth of the Marias River. By then the Blackfeet had tempered their dislike for these intruders because the Indians enjoyed the goods that traders brought with them. Besides, the American trappers had adopted the British trade systems the Indians knew in Canada. This was far more palatable to the Blackfeet than the "Big Knife" American trappers of a few years before who were interested only in trapping and ignored a viable trade relationship with Indians.

From 1840 to 1860, the three Blackfeet tribes became more distinct and their home regions better defined. The Bloods and North Blackfeet stayed north of the Canadian border and the Piegan lived south of the border. Although the Piegan Blackfeet were not involved directly in the Fort Laramie Treaty of 1851, the federal government named them as one of the tribes authorized to use that huge part of Montana north of the Missouri River and east of the Continental Divide. It was from this treaty that the eventual Blackfeet Reservation evolved.

In 1855, the first specific treaty between the United States government and the Blackfeet Nation was written. Called Lame Bull's Treaty, it was made with Washington Territorial Governor Isaac Stevens and was designed to stop tribal warfare and to define reservation boundaries. The Blackfeet along with their close allies, the Gros Ventre, were given almost two-thirds of eastern Montana. However, before long their reservation boundaries were reduced again. In 1865 and 1868, two so-called treaties excluding Blackfeet from lands south of the Missouri were drawn up by the federal government. Congress didn't ratify these agreements, but homesteaders flocked into the country in question anyway.

In 1870 the hostility between the Blackfeet and the U.S. government culminated in the Baker massacre. This incident was precipitated by a band of Piegans having killed a prominent settler, Malcolm Clarke, outside of Helena in the fall of 1869. The army decided to retaliate that winter, so Colonel E.M. Baker left Fort Shaw and went north to the Marias River and, in a surprise attack on January 23, 1870, killed almost all of Heavy Runner's band —mostly women and children, who were ill with smallpox.

The Blackfeet Reservation spreads eastward from Glacier Park and the eastern face of the Rockies or the so-called Rocky Mountain Front. Bruce Selyem

Although Baker was supposed to attack the band of Mountain Chief and not that of the peaceful Heavy Runner,

the massacre did stop the Piegans from making further raids on white settlements. The Piegan and Blackfeet continued to hunt buffalo as best they could on what remained of their lands north of the Missouri. However, their territory shrank again by President Ulysses S. Grant's executive orders of 1873 and 1874, which took away from the Blackfeet the land between the Marias River on the north and the Sun River on the south.

In 1877 the Bloods and the North Blackfeet signed Treaty Number Seven with the Canadian government, restricting

them to designated reservations in Alberta. The Piegan Blackfeet remained south of the 49th Parallel, occupying part of the vast reservation north of the Missouri and Marias Rivers.

Even though, in 1880-1881, the Blackfeet still had some successful buffalo hunts, their staff of life had been virtually eliminated. By the winter of 1882 the Blackfeet were destitute. They were forced suddenly to rely on their enemy, the U.S. government. That winter more than 600 Blackfeet died of starvation.

It was this desperate situation that led the Piegan leaders, White Calf and Three Sons to sit down with a United States treaty commission in 1887 to again sell part of the reservation for survival needs. The Sweetgrass Hills Treaty was agreed to and was ratified by Congress in 1888. This land agreement broke up the big northern Montana Indian reservation and set up the reservations of Fort Peck, Fort Belknap and Blackfeet with more or less their present-day borders.

From a reservation that once took in almost two-thirds of Eastern Montana, the Blackfeet now found themselves on a small piece of land in the northwestern corner of Montana's Great Plains. In return the Blackfeet got tools, equipment and cattle to help them become self-sufficient as farmers and ranchers. However, the nearly nomadic hunters did not take to farming nor was it a lucrative occupation on the marginal land of the reservation. Once again, in 1895, the federal government offered a treaty and took more Blackfeet land, seeking valuable minerals in the western portion of the reservation in what is now Glacier National Park.

George Bird Grinnell, a friend of the Blackfeet, and two other officials made up the treaty commission. After heated discussion the Blackfeet were pressured into selling the scenic and revered portion of the reservation. When minerals were not found, this land in 1910 became the part of Glacier National Park from the Continental Divide to the boundary of the reservation.

By the time the Great Northern Railroad was built across the reservation in 1890-1891, the Blackfeet bore little resemblance to the fiercely proud and majestic tribe that had dominated the Montana plains only a few decades before. With no buffalo, a reduced land base, the iron horse cutting the reservation in two and non-Indian trespass for cattle grazing, mining and timber cutting, the Blackfeet at the turn of the century were in a sad state of affairs.

Even though most Blackfeet and non-Indian observers recognized that the reservation lands were far more conducive to raising cattle than to farming, Indian agents continued to try to turn the Blackfeet into a farming people. Agents argued that a sedentary family farm life was the Blackfeet's key to individual self-sufficiency and that, with irrigation, the arid plains could be made productive. In 1907 the U.S. government gave the Blackfeet the authority to allot lands to individual families on the reservation, and a year later, it started building a large irrigation project. The allotment process was completed in 1911 and was bitterly contested by recalcitrant tribal members. Finally in 1919 President Woodrow Wilson signed legislation repealing the 1907 Blackfeet allotment act, which returned all surplus lands to the tribe. Without Wilson's intervention the tribe and its members would have very little of the Blackfeet reservation today, because allottees were selling land to non-Indians just to survive.

Although big irrigation projects were proposed and allotment took place, by 1915 the federal government changed its farming policy on Blackfeet toward an emphasis on ranching. But by 1919, a drought eliminated any economic progress that had been started with reservation farming and ranching. By the early 1920s, the Blackfeet's fragile economy was in shambles with more than two thirds of their members directly reliant on federal handouts. A succession of Indian agents tried to get farming and ranching started again in the ensuing years. This included a Five Year Industrial Plan begun in 1921, based on farming, that produced some positive results. Oil was discovered also in 1921, but it was not seen as a great new economic self-sufficiency opportunity at the time. Timber harvesting also began, but provided little employment and income to Indians. Widespread poverty continued throughout the 1920s, and when Montana Senator Burton Wheeler visited the Blackfeet Reservation in 1928, he found deplorable conditions.

The Depression years brought employment and resource improvement through the Indian division of the Civilian Conservation Corps. The reservation's range and forests were improved, and more jobs were available than at any time since the creation of the reservation. The Blackfeet reorganized under the 1934 Indian Reorganization Act; the land allotment process was terminated, and there was no further wholesale disposal of reservation lands to non-Indians.

Vocational training programs and job placement efforts for Blackfeet tribal members who wanted to live off the reservation were promoted and instituted in the 1940s and early 1950s. There was some talk of federal termination of the reservation, but no real action occurred because the tribe continued to be in a dreadful economic state despite the fact that oil leasing and farming were beginning to bring in some revenue for tribal needs.

In 1964, a disastrous flood ripped down Two Medicine River, killing 30 Blackfeet and leaving hundreds homeless. This proved to be a catalyst in getting a huge new reservation housing program started along with a major

Top: *Early forestry crew on the Blackfeet Reservation.* Courtesy, Montana Historical Society.
Bottom: *Dedication of oil well.* Courtesy, Peter Red Horn

a.

b.

c.

d.

a. Giveaway at Heart Butte, 1945
b. Chewing Blackbone, 1962
c. Sweat lodge, no date.

d. Yellow Kidney, no date.
Photos courtesy of Montana State University Archives.

The Blackfeet Today

Population

As of August 1985, Blackfeet tribal enrollment figures showed that there were 12,711 tribal members with approximately 6,356, just over half, living off the reservation. Enrollment is determined by blood quantum, with one-fourth being the minimum requirement.

Reservation Lands

The reservation encompasses 1,462,640 acres with a little more than 555,000 acres or 38 percent of the reservation owned by non-Indians. The rest is either allotted to tribal members or is owned by the tribe.

The reservation once was covered by glaciers from the Wisconsin Glacial Period. Remnants of old glacial waterways, and benches, are easily seen throughout the reservation. The low point on the reservation is 3,400' and the highest is over 9,000'. Average rainfall varies from 12" a year to 120" a year in the mountains near the Continental Divide. However, the mean annual precipitation across the reservation is 15". The mountains to the west provide approximately a million acre feet of surface water. Major creeks such as Badger, Birch, Two Medicine and Cut Bank wind their way through the reservation as do the Milk and Marias Rivers.

Tribal Government

The Blackfeet formally call themselves the Blackfeet Indian Nation. They organized their government in 1935 under the Reorganization Act of 1934 as a business corporation and a political entity. Its tribal business council originally had 13 members but now has nine members, who are selected from four different districts on the reservation: Browning, Heart Butte, Seville, and Old Agency. Council members are elected for two years, and their terms are not staggered, which tends to cause problems of leadership continuity as wholesale changes in tribal leadership can occur every two years. An executive committee as well as a series of other committees administer the various functions of the tribe. These committees are all headed by a tribal business-council member. The tribal chairman is elected through a general election to a four-year term of office.

industrial development program. The effects of Great Society programs then were felt on the reservation. They provided temporary relief in certain areas of tribal life as schools were built, hospital facilities improved and adequate housing was made available to more tribal members. The Community Action Program, Neighborhood Youth Corps, VISTA and Senior Citizen programs provided assistance to the tribe, as did a series of Economic Development Administration projects. All of this, plus the increasing economic impact of oil and gas revenues, have provided hope to the Blackfeet. Today, the Blackfeet still face severe unemployment problems and fundamental issues regarding treaty and water rights. But thanks to oil and gas and improving tribal leadership, the tribe is in a position to realize a bright future.

Tribal Budget

The total budget on Blackfeet is approximately 11 million dollars. Approximately 5 million dollars comes from oil and gas revenues and agricultural land leasing.

Natural Resources

Agriculture

Since the Blackfeet were first confined to a reservation, the federal government has encouraged them to become farmers and ranchers. But the tribe has never had an easy time adjusting to this lifestyle in part because of the extreme climate and semi-arid land on the reservation. Between 14,000 and 16,000 head of cattle were on the reservation in 1984, yet at one time there were as many as 40,000. However, most cattle today are part of a large non-Indian leasing program. Such a small herd relative to carrying capacity is due in part to the poor cattle market and to lack of tribal activity in promoting the cattle business.

Blackfeet tribal and allottee farming is mainly in barley, wheat and hay crops. Irrigation likely will dictate the amount of farming that will occur on tribally owned and allottee lands. The availability of water and the uncertainty regarding tribal water rights is another important factor. When the water issues are resolved, farming, despite the climatic conditions, could be far more significant than it is now.

Forest Resources

Approximately 10 percent of the reservation is timbered and only 40,077 acres are classified for commercial use. This forest is primarily lodgepole with some spruce, Douglas fir, alpine fir and limber pine. Today, the forest provides seasonal employment for up to 70 tribal members. The tribe realized about $18,000 in fiscal year 1983 from a harvest of 2.3 million board feet of timber.

Before 1945 little logging occurred and most was of dead falls for use by tribal members. In that year, the first forest-management plan was put together. It suggested an annual cut of slightly more than 1 million board feet a year. In the 1972 forest management plan, a more accelerated cutting plan was suggested, with as much as 6 to 12 million board feet a year to be harvested. In 1980 this was reduced to 3 million board feet per year. Obviously, timber is not a large resource on the reservation. Furthermore, the distance from markets and recent market fluctuations in the forest products industry have prevented the tribe from cutting at the maximum end of its allowable cut. Nevertheless, and despite fickle markets, the tribe has been trying to attract a wood-products manufacturing company to the reservation.

In the fall of 1984, a fire consumed 3,400 acres of Blackfeet timber. This drastically changed the total amount of the tribe's commercial forest acreage, and it demonstrated how fragile a resource a small timber base can be.

Top: *A 1984 Blackfeet Tribal Council meeting in Browning.*
Bottom: *Browning.* Michael Crummett photos

Oil well on Blackfeet reservation, Glacier Park in background. Michael Crummett

Wildlife Resources

Because the reservation includes both mountains and high plains, there is great diversity in wildlife populations. Elk, deer, antelope, mountain goat, black and grizzly bear, mountain lion and some bighorn sheep are found on the reservation. Strict regulations have been enacted covering non-tribal members, who are allowed only to hunt upland birds and waterfowl. There is a Wildlife Protection Office and some regulations regarding tribal members have been instituted. These are not well enforced and have allowed overhunting and lower than normal populations of big game animals. There are excellent sport fisheries on

Blackfeet, particularly in Lower Two Medicine, Lower St. Mary's and Duck Lake. Trout, salmon, grayling and northern pike are found on the reservation. All are subject to good tribal regulation and have been managed well.

Oil and Gas Resources

Oil was discovered on the reservation in 1921 but did not become a major economic factor until after World War II. Most of the oil reserves are found on the eastern edge of the reservation in the Cut Bank and Reagan Fields. However, oil was recently found near the western boundary at Two

Medicine and East Glacier. As of 1982, 238,000 acres of land were under a total of 920 leases. At that time, there were 643 producing oil wells and 47 producing gas wells. Production exceeds 50 million barrels a year.

As much as 90 percent of the annual income of the tribe is from oil and gas. Therefore, the demand and price for oil and gas greatly affect the tribe's economic situation. Some of the largest energy companies in the world, including Chevron, ARCO and Union Oil of California, have oil and gas leases on the reservation.

Oil and gas leasing practices on the reservation have not favored the tribe. However, a new leasing contract with Damson Oil in 1975 made leasing much more advantageous to the Blackfeet. As a result of this contract, the tribe is allowed to participate in management decisions and profit sharing. In return the tribe assumes some of the financial risks. The Damson contract has encouraged the Blackfeet to ensure that other oil and gas leases involve the tribe and that royalties and bonuses are more equitable.

In 1981 some discrepancies were uncovered in the accounting of how much oil was being taken off the Blackfeet reservation. At the time, oil production logs were left solely to the oil and gas companies. However, a much publicized case of "missing run tickets" made the tribe realize how much it needed to monitor closely exploration

Lower Two Medicine Lake straddles the reservation-Park boundary. Bruce Selyem

and production. Today the tribe's oil and gas office has access to all seismic data, monitors all seismic activity and keeps a close watch on all production. The office also has employed a tribal elders committee that monitors all lease sales and seismic activity, so that sacred and religious sites, important in Blackfeet history and traditions, are not damaged.

Besides all of this monitoring the Blackfeet have several joint ventures with energy companies. They also have developed their own venture based on geological, seismic and production information gathered from past exploration and production activities, so that they can promote their own expertise for profit with oil companies that are entering into new leases on the reservation.

Other Mineral Resources

More than 3 million tons of sub-bituminous coal are estimated to be located on the reservation. Although this is adequate for domestic use, it is not enough for any sizable commercial mine. (For example, Westmoreland Resources on the Crow ceded strip has the capacity to mine 11 million tons per year for at least 20 years.) Bentonite (an adhesive) and titaniferous magnetite (used in the hardening of steel) have been found, but due to poor markets, accessibility and the limited size of the reserves, there has been no development.

Tourism and Cultural Celebrations

The proximity to Glacier National Park provides a unique opportunity for Blackfeet people, in that more than 2.3 million people drive through the reservation each year while visiting Glacier National Park. There are tribal campgrounds such as Chewing Black Bone and Red Eagle, but most tourist facilities in and around the entrances on the eastern park boundary are owned by non-Indians. The Museum of the Plains Indian, at Browning, has excellent dioramas of ancient plains Indian life. The reservation has several buffalo jump sites. With approximately 175 miles of rivers and streams and eight major lakes, the reservation also has great potential for more recreational and tourist development.

The annual Indian celebrations on Blackfeet are highlighted by the North American Indian Days Celebration (mid-July). At least four rodeos, the largest being the Babb Rodeo over the 4th of July weekend, take place on the reservation. Smaller Indian celebrations occur at Starr and Heart Butte in late June and early July, respectively. All of these events involve dancing, singing, drumming, stick games, give-aways and rodeos.

64

Opposite page:
Top: *Grand entry, Native American Indian Days, a major Blackfeet celebration.*
Bottom: *Blood Indian, one of three major divisions of the Blackfeet nation, with travois.*
This page:
Above left: *Deer Clan tipi, Native American Indian Days.*
Above: *Otter Clan tipi.*
Left: *Seal of the Blackfeet Nation.*
Michael Crummett photos

Education

The three public elementary school districts and one high school district on the reservation are controlled by elected school boards with the majority of members being Blackfeet. The public high school is located in Browning. The BIA maintains a dormitory for high school students who come from poor home situations or live in remote parts of the reservation. The Blackfeet Community College in Browning, established in 1976, is in its final stages of accreditation. Progress in education has been helped greatly by federal legislation passed in the 1970s including the Indian Education Act, the Indian Self-Determination Act, the Community College Assistance Act, the Elementary and Secondary Educational Program Act and the Impact Aid Program. Still, the Blackfeet students lag behind national averages. For example, the 1980 census showed that in Glacier County, which includes much of the reservation, approximately 5 percent of Indians who were 25 years or older had a college degree, compared to 18 percent of the non-Indians living in the county. Severe reductions in federal funds for education in the past few years have raised concerns about the quality of education on the Blackfeet Reservation in the future and the variety of programs that can be offered, such as vocational education and the community college.

Economic Development

With the median family income at a little more than $5,000 annually (compared to Montana's statewide average of some $18,000) and with unemployment ranging from 60 to 70 percent, it is easy to understand why economic development is a high priority of the Blackfeet Nation. The only significant employers of Blackfeet tribal members today are the tribe, the school system, the hospital and the Blackfeet Indian Writing Company. The latter is a tribal enterprise, located in the tribe's industrial park at Browning. The firm originally started with help from the Small Business Administration in the early 1970s and today employs nearly 100 tribal members. The idea of making pencils was attractive to Blackfeet leaders because of the availability of wood and because it was a labor intensive industry. The company's total daily production exceeds 300,000 pencils, 100,000 ball-points and 60,000 markers.

The tribe has been developing annual comprehensive economic plans since 1972. Early plans called for development of an industrial park, recreational campgrounds, better education facilities, new hospital, and expanding the land base of the tribe. All of these initial goals met with moderate to excellent success. Neverthe-

The Sweetgrass Hills, lost to the tribe by treaty, on the horizon from the Palookaville Road. Bruce Selyem

less, unemployment remains high. So in a recent assessment of tribal needs in 1984, economic development was the first priority. Others, in order, were community services, housing, education and natural resource development. The tribe's most recent economic development plan has a specific goal of creating 500 new jobs for tribal members by 1989. Natural resource development is one of the tribe's preferred approaches. Ideas include water development, wind energy, an expanded farming and cattle base, more intensive timber management and development, and more oil and gas production.

Another hope for employment is securing Department of Defense contracts for the tribe's new electronics company, patterned somewhat after A&S Industries on Fort Peck Reservation. The tribe also has plans for a log home sawmill and recently announced a plan for a large all-season resort facility located on the shore of St. Mary's Lake. There is hope that such a facility could be constructed by 1988 when Calgary, just a few hours to the north, hosts the Winter Olympics.

Lack of capital is the main limitation on these projects. In the fall of 1984, Browning's only bank closed, which set back individual economic development efforts because tribal members and the tribe have to go off-reservation for loans. The tribe wants to develop a capital revenue fund of

its own, possibly with oil and gas revenue monies. However the tribe's per capita payments policies make such action difficult.

Looking to the Future

The Blackfeet Nation must resolve the reservation's extremely high rate of unemployment even though the lack of capital is a significant barrier to economic development. Furthermore, the problem of a very small managerial pool among tribal members often makes new economic projects only marginally helpful in that they can only employ the unskilled labor force on the reservation.

The other high priority issue for the tribe is to clarify its rights to land, water and timber on and near the reservation. For example, there is still a rights and ownership issue regarding the eastern portion of Glacier National Park and the tribe's claim to timber there. The 1895 agreement ceding the eastern portion of Glacier Park retained the tribe's rights to fish, cut wood, hunt and graze on that land. The federal government today claims that those rights were lost when the land was made into a national park in 1910.

Another unresolved land issue has to do with the ownership of a portion of Lewis and Clark National Forest just south of the reservation. This jurisdictional issue between the federal government and the Blackfeet Nation has led to a negotiated proposal to manage jointly approximately 12,000 acres of the forest. A significant timber resource, important water rights, oil and gas reserves and substantial wildlife populations are at stake.

Another issue that will become more and more important to the tribe has to do with the ownership of valuable agricultural land on the reservation. A large agricultural corporation recently was sodbusting a substantial number of acres of the non-Indian lands within the reservation. Although this has been halted temporarily, the tribe is particularly worried that such sodbusting will resume and it would like to buy back as much of these prime agricultural lands as possible. There is also growing friction about the use of Birch Creek between the tribe and the two Hutterite colonies that own and farm approximately 15,000 acres of land within the reservation boundaries.

Perhaps the most important natural-resource issue facing the tribe is ownership of the water on the reservation. The tribe has not submitted to adjudication with Montana's Water Compact Commission. Although all other tribes on Montana reservations are proceeding with such negotiations, the Blackfeet have steadfastly refused to do so, because they have adopted an aggressive water code stating their belief that they own all of the water flowing through the reservation. In 1979 the Bureau of Indian Affairs contracted with the Helena engineering firm of Morrison-Maierle for a baseline study that showed much of the reservation to be suitable for irrigation. This report assumed from historical documents that the water in the Milk and St. Mary's Rivers belonged to the tribe. Because of these results, the Department of the Interior commissioned a new study. Furthermore, when filing water claims for the Blackfeet with the state of Montana, the federal government refused to include the Milk and the St. Mary's Rivers because of the Bureau of Reclamation projects located downstream from the reservation on both of these rivers. One of the outcomes of these federal actions was that the tribe formally resolved to provide no cooperation whatsoever in the new study.

Other issues that face the tribe are political. For one, the Blackfeet Reservation crosses the boundaries of two counties, which has prevented the tribe from having a fair impact on county politics. The tribe would like to see the county boundary lines redefined so that the reservation is in one county. Another political issue that needs to be resolved is that tribal elections are held every two years for everyone except the chairman. This potential for the lack of political continuity has stymied economic development and other important tribal planning projects.

The Blackfeet have been at the forefront on the issue of taxation. Can a tribe tax oil, gas and other property within reservation boundaries, or can the state tax such minerals and other properties? This is particularly important for the Blackfeet, as sources of federal money are rapidly shrinking. On June 3, 1985, the United States Supreme Court ruled in favor of the Blackfeet's position that the tribe and not the state can tax oil and gas royalties on non-Indian lands within the reservation's boundaries. This court case symbolizes a major issue to all Montana tribes, because of its bearing on the funding of tribal governments. However, the decision has been initially interpreted as addressing only taxation of royalty income, and not whether the state can tax non-Indian producers on reservations. Further court debate is sure to follow.

Although the Blackfeet's future remains uncertain, their substantial natural resources, relatively large population and aggressive posture regarding sovereignty and rights issues, make the tribe's future brighter than those of many of their tribal neighbors.

Stick game. Bruce Selyem

Hand Games or Stick Games. *An Indian sport that dates back to the 1880s when the buffalo had all but disappeared, the hand game is a favorite pastime of all Montana tribes. Each reservation has a series of tournaments each year, often with teams from other reservations.*

Roger Clawson of the Billings Gazette *best describes hand games this way: "They are part poker psychology, part ritual and medicine-making, part pep rally and totally sociable." Basically it is a game of hiding and guessing. A member of one team hides an object in one hand or another. A member of the opposing team guesses which hand. The games have a captain or a medicine man who has been given the right to organize and lead a team. Such teams have anywhere from 10 to 40 players,* *who are both men and women, and sport similar colors and dress.*

Accompanying the action of each team are singers to chant and drum their team to victory. At least 20 women with rattles follow the tempo set by the drums. Several players who have purchased the right to guess complete the team.

The game begins with 14 sticks or bones on the floor between the two teams and ends when one teams has picked up all 14 bones. The game between two teams could continue all night, as there is no time limit.

Along with the fun and competition, there are usually prizes that would reach as high as $5,000 or more during the tournament. In addition, individuals in the audience wager hundreds of dollars on side bets.

Cut Bank Pass, one of the main east-west routes over the mountains for raiding and war parties. Bruce Selyem

And How Did the Government Acquire the Land for Glacier National Park?

At a time when mining exploration was still a major factor in the selling of the west, precious metals discoveries in the Little Rockies on Fort Belknap and just east of the Continental Divide on the Blackfeet Reservation, precipitated the establishment of a three-man commission which was to return these areas to the public domain by buying them from the Indians. The commission first went to the Blackfeet to negotiate for their mountain lands, lands that today are in Glacier National Park, north from the Northern Pacific Railroad to the Canadian border and east from the Continental Divide to the present western boundary of the Blackfeet Reservation. The head of the U.S. commission was none other than George Bird Grinnell, naturalist and long-time friend of the Blackfeet and other western Indian tribes.

At the outset of the negotiations, the commission offered to purchase the mountain lands for $1 million. The Blackfeet, smarting from previous takeovers by the federal government and by what they thought was a pittance settlement for the Sweet Grass Hills in the Treaty of 1888, were adamant about getting a better price. They asked $3 million. Many tribal members didn't want to sell at all, but they were completely dependent on the federal government and had no money left from the 1888 Treaty, so tribal leaders were not in a good negotiating position. Nevertheless, for the first few days they held firm with their demands — as did the commissioners.

At one point, Grinnell told the Blackfeet leadership that they were asking three times what those mountains were worth, and that he did not want to go back to Washington and have Congress laugh at the Blackfeet for demanding so much money. It was important, he said, for the tribe to get the one million dollars, so that their children could go to school and so the tribe would be able to buy cattle to become economically self-sufficient. He sought to compliment the Blackfeet by saying:

"You have improved so much from being a savage people, that I want to see you are helped for ten years more by another agreement, you will then not want any more help. You will be able to walk alone, like the white man. The only difference will be the color of your skin. Try to think of things carefully, and let us know whether we are to go or to stay."

With that, the Blackfeet leaders were told to go and talk about the agreement among themselves. They returned, adamant about their $3-million demand. The negotiations were dissolved and the U.S. Indian agent, George Steele, and a local Indian trader, Joe Kipp, talked long and hard with the Blackfeet. They eventually got the tribal negotiators to accept a compromise figure of $1.5 million, to be paid over a 10-year period, with 4 percent interest.

The Blackfeet apparently took Grinnell's comments to heart. However, largely because of the leader Big Brave, the tribe retained hunting, fishing and timber-cutting rights on the sold land. This later became an issue of contention, after the land received national park status in 1910. But Article I of the agreement, signed by the tribe and ratified by the United States Congress, said that the tribe had reserved the right to "cut and remove ... wood and timber for agency and school purposes and for their personal uses for houses, fences, and all other domestic purposes ... to hunt upon said lands, and to fish in the streams, so long as the same shall remain public lands of the United States."

The Blackfeet still claim that they have timber and hunting and fishing rights in the park. The U.S. government maintains the Blackfeet held those rights until Glacier was made a national park after no minerals were found in the "ceded strip." The government claims that the national-park legislation takes precedence over the treaty. So, the Blackfeet currently don't hunt, fish or cut timber in the eastern portion of Glacier Park, nor do they get a percentage of the park entrance fee. Only time and possible litigation will determine whether the Blackfeet still have any rights to this portion of Glacier National Park.

Top: *Eagle staff on Rocky Boy's Reservation.*
Right: *Evening dances, Native American Indian Days.*
Michael Crummett photos

Eagle Feather

Soaring high and alone, the eagle is the symbol of power, courage and freedom to Indians. It is a sacred bird, viewed by many as the messenger from the Great Spirit. Therefore, the feather, particularly the fore feather or tail feather of an eagle, is a sacred symbol, and many ceremonial costumes and warrior paraphernalia include eagle feathers in their design.

The federal Bald and Golden Eagle Protection Act makes it illegal for non-Indians to possess eagle feathers, and it's illegal for all people, including Indians, to kill this rare and endangered species or trade in eagle parts. Yet eagle feathers continue to be in high demand among Indian tribes and in 1983 the Fish and Wildlife Service uncovered the killing of 200 to 300 bald eagles on and near a wildlife refuge in South Dakota. These eagles were used to supply the black market trade in Indian artifacts. Many people, including Indians, were arrested.

Earl Old Person

Earl Old Person is one of the most highly respected and honored Indian leaders in the west. A full-blood Piegan, he was born in 1929 on the Blackfeet Reservation. He grew up in the community of Starr School and graduated in 1936 from Browning High School where he had been an outstanding basketball player.

Old Person has spent all his life representing the American Indian and specifically, the Blackfeet. His easy-going nature and his willingness to communicate with all kinds of people have made him popular with people from all walks of life, but many a non-Indian has been brought up short by Old Person's determination to promote and protect Indian rights and interests.

A staunch traditionalist, he speaks fluent Blackfeet and is an excellent traditional dancer. His Indian name, Cold Wind or Changing Home, was given to him by his grandfather.

Old Person worked for the Plains Indian Museum in Browning before going to work in 1953 with the Land Department and then the tribe's credit program. At that time he also became the Blackfeet tribe's official interpreter for those members who could not understand or speak English. He still plays that role today.

At the age of 25, Old Person was elected to the Tribal Business Council and has served continually for more than 31 years. When first elected, he was the youngest person ever to be elected to such a position. In 1964 he became chairman of the Business Council and has held that position since except for two years in the late 1970s. He also has served as president for a variety of organizations throughout the country, including the National Congress of American Indians and the Affiliated Tribes of the Northwest. He has served on more state and national committees and organizations than any other Indian leader in the Northern Rockies. These include the Board of the National Indian Bank, National Council of Indian Opportunities, Governor's Task Force on Indian Affairs, National Advisory Council on Aging. He was chairman of the reorganization of the Bureau of Indian Affairs in 1977. It's no wonder that he was elected lifetime chief of the Blackfeet Tribe in 1978.

In looking back over the years that he has been on the Business Council, Old Person is particularly pleased with his involvement in obtaining a new hospital, as well as in getting an adequate claim settlement for the Sweetgrass Hills Treaty of 1888. He is proud of the Blackfeet Writing

Earl Old Person. Michael Crummett

Leonard Mountain Chief.
Michael Crummett

Company, where he currently is Chairman of the Board of Directors. Old Person believes that unemployment is the tribe's number one social issue and that if unemployment does not decrease, the tribe's future is bleak.

Old Person believes that the most critical natural resource issue is the tribe's water rights, and he said, water is "the lifeblood of the reservation." He, along with most of the present Blackfeet leaders, is still angered about the government's attempt to deny the tribe water rights on the Milk and Marias Rivers.

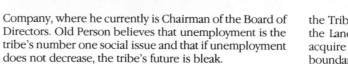

Leonard Mountain Chief

One of the most colorful Indian leaders in Montana, Mountain Chief was born in November 1939 on the Blackfeet Reservation. The great-grandson of the last Blackfeet war chief, Mountain Chief, Leonard is a staunch traditionalist who lives in Heart Butte, known since the beginning of the reservation as the most traditional community of Blackfeet.

Mountain Chief received his graduate equivalent diploma in 1955 before serving in the Navy for a year and a half. He has worked for the tribe for more than 15 years in various capacities.

His great-grandfather gave him his eagle forefeathers when he was two years old. "That's something you have to earn," Mountain Chief says, and he feels that now he has, because of his time in the Navy and his three elections to

the Tribal Business Council. He was also the chairman of the Land Board for the Tribe and currently works to re-acquire non-Indian lands within the reservation's boundaries.

Mountain Chief is known as a great old-time fiddle player, and he competes all over the country. "I try to set an example for young Indian people that I, an Indian, can go out into the other world and succeed with my fiddle." Mountain Chief tells Blackfeet youth that self-esteem and a viable future for Indian people go hand-in-hand.

Mountain Chief believes that the tribe must resolve the unemployment situation through a variety of economic activities, including agriculture. "Ranchers used to be the backbone of the reservation," he said, adding that it is not so today and may not be again, unless the tribe has more capital and the cattle market recovers.

"We need Indian people in money-making businesses on reservations," he said and he's not pleased to see all the businesses just outside of Glacier being run by non-Indians. "Managerial skills are something we need more of within our people," Mountain Chief says. "Then the non-Indian Glacier 'strip' would not happen."

Mountain Chief believes the Blackfeet future could be very bright if "we have the right people in good leadership." He said that the sooner the Blackfeet quit relying solely on the federal government, the better off the tribe will be. That's why he is so adamant about wanting tribal members to establish and maintain their own businesses. Although Mountain Chief is a traditionalist and promotes Blackfeet identity, he strongly believes that Blackfeet can't go on in isolation from the rest of the world.

Myrna Galbreath.
Michael Crummett

George G. Kipp. Michael Crummett

Phillip Roy. Michael Crummett

the freights and taking temporary construction jobs. He found an important job during the oil and gas "mini-boom" in the late '70s and soon after became tribal coordinator and the director of natural resources.

Kipp has been instrumental in reorganizing the oil and gas leasing activities on the reservation and changing the accounting systems so that the tribe knows more about oil and gas production figures.

Until recently, Kipp did all the accounting for reservation oil and gas extraction. He also assisted in planning other natural resource development activities.

Although recently having resigned the directorship, mainly because of internal politics, Kipp says he is proud that the oil and gas program has become one of the most stringent in the country for accountability by energy companies to tribal governance.

Phillip Roy

One of the toughest and most aggressive advocates for Indian people in Montana, Phil Roy has served as general counsel for his Blackfeet tribe since 1971, easily the longest tenure in the state for a tribal attorney.

Born in Browning in 1938, Roy worked as a laborer for the Great Northern Railway and a variety of construction companies after high school. He was graduated from Gonzaga University in 1960 and obtained his law degree from the University of Montana in 1963.

Phil's advocacy for human rights became known statewide when he was appointed director of the state Economic Opportunity Office in Montana in 1969, where he served for two years before becoming the Blackfeet tribe's attorney. He also has served as general counsel for Fort Belknap and Rocky Boy's tribal governments. Today Roy works full time maintaining and protecting the rights of the Blackfeet tribe and its individual members. He, along with his wife and four children, are proud to be living in Browning with fellow tribal members.

Roy immediately captivates a visitor to his law office with stories of the latest complex legal efforts against the Bureau of Indian Affairs, oil companies, sub-dividers, and the U.S. Forest Service. But he says he enjoys playing a low-key role as the tribe's legal resource even though he could have pursued his legal career to more visible state and national levels. Both adversaries and friends alike give him unusually high marks for his commitment to the betterment of the Blackfeet.

Myrna Gailbraith

One of the few Blackfeet women to be elected to a tribal leadership position, Myrna Gailbraith currently serves as member and Secretary of the Blackfeet Business Council. No one on the Blackfeet Reservation today knows more about the tribe's day-to-day operations than Gailbraith.

Born in 1940 and educated in Browning, Gailbraith attended college for a year, and returned to the reservation to work for the tribal court. Soon thereafter she participated in the Bureau of Indian Affairs relocation program and was sent to California for training in bookkeeping and auditing. She served as an auditor for Mutual of Omaha before returning home to work at the high school. She later became a counselor at one of the housing projects on the reservation.

Gailbraith is also on the Housing Authority Board and is actively involved in the tribe's home-improvement program. She said she believes that adequate housing is essential for tribal members to defeat low self-esteem.

A mother of four, Gailbraith decided to run for the Business Council in 1984 because, as she put it, "I want to change the system. I've been on the other side; I know what the people aren't getting." Her spirit and her work experience have made Gailbraith an excellent new council member as well as a superb role model for Blackfeet women.

Gailbraith believes the biggest issue facing the tribe is a psychological one. "We must believe in ourselves" she said. She said she hates welfare but thinks it may be a necessary evil for now. "Welfare can take the spirit out of the people."

George Gerald (G.G.) Kipp

Kipp typifies many Indians in their 30s who were in school during the tumultuous days of the late '60s. A staunch traditionalist who often goes by his Indian name, Eagle Flag, Kipp was born on the reservation, but because his father was in education, he lived in many different places throughout the West. He attended Flandreau Indian School in South Dakota and then went to Haskell Junior College in Lawrence, Kansas, the University of California at La Jolla, U.C.L.A., University of Montana and Northern Montana College. Kipp drifted in the early '70s, often riding

CHIPPEWA-CREE

Tribal Histories

Nestled in the foothills of the Bearpaw Mountains, and extending north toward Old Fort Assiniboine, is Rocky Boy's Reservation. Established in September of 1916, it is the newest reservation in the state. At the time, it went against all federal Indian policy, which advocated termination of the reservation system and assimilation of the Indian into western civilization.

Rocky Boy's Reservation, like many other reservations, has two tribes residing on it — bands of both Chippewa and Cree.

The Chippewa are from the largest of the Great Lakes tribes. Algonquian in language, bands of this tribe dominated the area from Lake Huron west to Northern Minnesota. They were nomadic and first encountered white fur traders in the Great Lakes in the 1600s. Slowly the Chippewa began to move west when the furs in the Great Lakes region became depleted. By the mid-1700s, most Chippewas were on the western edges of the Great Lakes region, but some bands had gone to the Turtle Mountains in North Dakota, and some had joined their Cree neighbors to the north in Canada. Both the Turtle Mountain Chippewa and those who went to live with the Cree changed their way of life toward hunting the buffalo.

It is not known exactly when the Chippewa came from the Turtle Mountain Region into Montana. More than likely, this happened well after 1875. Most historians believe that the Chippewa came to Montana under Chief Rocky Boy (Stone Child), or accompanied Chief Little Shell and his Chippewa band. They probably left the Turtle Mountain country because the designated reservation was not big enough and they believed they had been short-changed and left out of the negotiated settlement of the so-called "ten-cent treaty" in 1892, which involved selling one million acres of Turtle Mountain Reservaton for $90,000 (see Little Shell history).

As for the Cree, they were also found in the Great Lakes country, but far to the north in the vicinity of Lake Winnipeg and Lake of the Woods. Also of Algonquian dialect, the Cree were mainly of Canadian descent and bands were found as far east as Labrador. The Cree began to move westward in the mid-18th century and allied themselves with the Assiniboine and became a major force on the Great Plains. They too followed the buffalo, and eventually encountered Sioux and Blackfeet around 1800.

Initially the Crees had a near monopoly on guns and horses and, therefore, had a decided advantage over their Blackfeet rivals. By the mid-1800s, however, the Blackfeet also had obtained horses and guns and the Crees' influence became more limited.

Smallpox devastated the Cree as it did so many other tribes and they suffered with the decline of the buffalo. After the Treaty of 1818, in which the Canada-United States boundary was established, many people south of the border thought that the Cree were Canada's problem. Despite United States and Canadian efforts, many roving bands, particularly under the leader Big Bear, wouldn't stay north of the border and continued to pursue the few remaining buffalo south of the line. Big Bear refused to sign treaties until 1882, when he signed the Canadian treaty that guaranteed his band rations.

The Cree continued to wander and refused to settle on a reservation. Big Bear then made the fateful mistake of aligning with the Metis under Louis Riel. Riel was seeking recognition for the Metis, who were Canadian-Indian mixed bloods. In March of 1885, after repeated attempts at gaining recognition, he announced the establishment of a Metis province on his own. Thus began an armed rebellion against the Canadian government that lasted two months. Actually, Big Bear's band played only a supporting role, but still he was jailed for three years. His son, Little Bear, was more active as was another sub-chief, Wandering Spirit. Wandering Spirit was hanged, but Little Bear escaped with approximately 200 of Big Bear's band and came to the United States.

Unwanted by Indian and white alike, Little Bear and his band of Cree began to wander from town to town and from reservation to reservation. Little Bear thought that his group could settle with the Flathead in the Bitterroot but were rebuked. Therefore, his band usually camped in the winter near Fort Assiniboine and in the summer roamed the state in search of food and work.

In 1889, when Montana was given statehood, there was an immediate clamor to send the Crees back to Canada. In 1896, Little Bear, in defiance of the state law outlawing the sun dance, held the sacred religious ceremony just outside of Helena. The band was deported, but they came right back into Montana by late fall of the same year.

Over the next 20 years, both Rocky Boy's band and Little Bear's band roamed the state, rejected and destitute.

Montana residents wanted them away from the outskirts of towns; citizens suggested putting them on the Flathead Reservation, then on the Blackfeet Reservation and later on the Crow Reservation. None of these proposals worked, and in 1908 the Chippewa-Cree bands were a pathetic group. A coalition of Montana residents recognized their destitute situation and began to demand a reservation for these "homeless" bands. A move was afoot to establish the reservation somewhere in Valley County (Glasgow), and a proposal surfaced to carve out 11,000 acres northeast of Babb on the Blackfeet Reservation.

An allotment was made for the Chippewa-Cree on the Blackfeet Reservation, but most refused the allotments and by 1911 were all back on the outskirts of Helena. In 1912, a proposal was made to set aside 92,000 of the 160,000 acres of the Fort Assiniboine military reservation. Havre residents wanted no part of this idea; so it was thwarted again in 1913, even though the bands by then had taken up semi-permanent residence on the military reservation.

Meanwhile, the two bands were viewed differently by Montanans. Rocky Boy's people had the image of being good workers who did not engage in petty theft. This was not the case for Little Bear and the Cree, therefore efforts were concentrated on helping Rocky Boy, with little assistance planned for Little Bear.

Finally, in 1915, after the bands had resided on the military reservation for more than a year, another proposal surfaced to put the Chippewa and the Cree on the southern and westernmost part of former Fort Assiniboine. Only 55,040 acres were suggested this time, and an 8,880-acre park (known today as Hill County Park) was put between the tribes and Havre to create as much separation as possible between Havre residents and tribal members.

In April 1916 Rocky Boy died. He had gotten along well with whites and as a result played an instrumental role in obtaining the reservation that would bear his name. President Woodrow Wilson signed an executive order on September 17, 1916 creating Rocky Boy's Reservation. Ironically, the 451 initial members of the reservation were by then under Little Bear's leadership.

During the first years after the creation of the reservation, the Bureau of Indian Affairs administered Rocky Boy's from Blackfeet and then from Fort Belknap. The Chippewa-Cree had great difficulty adjusting to the sedentary life after the nomadic one to which they had become accustomed over the years. Therefore, the concept of self-sufficiency was extremely difficult to implement. This was accentuated because plentiful employment could be found off the reservation in the summer, when tribal members were supposed to be hard at work trying to learn and to practice agriculture on their tribal lands. But, in the winter when employment was most needed, it wasn't available.

Above: *Little Bear, 1896, leader of a landless band of Cree, who eventually were settled on the old Fort Assiniboine military reserve.* Courtesy, Montana Historical Society

Below: *Rocky Boy led his Chippewa band during 20 years of wandering before the reservation bearing his name was established in 1916.* Photo courtesy, Museum of the Rockies

In the Bear Paw mountains, on the southeastern edge of the Rocky Boy's Reservation. Michael Crummett

Unfortunately, the result was that rations contributed increasingly to their existence. Despite the reservation's bleak semi-arid landscape, the first agricultural efforts began to bear fruit. However, a severe drought beginning in 1917 nullified self-sufficiency through agriculture. Rations became the way of life and reduced Little Bear to the role of beggar. His following was ill-fed with little or no housing, poor clothes and no schooling.

As the drought subsided, bad farm prices became another obstacle to agricultural self-sufficiency. All during the 1920s, Rocky Boy's Reservation was in a disastrous situation. Increasing conflicts with the Bureau of Indian Affairs made things even more difficult. This became critical when Congress appropriated only one-third of what the Indian agent at Rocky Boy's wanted. By 1928, 200 of the tribal members lived off the reservation in the summer

trying to find work, but came back in the winter. It was almost as if things hadn't changed since before the reservation was established.

Fortunately, the federal Merriam Report in 1928 began to change things for the Chippewa-Cree as well as for other Indians in the country. In spite of all of the problems with allotment on other reservations, tribal members at Rocky Boy began demanding the allotment of their lands. By this time the BIA had realized from its experience on other reservations that allotment wasn't working. The Bureau delayed going through with the process and the allotment practice was abolished in 1934 with the passage of the Indian Reorganization Act.

During the 1930s it became obvious that Rocky Boy's Reservation could not support all of its enrolled members. The government did not know how to deal with this reality,

other than to try to figure out a way to expand the reservation. During the New Deal, under John Collier, 90 percent of the Chippewa-Cree were employed through the Indian Emergency Conservation Program. This infusion of federal funds delayed the inevitable need for the Chippewa-Cree to increase their land base. Another drought hit in 1936 and more and more of the Little Shell band of Chippewas began to come onto the reservation, making it even more obvious that the reservation couldn't fully support its tribal residents. By the end of 1936, the reservation population totaled 855, including 250 non-enrollees.

Some land expansion did take place in the late 1930s, and in 1937 a 78,000-acre acquisition was proposed. Congress never funded it, and it wasn't until 1947 that an additional acquisition of 45,523 acres was made. However, a condition was attached — that 414 of Montana's landless Indians be added to the tribal rolls, swelling the total reservation population to approximately 1,500.

After World War II, the termination policy led to Rocky Boy's Reservation coming under a consolidated jurisdictional arrangement, with the Bureau agency located at Fort Belknap. It remained there from 1947 until 1965, when it was returned to Rocky Boy's Agency. Other than that, reservation life remained about the same.

In 1949, enrollment was slightly fewer than 1,200, with 50 percent of the enrolled members living off the reservation for employment (and survival). The basic problem of too many people and too little land had not disappeared. Moreover, those who stayed on the reservation were in such destitute condition that a Rocky Boy's Rehabilitation Bill was introduced in both houses of Congress. It died in committee because of lack of support.

As the Chippewa-Cree faced the government's new era of self-determination in the 1960s, they found themselves with a land base that had doubled since 1916, and a population that had tripled. Most members lived from day to day, with no clear thought about the future. As Montana State University professor Tom Wessel so eloquently stated, "The government has treated Rocky Boy's as an outdoor asylum for social deviants, who hopefully someday would assimilate into the western world."

Wessel's analysis concluded that the BIA never clearly saw Rocky Boy's as a community or as an economic entity and allowed the reservation to drift without definition or direction. Therefore, the descendants of Little Bear and Rocky Boy deserve all the credit that the reservation still survives.

Now the reservation has a new attitude about its future. The following description of life today at Rocky Boy's reflects the determination of the Chippewa-Cree people to have a home and a place to maintain their culture.

Fall cattle drive on the reservation. Michael Crummett
*Chippewa-Cree Ski Area at Baldy Butte, Bearpaw
Mountains. One of two tribally owned ski areas in the
country.* Photo courtesy of Montana Intertribal
Policy Board

Rocky Boy's Reservation Today

Factual Information

As of December 1984, tribal enrollment was 3,108 members. About 40 percent of these people live off the reservation. Enrollment on the reservation is governed by the tribal constitution, which requires that enrolled members have one-half Indian blood. If one's parents live on the reservation, any level of Indian blood quantum entitles one to enrollment. However, members can be stricken from the rolls if they are gone from the reservation 10 years or more. The reason for this stipulation has to do with the reservation's limited size and resources to handle a large enrollment.

Reservation Lands

The reservation has grown from 55,040 acres to approximately 108,015 acres today. It is totally owned by the tribes, with no allotments. Tribal members can have assignments of one to 160 acres, which can be made to a tribal member for his or her life. Such assignments are viewed as temporary, and are not inherited. One third of the reservation is in the Bear Paw Mountains and two-thirds can be described as plains and foothills. The elevation ranges from 2,500 feet to 6,916 feet at the top of Mount Baldy in the Bearpaws. Precipitation ranges from 12" to 40" per year. Most of the reservation land is semi-arid.

Government

Rocky Boy's tribal members acted swiftly to be organized under the Indian Reorganization Act of 1934 (IRA). In the fall of 1935, only seven of 179 voters elected not to reorganize in a way that was consistent with the constitutional form of government promoted by the IRA.

Today there is an elected tribal business committee of eight and an elected tribal chairman, all serving staggered four year terms. Business committee members also serve on the various committees of tribal government. Therefore, being a tribal business committee member is a full-time job.

Tribal Budget

In fiscal year 1985, tribal government operated with a $491,000 budget. Only $200,000 comes from general revenues, of which $50,000 is from leases or tribal agricultural activities. The rest of the tribal budget comes from indirect costs stemming from the many federal programs that operate on the reservation. In fiscal 1985, the total budgets for federal programs operating on the reservation were just over $5.7 million.

Natural Resources

Much like the Fort Belknap Reservation, Rocky Boy's Reservation has few natural resources of economic consequence. Although the reservation is located in an aesthetically pleasing setting, it is not a place where self-sufficiency can be achieved through the abundance of natural resources.

Agriculture

Lack of irrigation, and the rolling terrain, have limited grain production on the reservation. The tribes do operate Dry Fork Farms through a Business Development Committee. Here, approximately 4,500 acres are under wheat and barley production. In 1984, production figures for winter wheat were 15 bushels an acre and for spring wheat, 13 bushels an acre. These figures are low because of the severe drought of 1984, which also affected hay production. Only 800 tons of hay were produced in 1984, compared to the usual 1,600 to 2,200 tons.

In the 1930s the tribes had approximately 600 head of cattle, but today the herd is down to 200 head, even though there is plenty of grazing land to support a much larger one. Lack of capital and a poor economic market have thwarted attempts at expansion.

Forest Resources

During the early days of the reservation, timber was an important part of the reservation's economic activities. The government operated a sawmill from 1927 to 1938. The BIA throughout that time promoted forestry because of the relatively high quality of lodgepole, Douglas fir and ponderosa found on the reservation. Today total forest acreage on the reservation is estimated at 20,532, of which only 12,552 acres are commercial. The huge Mount Sentinel fire of 1984 consumed 10 percent of all the reservation's lands, including a great deal of its commercial forests. Because the forests are isolated from markets, no harvesting has taken place for several years. Small post and pole operations are likely to be the most profitable uses of the reservation's timber resource.

Wildlife

Big-game species are not plentiful even though good habitat is available. A herd of approximately 70 elk move on and off of the reservation in the Missouri River Breaks country. Small populations of mule and white-tail deer are scattered across the reservation and there are plenty of pheasant, grouse and beaver. Although the tribes employ a full-time game warden who tries to enforce the spotty regulations, wildlife populations are not likely to change significantly until the regulations are made more comprehensive and the tribes make wildlife a priority.

Mineral Resources

In 1931, the Bear Paw Mining and Drilling Company signed a 20-year lease with the tribes, to mine gold, silver, zinc, lead, copper and vermiculite. Even though the lease shows that a royalty should have been paid to the tribes, payment was never made and in 1945 the BIA cancelled the lease. There are no active mines now, although there has been some exploration for uranium.

Gas has been discovered on the reservation and the tribes have had a gas contract with Montana Power Company since 1967. The reservation has seven producing wells, with 12½ to 16-2/3 percent royalty payments. A new agreement recently was negotiated that will increase the royalties to 20 percent after payout (after drilling and constructions costs are paid). A new lease agreement has been completed with Southwest TAL Corp. for a five-year exploration period. However, no bonus or advance payments will be made because the lease is a highly speculative one.

Recreational Resources

The tribal business committee has established the Chippewa-Cree Tribal Recreation Area to take advantage of the scenic beauty and high relief of the Bearpaws. The main feature of this area is the Baldy Butte Ski Resort. The ski area boasts some of the best powder in the West, but the powder tends to arrive in "big dumps" followed by long dry spells. The ski area is open on weekends and the chair lift is run by tribal members. The tribes hope to operate the recreation area year-round with hiking, fishing and camping in season. More than 40 campsites already have been established. Unfortunately Baldy Butte Inn at the base of the ski area burned down in 1983. Nevertheless, tribal leaders see the Baldy Butte area as an important economic asset in the tribes' economic future. The essential missing ingredient is large numbers of people living in the vicinity to make such an enterprise economically viable.

Top: *Rocky Boy's Reservation from the Bearpaws*. Photo courtesy of Montana Intertribal Policy Board
Bottom left: *Rocky Boy High School cross-country team*. Michael Crummett
Bottom right: *The Rocky Boy's Reservation has seven producing gas wells*. Michael Crummett

Natural Resource Issues

A major concern facing the tribes is how to make the best use of their natural resources and at the same time promote the tribal goal of self-sufficiency. With so few resources and with timber having been severely depleted by fire, the future economic self-sufficiency on Rocky Boy's Reservation is precarious.

The tribes' Natural Resources Department is making a major effort to oversee and manage the resources to the greatest extent possible. Currently, the department is doing an exhaustive inventory of its resource base, which includes computerizing all of its natural resource records. This natural resource inventory is being funded partially through the government and through the tribes' meager

revenues from current natural resource development. The department recently negotiated the Southwest TAL Corporation's five-year drilling program, and is responsibile for attempting to reforest the huge 1984 burn area.

The number-one natural resource issue on the reservation is water rights. Because the tribes do not have a major body of water on the reservation, they are trying to assert claim over all waters that originate there, mainly Box Elder, Big Sandy, Sage, Duck, Camp, and Beaver Creeks.

Another major environmental issue has to do with land acquisition. The tribes are negotiating with the state of Montana and the Bureau of Land Management to acquire state and BLM lands within the reservation or adjacent to it. All of this and more is needed for the tribes to have a more adequate land base.

Left: *The Rocky Boy buffalo herd.* Michael Crummett
Right: *Sunset over Rocky Boy's Reservation.* Michael Crummett

Sweat lodge on Pryor Creek, Crow Reservation. Michael Crummett

The Sweat Ceremony

The sweat ceremony is a sacred religious ritual providing tradition-minded Indians what they believe is an opportunity to communicate directly with God. It's a simple, straightforward ritual of prayer for loved ones, those who are ill or those about to take on a major challenge. "Traditionals" attend a "sweat" much as non-Indians go to church. Some partake in such a ritual a few times a year and some nearly every day.

The ceremony takes place in a lodge that has been blessed by a tribal medicine man to make it a spiritually acceptable place of worship. The dome-shaped lodge is constructed of willow saplings and is approximately four feet high. Covered with blankets, skins and any other material that can help retain the steam, it will accommodate four to 12 people, who sit or lie around a rock pit in the center.

Worshippers place heated rocks in the pit and close the skin-covered opening, creating total darkness. Prayers begin the ritual along with the burning of sweetgrass, as smoke is believed to be one way of communicating directly with God. The hot rocks are sprinkled with water while the ceremonial leader leads the rest in prayer and song. There can be as many as four periods of praying in a sweat ceremony. During each period more and more water is sprinkled over the rocks, driving the temperature within the lodge to well over 200 degrees. After the prayer ritual, which can last one or two hours, the participants cool themselves in a nearby creek or, in winter, the cold air or a water hose suffices.

On some reservations, such as Rocky Boy's, people wear clothes during the sweat. Other tribes do a sweat in the nude. Some allow only men in the sweat lodge but most tribes involve men and women in the ceremony.

Despite tribal variations, the sweat ceremony is one of the spiritual realities of every-day, traditional life. Its simplicity and religious reverence make it a moving and unforgettable experience for non-Indians who are invited on occasion to participate.

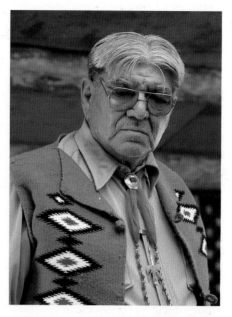

Feasting inside the Native American Church at Rocky Boy's Reservation.

Above: *The half circle of sand represents the story of birth to death in this Native American Church ceremony.*
Right: *Bill Denny, Sr., brought Native American Church to the reservation.*
Michael Crummett photos

Native American Church

The Native American Church, or Peyote Cult, is active on most reservations in Montana. The cult or religion didn't fully develop with the Plains tribes until the 1880s, when it helped Indians through the drastic cultural changes they were having to make because of the disappearance of the buffalo and the Indians' dependence on the federal government.

A nativistic movement, the church was fully developed as we know it today by the Kiowa and Comanche tribes far to the south, and it came when the ghost-dance movement was emerging among the Sioux nations. In contrast to the ghost dance, the Native American Church promoted a philosophy of conciliation and resignation instead of a philosophy that was threatening to white supremacy. The Native American Church is a highly individualistic religion with the primary purpose of promoting the search for personal power. The religion and its rituals replaced the vision quests common among Indians before the 1880s.

The Northern Cheyennes were the first to bring the peyote ritual into Montana in 1904, and the Crows quickly adopted it and helped make it available on Rocky Boy's Reservation by at least 1934. Indian agents had resisted the Native American Church from its beginning until John Collier became Commissioner of the Bureau of Indian Affairs in 1933. He reversed this "outlaw" policy and promoted the Indian's right to choose his own religion. It wasn't until 1944 that the Native American Church received its official charter from the United States Congress. Today the Church has the largest membership of any Indian religious group in the United States.

The church, like any other religion, has a ritual, a doctrine and an ethical code. On Rocky Boy's Reservation the church has a building, but the ritual does not need to take place in a formal church structure. The ritual is performed inside with a straight-flamed fire at the center of a circle and a moon-shaped altar to one side. The meeting or service is held at night and is usually from 11 to 12 hours in length. All meetings have some kind of a purpose, such as honoring a loved one, praying for the sick, or commemorating a tribal holiday. A major part of the ritual is praying for life, health, luck, freedom, peace and happiness, accompanied by singing and drumming. Preceding a long period of contemplation, church members consume peyote, which is a type of cactus that comes mainly from Texas and is hallucinogenic to many.

The doctrine of the peyote cult is founded in the fundamental belief in power, spirits and various incarnations of power. It is believed that power is essential if one is going to be successful and healthy, and that peyote has such power. It is through the ritual that this power is conveyed to those involved and to those for whom the meeting is called. The ethical code, or the peyote road, has four rules: brotherly love toward all, care of family, self-reliance and avoidance of alcohol. There is a strong and fundamental belief in God, morality, industry, charity and appropriate living underlying these basic rules.

The night-long prayer meeting is followed by a morning feast. Church members then go their way and reconvene for a specific need.

Many believe that the Native American Church has emerged as an important force in promoting intertribal solidarity. It also has been given credit for bringing tribes together, and providing a common ground for traditional and transitional Indians. Its supporters think that it has been helpful in assisting Indians with transitions from native cultures to today's way of living.

Some Indian traditionalists are very much opposed to the religion because it is not an old one. There's little question that it's not an easy religion because the peyote itself is so bitter and can cause sickness, and only the hardy can sit for ten to twelve hours at a time. Most active members of the church say that one has to experience the ritual in order to find out about the peyote cult and how it can promote a purposeful life and higher self-esteem.

John Windy Boy

John Windy Boy. Michael Crummett
Rocky Stump. Michael Crummett

development. He believes the Chippewa-Cree Development Committee Company was an essential step in securing economic enterprises for the reservation. He emphasizes the success of the small, new propane company and hopes that the ski and recreation area will begin soon to realize its economic potential.

Windy Boy has been available to the new chairman, Rocky Stump, who has high praise for him and wants Windy Boy's assistance.

Senator John Melcher said on the eve of John Windy Boy's retirement, "He has given the best of his life to make the sun shine for his people."

Rocky Stump

The newest tribal chairman in Montana, Rocky Stump was born in 1935 and raised on Rocky Boy's Reservation. A full-blood Indian of predominantly Cree ancestry, he is fluent in the Cree language. He attended Parker and Haystack Bureau of Indian Affairs schools on the reservation but never finished high school.

He left the reservation before reaching the age of 20 because he could not make a decent living. He worked on a ranch for five years picking rocks and baling hay, before joining the army. Rocky spent 28 months in the Far East and saw action in Korea. When he was discharged, he came back to again do ranch work, but could not support his wife and six children. Stump and his family returned to the reservation to take advantage of Indian Health Service care and other amenities, while he worked in the CETA program. Eventually he found employment in the tribe's housing authority and spent four years as a maintenance person. He also did maintenance work and drove buses for the elementary school.

In 1980 Rocky won a seat on the tribal Business Committee and almost immediately became vice-chairman. In 1984, with tribal elders solidly behind him, Rocky ran for chairman and won by 100 votes.

Over the last five years Rocky has been a dedicated tribal leader. He has worked particularly hard at developing the tribes' agricultural enterprise, Dry Fork Farms. With Economic Development Administration assistance, this farming project includes dry-land farming and ranching with a small tribal herd of 200 cattle. He thinks Dry Fork Farms will be instrumental in lowering unemployment.

John Windy Boy

One of the great unsung leaders of Indian people in Montana over the last two decades, John Windy Boy retired in November 1984 after more than 15 years as tribal chairman of Rocky Boy's Reservation.

A 15/16-blood Chippewa-Cree, Windy Boy was born in March 1925 on Rocky Boy. Although he attended Bureau schools on the reservation, he never did receive a high school diploma. He was employed as a cement-finisher in construction work for more than 23 years before he was elected in 1966 to the tribal Business Committee. Three years later he was elected tribal chairman.

Windy Boy is a great family man; he and his wife have nine children, many of whom still live on the reservation. He is fluent in his native language and has been a leader in maintaining the tribal traditions of his people, frequently seeking the advice of tribal elders.

Windy Boy immediately points to the new Indian Health Service Clinic, the Senior Center, the community building and the facility to house the tribe's police and tribal court as his successes during his tenure. John also is pleased that the tribe was able to contract many programs with the Bureau of Indian Affairs, but most of all, he points with pride to the emergence of education on the reservation. He is particularly pleased that a contract high school was established, and enjoys pointing to the tribal building which has been converted into the high school — leaving the tribal administration in the basement of the alcoholic treatment center.

Perhaps his greatest disappointment has been watching the effects of federal budget cuts in the areas of tribal health care and education. Because the tribe has few natural resources and owns little land, the federal government has played, and will continue to play, a critical role in the economic and social well-being of the tribe, and Windy Boy is discouraged to see the federal government abandoning so many Indian programs.

Looking to the future, Windy Boy is pleased that the tribe is doing all it can in long-term planning for economic

"We've got to bring more jobs onto the reservation to resolve our 80 percent unemployment problem," Stump said. As tribal chairman he would like to expand production at Dry Forks Farms and rehabilitate the burned-over forest and to get better housing on the reservation. Stump also plans to keep education as the number one tribal priority and to find a way to build a new high school.

Another major issue for Stump is to negotiate the tribes' water rights with the Montana Water Compact Commission.

Stump has dedicated himself to learning how best to fulfill his new leadership position, and he has benefited greatly from a close working relationship with the retired chairman, John Windy Boy, which helped a smooth transition in tribal leadership. Despite his busy schedule, the chairman still takes time to pursue his favorite pastime, rodeoing. Rocky specializes in calf-roping and team-roping.

Ron Swan

Daryle Wright

Peggy Nagel

Ron Swan & Daryle Wright

Ron Swan and Daryle Wright work as a team on Rocky Boy's Reservation, managing the tribes' precious natural resources. Swan is the Director of Natural Resources for Rocky Boy's Reservation. Born in 1949 at Fort Belknap, he is Chippewa and Cree. He graduated from Box Elder in 1966, drifted for a few years and worked for three summers in Yellowstone National Park. After taking vocational training as a forestry technician in Missoula, he went on to the University of Montana to pursue a degree in social welfare. Upon returning to Box Elder and the reservation, Swan became the Economic Development Administration Coordinator and helped with the establishment of the Baldy Butte ski area on the reservation. In 1982 he became Assistant Director of Natural Resources and in 1984 took over the directorship.

Wright is the Water Resource Coordinator on the reservation. He was born in 1952 in Washington state, then moved to California and lived there through the eighth grade. He returned to the reservation in 1969 and earned his graduate equivalent diploma a year later. After two years at a junior college in California, Wright became involved in the confrontation between the federal government and the American Indian Movement at Wounded Knee and other Indian-issue activities in the early '70s. When he returned to Montana in 1975 he worked in the state's weatherization

program, settling back on the reservation in 1976 as an outreach worker for the Bureau of Indian Affairs. Soon he was involved in weatherization and solar utilization work. He promoted the construction of a solar greenhouse and directed the tribe's community garden program before becoming Assistant Director of Natural Resources in 1981. In 1982 he became Director of Natural Resources and was selected the tribe's employee of the year in 1984. Wright decided to let Swan take over the directorship so that he could concentrate all his energies on water because, to him, this is the most crucial natural resource issue for the tribe.

Peggy Nagel

Born in Great Falls in 1952, Nagel has more or less always lived on Rocky Boy. She is three-quarter Cree and the mother of two children. After graduating from high school in 1970, she attended Northern Montana College, University of North Dakota and then Northern Montana again, in pursuit of her bachelor's degree. She taught elementary school in North Dakota before returning to the reservation in 1979 as federal grants coordinator. Nagel left Rocky Boy's again to obtain her master's degree in school administration in 1982, returned to become adult education instructor and is now Education Director for the tribe.

"I feel fortunate to be home and employed," Peggy says.

She states with pride that education is the number-one priority on Rocky Boy's Reservation. That's not idle talk because Rocky Boy's Reservation has the highest percentage of college graduates of any reservation in the state. "We have people going back to high school right now and getting their Graduate Equivalency Diploma — people that I would have never dreamed of — mainly because education is so important to us." Nagel said education promotes self-confidence, which she expects will lead Rocky Boy's tribes to a brighter future.

Even though she can't speak Cree, she can understand it and spends as much time with her 85-year-old grandmother as possible learning about the past. This precious time has led Peggy to take strong stands about the tribes' elders. She says, "One of the most important things that we've still got to do is to take better care of our elders. Perhaps we need to develop cluster housing so our elders will have a decent place to live in their older years. We need to provide better health care for them than we are currently providing." Such comments from a 33-year-old reflect the priority placed by Indian people on elders. She said, "They have such a wealth of knowledge — it's enjoyable for me to be around them."

Nagel has a clear vision about the reservation's future and is not at all afraid to state it to anyone willing to listen. Given the small size of the reservation, she realizes that the tribes can't develop total self-sufficiency here. She believes that perhaps the reservation should be an educational and cultural center for Chippewa-Cree people and a place for them to live in retirement. She is opposed to the notion of leveling the hills for uranium or coal when the reservation is such a beautiful, spiritual place for the Chippewa-Cree. The land to her represents more than potential income. It's symbolic of her past and culture and it anchors her vision of the future.

Tribal Elders

A tribal elder, or senior citizen, within an Indian tribe, generally is perceived and treated with more respect and held in higher esteem than those of similar age in the non-Indian culture. They are seen as critical in maintaining the culture of the tribe, providing personal advice to tribal members, and giving important counsel on a regular basis to the tribe as a whole.

On most reservations a core leadership of traditional elders is sought out for the members' wisdom and they can be extremely influential in tribal matters. These traditional elders are held in higher esteem than other elders, because they have not been trained in non-Indian culture and have worked hard to practice their tribes' traditions in everyday life. Male and female elders are usually active in the traditional ceremonies such as sweats, the sun dance, clan meetings, and the Native American Church. They are the people who communicate stories, songs, ceremonies and common-sense advice to the next generation.

Most elected political leaders on the reservation claim they use elders extensively for advice. Former tribal chairman John Windy Boy on Rocky Boy's Reservation regularly involved elders in tribal council meetings their counsel on critical issues facing the tribe. Fort Peck tribal chairman Norman Hollow was recruited originally by tribal elders to run for tribal government and, in turn, has asked them to provide advice to himself and the tribe. Younger tribal members often mention their concern about elders and how they are treated on the reservation. Peggy Nagel at Rocky Boy's Reservation feels that an important tribal priority is better housing for elders there. She also tries to spend as much time as possible with older people because of their common-sense outlook on life as well as their eagerness to share the tribes' cultural history.

Art Rainingbird. Art Rainingbird is perhaps the most important elder and religious leader on Rocky Boy. Born in Havre in 1907, he is a full-blood with Chippewa, Cree and Blackfeet bloodlines. He never went to formal school, yet spent years with tribal elders learning about Indian ways and customs. A strong believer in traditional Indian lore, Art is the only person on Rocky Boy's Reservation who can bless the sweat lodges. He is also the only person who knows many of the old sun dance songs of the Cree. Today he is passing on the songs and chants to younger tribal members, including William Stump, Sr. It is in Stump's backyard that Art almost daily presides over an afternoon sweat.

Rainingbird is employed part-time by Rocky Boy's High School to help with their bilingual program. This includes teaching young Chippewas and Crees about old customs, songs and religious rites. His strong religious background and tribal knowledge were the subjects of a book written by a Montana State University professor, Verne Dusenberry, in the late 1950s. Today, Rainingbird is perhaps the most well known and respected Indian spiritual leader in Montana. Michael Crummett

Mary Ground. Perhaps the oldest Indian living in Montana, Mary Ground was born in 1883. A Piegan born near the Belly River in Alberta, Ground crossed to the United States on a travois when she was small. Her Indian name is Grass Woman. An adopted child, she attended elementary school at the Catholic Holy Family Mission on the reservation. Ground was 16 when she married. She became the mother of 14 children, whom she raised on a small ranch near Starr School. She is both a strong traditionalist and a devout Catholic. Today she lives in Browning with her many grandchildren and great-grandchildren. In 1978 she wrote Grass Woman's Stories, which contains 12 Blackfeet stories that she told to her granddaughter Cynthia Kipp. Michael Crummett

Estelle Lefthand Blackbird (left) and *Wanita Tucker* are two Assiniboine tribal elders. Tucker is 89 and Blackbird is 96. Blackbird, who is now blind and deaf, has a hard time communicating except in her native tongue. As for Tucker, she was born "when the cherries were ripe," and is not sure exactly when her birthday is. She was orphaned as a baby and raised by her aunt. Tucker knew no English before she went to school. She went to school voluntarily when she was old enough because she feared that the Bureau of Indian Affairs would take her away if she didn't, as had been the case with many of her friends. Once in school she wasn't allowed to speak Assiniboine, which made boarding school a most trying experience. Having lived in an old lodge throughout her early years, Tucker now wonders, "How did we ever make it through those old times?" She still shudders at the thought of regularly bathing in the creek in the winter.

Wanita and her husband, Joe Tucker, a logger, raised 11 children. She received honorable mention as Senior Citizen of the Year in Montana in 1979, and is proud to say she still has her own allotment.

Tucker is a respected tribal elder who is regularly sought out for advice. She is not at all defensive about her past and is very pleased to see young tribal members getting some education. But she declares that "young people today have it a lot easier than we ever used to." Michael Crummett

Louis Gingras. A Kootenai, Gingras is credited by some with being born in 1893, although other people (including Gingras) are not sure. He was born on the reservation, went to the mission school at St. Ignatius, then to Fort Shaw Indian School, and eventually attended Carlisle in Pennsylvania. Gingras has spent almost his whole life on the Flathead Reservation and is known as a great storyteller and communicator of Kootenai lore. Today, he lives with his relatives at Kicking Horse Job Corps Center near Ronan. Michael Crummett

Robert Yellowtail. Born in 1889, the year Montana became a state, Robert Yellowtail was for five decades the single most powerful member of the Crow tribe. He was not only tribal chairman for a time, but also the Crow Agency BIA superintendent for 12 years. Although controversial at times, Yellowtail has fought long and hard to save the natural resource base of the Crow tribe and to keep the tribe together. Faulted by some for supporting Yellowtail Dam and backing the general-council form of government that was established in 1947, Yellowtail is unquestioned in his concern and work for self-sufficiency and equality for Crow and all Indian people. Michael Crummett

CROW

Top: *Crow Indians swimming in the Yellowstone River (date unknown).* Courtesy, Montana Historical Society
Bottom: *Crow sun dance, 1941.* Montana State University Archives photo

Tribal History

The Crow, like the other plains tribes now in Montana, originally came from the Upper Midwest, that is the Mississippi Headwaters country as far north as Lake Winnipeg, Canada. Of the Siouan linguistic family, the Crow were part of the larger Hidatsa tribe and practiced a rather sedentary, agricultural lifestyle before they started to migrate west as early as the late 1300s. Their first migration took them as far as the Devils Lake country in northeastern North Dakota. After about 100 years, they slowly resumed their western journey, first entering what is now far eastern Montana and western North Dakota as early as 1600. They lived along the Missouri River and Yellowstone River bottoms, continuing a sedentary way of life raising crops and hunting bison, elk and deer. During this period, the Crow continued to be a part of the Hidatsa, who lived in earth lodges along the Missouri River primarily in what is now western North Dakota. The Crow, however, relied increasingly on hunting. Eventually they left the Hidatsa and moved into the Black Hills and eastern Wyoming, building a life around the buffalo.

When the Crow came into Montana in the 1600s, they lived along the headwaters of the Tongue and Powder Rivers, as well as along the Yellowstone. This territory remains their historic domain. Originally the Crow may have intended to move farther west, but they were restricted from doing so by the Shoshone, who had come into Montana from the Great Basin country to hunt buffalo.

When the horse first was introduced into the Great Plains Indian cultures in the 18th century, the Crow quickly became excellent horsemen and prospered. Their first meeting with Europeans probably came about 1740, but it wasn't until 1795 that a meeting of whites and Crow documented such contact. In 1806, members of the Lewis and Clark Expedition with Captain Clark spent more than a month in Crow Indian country and developed excellent relationships with Crow people. Shortly thereafter, the Crow's country was frequented by fur traders who also got along well with the Crow. This history of early amicable relations with whites led to a treaty of friendship in 1825 between the federal government and the Crow Nation.

The Crow in the Hidatsa language are called Absarokee, which literally means children of the large-beaked bird. Other tribes called Crows "sharp people," meaning that they were as crafty and alert as the bird, which was probably the raven. Also, in sign language, Absarokee was communicated by flapping one's hands as if they were a bird's wings in flight. Thus white explorers and traders applied the name Crow to this Montana tribe.

In the early 1830s, the Crow Nation divided into two groups, the River Crow and the Mountain Crow. The River Crow spent much of their time in the Judith and Musselshell River valleys, and the Mountain Crow stayed in the foothills and mountain country south of the Yellowstone River in Montana. The two groups frequently gathered for traditional ceremonies and they intermarried. In the late 1830s, the Crows were decimated by smallpox. It is estimated that as much as 20 percent of the Crow population was killed by the dread disease. This epidemic coincided with the white man's growing interest in the buffalo, which had brought the tribe and white buffalo hunters and traders into close contact. Crows, like so many Indian tribes, found themselves very vulnerable to many of the white's diseases, which continually reduced the Crow Nation well into the 1850s.

When the Fort Laramie Treaty of 1851 was signed by the Crow and many other plains tribes, Crow territory generally was recognized as the land encompassing southern Montana and northcentral Wyoming. The purpose of the treaty was to allow white settlers and prospectors to move through Crow and plains Indian country without being attacked. In return, the Indian tribes were to be given various annuities and trade goods. However, Congress changed the annuity payment from 50 years to 10 years and and gold was discovered in Montana, which brought more whites into the area. After more conflicts, another Fort Laramie Treaty was negotiated in 1868. This closed the Bozeman Trail that had gone through the heart of Crow country and set aside much of the area for the exclusive use of Indians. At the time, the Crow's major enemies were the Northern Cheyenne and Sioux, who also had encroached on Crow country. Thus the Crows were most anxious to sign the treaty as they believed that the United States government would help protect their territory from further attacks from these warring plains tribes. It is this treaty that forms the basis of Crow title to their reservation today, even though their boundaries have been modified substantially in later agreements with the federal government. Both the Mountain and River Crows lived on their de facto reservation after the 1868 treaty, with their agency being on the Yellowstone at Mission Creek eight miles east of Livingston. In 1869 the federal government began to "civilize" the Crows and encouraged them to become sedentary farmers. It was at this time that the famous Crow chief Plenty Coups emerged as a major leader and negotiator between the Crows and the federal government. He strongly promoted the importance of education and made the Bureau of Indian Affairs provide it.

Although the Sioux and Northern Cheyenne tried to get the Crows to work with them against the continuous stream of "white intruders," the Crows always resisted and remained friendly toward the whites. General Crook had 135 Crow scouts at the Battle of the Rosebud and George Armstrong Custer had six Crow scouts at the Battle of the Little Bighorn. Unlike other plains tribes, the Crow did not have a hostile relationship with the U.S., even though the government did little to make good on its promises to them.

Soon after the Battle of the Little Bighorn, the Crows had to negotiate with the federal government regarding the western portion of their reservation. The Crows were asked to give up the Upper Yellowstone River Valley, the Boulder River Country and the surrounding Beartooth Plateau in return for various annuities and agricultural implements. The United States wanted to open the valley bottoms to homesteading and the mountains to mineral exploration. Most importantly, the Northern Pacific Railroad wanted a route free of Indian harassment through the Upper Yellowstone country. Finally, in 1880 the Crows signed an agreement greatly decreasing the size of their reservation, but Congress didn't ratify it until 1882. Then, after nine years at its site three miles south of Absarokee, the Crow Agency was moved to its present location.

The next major development on the Crow reservation was land allotment. After the Allotment Act of 1887, the Crow tribe immediately applied for allotment status and the following year tribal members, including Chief Plenty Coups, began to receive their allotments. The allotment process furthered the trend of Crows becoming good agriculturalists, and the pattern continued into the early 1900s with only a limited interest in other economic pursuits such as timber harvesting. It was during this time that Chief Plenty Coups consolidated his leadership over

"Resting the herd," on Crow Reservation. Bill Yellowtail

Top: *Plenty Coups (1848-1932). At his death the Crow tribe voted that the term Chief of the Crow could not apply to another future leader.* Courtesy, Montana Historical Society

Bottom: *Plenty Coups' home.* Photo courtesy of the Montana Intertribal Policy Board

the Mountain and River Crows and continued his push for education and the gradual adoption of the culture of the white man.

After the turn of the century, a major continuing issue for the Crow Nation was compensation for land that had been taken earlier by the federal government. Furthermore, the federal government continued to want to acquire more tribal lands for homesteading purposes. They eventually acquired what is called the ceded strip north of the reservation in 1904. Also in that year, the tribe tried to sue the government for unjust compensation for lands taken in 1882 and 1891, but it wasn't until 1962 that the Court of Indian Claims awarded the Crow Tribe compensation on this matter. In 1905, 1910, 1915 and 1919, legislation was sponsored in Congress to open up the Crow Reservation to non-Indian settlement. In 1920 the tribe itself promoted Congressional legislation that divided what was left of the reservation into allotments for the rest of the enrolled members of the tribe. Most of this land was on the river bottoms rather than in mountain country. Unfortunately, many allottees from 1922 until 1962 sold their land to non-Indians, allowing much of the reservation's land to be no longer controlled by the Crows.

During the 1930s, the Crow reservation benefited greatly from New Deal programs. Reservation forests were improved. Several irrigation projects were started along the Bighorn, and a variety of land conservation measures were put into effect. All of these improvements helped the Crow continue to lead an agricultural way of life much like their ancestors 300 years before.

Perhaps the most important issue after World War II was the proposal by the Bureau of Reclamation to build Yellowtail Dam on the Bighorn River. The Mountain and River Crow, who had become more or less one group, split over this issue, with the Mountain Crow rigorously resisting construction. It was built nonetheless.

The Crow People Today

Crow Traditions

Crow traditions, unlike those of many other tribes, have remained a part of the Crow way of life even today. The Crow language is still spoken by 82 percent of the tribal members. This is a far greater percentage than in any other tribe in Montana. It is perhaps ironic that the Crow, who historically have been friendly to whites, have been the plains tribe that has been the most successful at keeping their traditions.

The Crow clan system is an excellent example of Crow tradition that has remained very much alive and well. As in almost all societies, the family is the primary unit of social organization, but the clan system is nearly as important in Crow culture. Several families are related in clans, with membership determined through the mother. In other words, children are members of families first, then they also are members of their mother's clan. Today, there are 10 clans: Whistling Water, Bad War Deeds, Greasy Mouth, Sorelip Lodges, Big Lodge, Newly Made Lodge, Peigan, Filth Eaters, Ties the Bundle, and Bring Game Without Shooting.

Naming ceremonies are often conducted by clan uncles. Furthermore, when a Crow makes an important decision, such as when State Senator Bill Yellowtail decided to run for the legislature in 1984, he sought out his clan uncles and asked them to pass judgment on his political desires. It wasn't until they approved, that Yellowtail began his campaign for the State Senate.

Characteristics of the Crow Clan system are described by Montana State University professor, Dr. Barney Old Coyote in this way:

1. Membership in a clan is matrilineal. One is born into a clan; one belongs to the clan of his natural mother for life, except in the case of adoption. An adoptee may claim membership to the clan of his or her adoptive mother while retaining his original clan membership.

2. No matter how remotely blood-related the families are within the clan, all clan members have a close sense of kinship and affinity. 3. The Crow clans are very competitive in sports, social and military affairs and activities. It is here that the Crow individual is convinced that he is first a clansman and second a tribesman. If he is a good clansman, then it follows that he is a good tribesman.

4. Between clan members there is a mutual concern, helpfulness and sharing of responsibilities. The needy, aged, and less fortunate members are generally provided with food, shelter, clothing and other needs by clan members. Furthermore, clansmen give each other comfort, moral support and protection when one member has difficulties or misfortunes.

5. Clan members must marry outside the clan. In a small population, this is eugenically sound.

Statistical Information

As of February 1985 there were 7,027 tribal members, of which more than 70 percent live on the reservation, primarily in the Bighorn and Little Bighorn River Valleys. Crow membership is determined by blood quantum, as stated in the Constitution. Before 1953, some enrolled members had as little as 1/64th Crow blood. An amendment to the Constitution required that those born after 1953 must have a minimum of one-quarter Crow blood in order to qualify for membership.

Pryor Gap. Michael Crummett

North of Pryor. Tom Dietrich

Reservation Lands

There are approximately 2,235,092 acres within the reservation's boundaries. The tribe owns 406,935 acres and allottees have title to 1,116,239 acres. 711,918 or 33.6 percent of the reservation is owned by non-Indians; most of this land is found along the river valleys and is definitely more productive agriculturally than what remains in Crow ownership. Outside the reservation boundaries to the north and east the tribe owns mineral rights on approximately 1.1 million acres of land whose surface rights were ceded to the government. This has proven to be most important with regard to coal development on the reservation.

Most Crow lands are gently rolling, semi-arid plains, except for the Pryor and Bighorn Mountains. Topographic relief varies from 2,900 feet to 9,000 feet. Average annual precipitation averages between 16" and 17" per year.

Form of Tribal Government

The Crow Tribe is one of two reservations in Montana that did not accept the provisions of the 1934 Indian Reorganization Act. It adopted its own Constitution in 1948 and has a general council form of government. The Council elects four officers for two-year terms. They are the Chairman and Vice-Chairman, Secretary and Vice-Secretary. What makes Crow government unique in the Western world is that all Crow women, 18 years and older, and all men 21 years and older are members of the Tribal Council. This unique form of pure "grass-roots" democracy has definite advantages and disadvantages. The Tribal Council (the entire tribe) meets quarterly with 100 members constituting a quorum. Proponents of this form of government say that it gives everyone a chance to be directly involved in Crow tribal affairs. Opponents believe that this form of government does not allow the tribe to forge ahead efficiently and effectively in a coherent direction in the areas of economic and resource development, environmental protection and social welfare. Instead, it allows tribal factionalism to dominate tribal affairs, a circumstance that tends to paralyze day-to-day operations and to forestall long-term development.

Besides the four elected members, several tribal committees are responsible for the day-to-day operation of the tribe. These include committees for law and order, enrollment, education, credit, health, oil and gas, industrial development, land purchase and recreation. An executive committee attempts to coordinate these efforts and it establishes the agenda for full Tribal Council meetings. The agenda-making power gives the executive committee clout in determining what takes place at council meetings because items at the end of the agenda often are not discussed because of lack of time.

Tribal Budget

In fiscal year 1985, the Crow Tribe's budget was approximately $1.6 million. Overall budgets, including various federal programs on the reservation, totaled approximately $10 million. The tribe has a substantial source of revenue from oil and gas leases, agricultural land leases and from Westmoreland Resources' Absaloka Mine on the ceded strip northeast of the Reservation. More than $1 million of the tribe's annual revenues go into per-capita payments made in December, August and April of each year. These three payments total $150 per tribal member annually. Most of the per-capita revenue comes from the Westmoreland contract, which stipulates that 60 percent of the royalties go to such annual payments.

Natural Resources

Although the Crows control only 67 percent of their land base, they are fortunate that it is rich in natural resources. The major natural resource is the billions of tons of sub-bituminous coal reserves found on the eastern portion of the reservation. Besides coal, great potential exists for oil and gas and the reservation has some timber and good dryland farming and grazing lands. Furthermore, the Bighorn and Little Bighorn Rivers provide a substantial water-resource base. These natural resources play a very important role in the tribe's planning for economic self-sufficiency.

Agricultural Lands

Almost all of the Crow Tribe's land is classified as irrigated, dryland farm or grazing land. Most of this land is leased to large non-Indian interests, such as the Scott Land and Cattle Company or the First Continental Corporation. There are more than 7,000 agricultural leases on the Crow Reservation, of which some 4,000 are overseen through a land management program by the Bureau of Indian Affairs. The others are called "competent" leases — leases that allottees can negotiate on their own, without approval of the BIA. Once negotiated, they have to be filed with the Bureau of Indian Affairs but the bureau has no say in their management. Competent leases are unique to the Crow tribe and complicate management of lands within the reservation's boundaries because there is no coherent land management system, despite the fact that reservation lands are divided into management units on paper. Approximately 1.2 million acres are leased as grazing land with another 150,000 acres leased as dry-land farming, primarily for alfalfa and wheat. There are roughly 30,000

Fishing on the Bighorn River has been the subject of sportsman-tribal controversy. Michael Crummett

leased irrigated acres, owned by the tribe and allottees, that mostly are used to grow corn and sugar beets. Since most of the acreage leased on the reservation is allotted land, tribal income from agricultural leases in 1984 brought in only about $500,000.

The Crows have a sporadic land acquisition program. 10,000 acres were purchased in 1983 and none were acquired in 1984 and 1985 because of the need to pay off loans for previous land purchases. Money used in land purchases comes from the following sources: 70 to 75 percent of leasing revenues, 20 percent of the Westmoreland royalty and 30 percent of the Shell royalty if and when the company begins to mine coal. Priorities in acquisition are to purchase lands along the Bighorn River, followed by irrigated tracts, lands situated for tribal consolidation and tracts with highly fractionalized ownership.

Wildlife and Fisheries

Although Crow Reservation has excellent wildlife habitat, only small populations of elk, deer and antelope are maintained, primarily because of the lack of comprehensive wildlife management ordinances and thorough enforcement programs. In the 1950s and early 1960s, the Bighorn Mountain portion of the Crow Reservation had one of the finest elk herds in the Northern Rockies. Today, greater access by four-wheel drive vehicles and lax enforcement of wildlife laws have drastically thinned the elk herd. Night hunting is no longer allowed, but the lack of enforcement has hampered the possibility of a significant increase of ungulates throughout the

reservation. The tribe has an enclosed buffalo herd, which supplies meat for celebrations and other tribal purposes.

The reservation has no commercial fisheries, but the Bighorn River below Yellowtail Dam is one of the most outstanding fisheries in the United States. A recent Supreme Court ruling gave control of these fisheries to the Montana Department of Fish, Wildlife and Parks. There is also a substantial walleye fishery in Bighorn Reservoir. The upper reaches of the Little Bighorn River and Rotten Grass Creek also support good trout populations for recreational fishing.

Forest Resources

Of approximately 117,284 acres of timber land, 47,630 acres have been classified as commercial grade. The predominant forest species are lodgepole, Douglas fir and ponderosa pine.

In the early days of the Crow Reservation, timber harvests were insignificant. Perhaps 15 timber sales were made in the 1920s, none of them large, and timber sales in the 1930s and 1940s averaged only 300,000 board feet per year. Recently, an intensive forest management plan for the Crow tribe was completed, but the tribe has yet to realize income from timber sales. The modest sales that do take place are on allotted lands, with revenues going to individual allottees.

Coal Resources

Coal has been mined periodically on the reservation since the 1920s. Most of the early mining took place near the reservation's border with Wyoming. Today the large Westmoreland Resources' Absaloka Mine on the ceded strip of the reservation reflects the nature of the coal resource that underlies most of the eastern part of the reservation. The Absaloka Mine first started stripping coal for shipment to midwestern markets in 1974. Today, it has mined more than 40 million tons from the Rosebud-MacKay seam and the Robinson seam. These seams total 58 feet of thickness and have averaged about 90,000 tons per surface acre. The mine has the capacity to supply 11 million tons of low-sulfur, sub-bituminous coal annually. Only 4 million tons of coal was mined in 1984, following the current soft market for coal, but this is projected to increase to approximately 7 million tons by 1986.

A subsidiary of Shell Oil Company has signed a 40-year lease with the Crow tribe to mine coal near Youngs Creek in the southeastern part of the reservation. Although no construction has started on the mine, the lease stipulates that a guaranteed royalty of at least $1 million per year will be paid to the tribe starting in July 1986. If constructed, the operation will strip-mine four different seams that are from

10 to 48 feet thick. If the poor market for coal continues, Shell has the option of giving the lease back to the tribe along with a $5 million penalty.

Gulf Resources also has a coal lease on the reservation, as does AMAX. The latter company is in the process of reconsidering its lease and returning it to the tribe.

Oil and Gas

Oil and gas has been produced on the Crow reservation since the 1930s. Currently, there are 32 stripper oil wells and 4 gas wells. In 1984, tribal lands produced approximately 18,000 barrels of oil, with a little more than 25,000 barrels of oil produced on allottee lands. This production realized approximately $100,000 in revenues for the tribe, with the royalties being constant at 12.5 percent. The wells are found in the Ash Creek area on the southern boundary of the reservation and in the Soap Creek area in the south central portion.

Oil and gas exploration continues on the Crow Reservation. In early 1985, 20 companies had 709 oil and gas leases. These companies included ARCO, Quantas, and Mobil along with many smaller operations. The ARCO exploratory lease reflects much better leasing arrangements than those agreed to by the tribe many years ago. Not only is the bonus for signing the lease much higher per acre, but also the contract includes scholarship money, guaranteed employment and a 20 to 22.5 percent royalty if oil is found.

The 1982 Minerals Development Act has allowed the Crow tribe to enter into several non-standard lease agreements. Perhaps the most innovative lease was signed late in 1984. It outlines a joint-venture agreement between the tribe and a subsidiary corporation of O'Hare Energy Company. This agreement gives the tribe 51 percent ownership of the partnership in what is called Raven Oil Company. The O'Hare subsidiary will have 49 percent and would provide all exploration costs. In addition to being a majority owner of Raven Oil, the tribe will be paid lease rental fees and bonuses and a 13 percent royalty on production. Raven Oil's exploration program started in the spring of 1985.

Other Mineral Resources

Uranium, bentonite, gypsum, limestone and dolomite have all been found on the reservation. Uranium once was mined on the southeastern side of the Bighorns, but today there are 20 abandoned mines and no plans for uranium activity. Midland Paint at one time leased 2,500 acres of tribal lands near East Pryor Creek for bentonite, but no mining has occurred.

Recreation Resources

Bighorn Canyon National Recreation Area is the Crow Reservation's largest recreational resource. Yellowtail Dam, completed in 1968, backs up the 71-mile-long Bighorn Lake with 1,375,000 acre-feet of water-storage capacity. The 520-feet-fall dam is the highest in the Missouri River Basin. It originally was developed for power, irrigation, flood control and recreational purposes. The recreation area is managed jointly by the National Park Service and the Crow tribe.

Nationally, the most famous natural resource on the Crow Reservation is the Bighorn River and its fishery of huge rainbow and brown trout. This fishery did not exist until Yellowtail Dam was built, creating below it a 12-mile stretch of the Bighorn River with cool, nutrient-rich water.

The tribe has designated two segments of the Bighorn and Pryor Mountains as lands sacred to Crow traditions and culture. These areas are off limits to development and, in a sense, are wilderness lands.

The most significant historical resource on the Crow Reservation is the 800-acre Custer Battlefield, located a mile south of Crow Agency and just off Interstate 90. Over 250,000 visitors come here each year to learn more and to reflect upon that famous battle and the events that surrounded it.

Water Resources

Two substantial rivers, the Little Bighorn and the Bighorn, flow through the reservation. Although the Bureau of Reclamation owns and operates Yellowtail Dam, the Crow claim enough water within the reservoir to satisfy the present and projected industrial and residential needs of the reservation. The tribe also has been given the right to construct a hydroelectric facility on the afterbay below Yellowtail Dam. The potential Crow water resource has not been thoroughly inventoried. A consulting firm in Billings is developing baseline water-resource data for the tribe. This will be used in upcoming water adjudication proceedings with the state of Montana.

Because both the Little Bighorn and Bighorn Rivers originate in Wyoming, some question arises regarding Wyoming water rights to these two water bodies. This has become a serious issue on the Little Bighorn, because the state of Wyoming is currently looking into the possibility of diverting its upper reaches into a reservoir for industrial purposes. Thus, Crow water rights involve Wyoming, Montana and the federal government; the interjurisdictional complexity will take years and millions of dollars in legal fees to resolve.

Christmas tree lumberjack, Heywood Big Day. Michael Crummett

Economic Development

Unemployment on the Crow reservation is certainly at least 60 percent and the tribe believes that the figure is closer to 85 percent. Small economic development efforts in the late '60s and early '70s, such as SunLodge and the Bighorn Carpet Company, were failures because of bad management and poor economic planning. Today most of the economic development on the reservation stems from the tribe's natural resource base, particularly coal, oil and gas.

The Crow tribe has not been at a loss for large-scale economic development plans. For example, the tribe has formed the Crow Development Corporation, which has had as its major objective constructing a coal-fired power plant. This proposed 1000-megawatt facility would cost over $1 billion. The tribe envisions such a project as a joint venture with a large energy corporation and hopes to have it built before the year 2000. Finding capital to undertake such a project is a major stumbling block, as is the fact that the demand for electricity has not increased significantly in the Pacific Northwest over the past several years. A further limitation is the Class I air designation on the Northern Cheyenne reservation just east and downwind of most of the best locations for such a generating facility.

The Crow tribe also has worked with Pacific Coal Gasification Company in assessing the feasibility of developing a synfuels plant on the reservation. With Council of Energy Resource Tribes assistance and money from the Department of Energy, a $3.7 billion plant has been proposed. However, synfuels technology has not developed to the point that such a plant is economically feasible at this time. Besides, the tribe has some underlying concerns about how many non-Indians would be brought onto the reservation to help construct and operate such a huge facility. With these issues in mind, in the spring of 1984, the Crow tribe received a $500,000 federal grant to prepare an application to the quasi-federal Synthetic Fuels Corporation for a scaled-down version of the original synfuels proposal. Today the tribe is studying a version that would produce 125 million standard cubic feet of synthetic gas per day, one-half the capacity of the earlier proposal.

The biggest employer of Crow people is the United States government, through the Bureau of Indian Affairs, the Public Health Service and the National Park Service. The Westmoreland lease has a provision that half of those employed at the mine site must be Crows; 40 members of the tribe work at Westmoreland at the present time. Other than tribal government, Crow employment is in small businesses and agriculture.

Left: *Dance arbor before dances at Crow Fair.* Michael Crummett 1979/Montana Folklife Survey photo
Right top: *Hand games at Crow Fair.* Bill Yellowtail
Right bottom: *Recording a music session.* Michael Crummett

Crow Celebrations

During the third week of August of each year, the Crow Fair celebration and PowWow takes place. This is easily the largest Indian celebration in Montana. Indians from throughout North America converge at Crow Agency, which becomes for a few days the "Tipi Capital of the World." The celebration features daily parades, dances, a rodeo, feasts, giveaways and a festive time for all.

In April and May, the Crow tribe sponsors a series of hand game and stick game tournaments, which involve teams from the various districts throughout the reservation. Some teams are also invited from other reservations, such as the nearby Northern Cheyenne. These games take place in the wooden octagon house at Crow Agency, where fascinated spectators watch teams hiding an object, usually a bone, in one hand while members of the opposing team try to guess which hand holds it. The games are a form of gambling, and much money changes hands in betting.

Education

"Education is your most powerful weapon. With education you are the white man's equal; without education you are his victim." This was Chief Plenty Coups' advice to his tribe in the late 1800s, and the tribal leadership has never forgotten. Education has always had a high priority on the reservation. Unlike many other tribes, the Crows have not had a federally run Bureau of Indian Affairs school or contract school on the reservation since 1920. All education has been conducted through public school systems.

The high schools on Crow Reservation are in Lodge Grass, Pryor, and nearby Hardin. Both the Lodge Grass and Pryor High Schools are controlled by Indian school boards but this is not the case in Hardin. Coal mining at Decker, just off the reservation, and at Westmoreland on the ceded strip, has made the Hardin and Lodge Grass school systems two of the wealthiest in the state.

a.

c.

d.

e.

Crow Fair: a. giving away blankets and horse; b. parade float; c. beating the heat on parade day. d. the late Bill Yellowtail, Sr. Bill Yellowtail photo *e. New Year's dance at Pryor.* Photos a, b, c, e: Michael Crummett

b.

Little Bighorn Community College is an all-Indian community college operating at Crow Agency. In the spring of 1985, it had approximately 58 full-time-equivalent students. Crow educational leadership estimates that seven or eight Crows a year now graduate from four-year colleges. In the 1970s as many as 20 Crow tribal members a year were receiving college degrees but because of the high cost of education and reductions by two thirds in federal money available to Indian students, fewer can afford to complete four-year degrees. This is frustrating to Crow people, since they know that many more tribal members could and should be attending college. It is important to add, though, that a trust fund was set up by the Bureau of Reclamation with revenues from Yellowtail Dam to help the future of the Crow tribe. In 1984-1985, $75,000 was used from this trust fund for higher education scholarships for tribal members.

Major Issues Facing the Crow Tribe

Restructuring Tribal Government

Many Crow tribal leaders believe that the greatest issue facing the tribe today is its general council form of government and that no major resolution of economic issues can occur until their tribal government becomes more effective. The current tribal chairman, Donald Stewart, is one advocate of council reform. "Now we would be lucky to get one good resolution passed in a year," he said. "This would not be so if we had a 12-person representative council."

In 1981 a grassroots organization called Crow United tried to set up a study commission to develop a more effective governmental structure for the Crow tribe, but the proposal to establish it lost by 22 votes. Since then it has not been a seriously discussed agenda item at quarterly council meetings.

The tribe's recurrent fiscal problems are a good example of how Crow governance affects such items as handling the Crow Fair money and law-and-order money. The tribe constantly finds itself in the position of having to explain fiscal irresponsibilities. Some government analysts believe that this is a result of the fact that despite "pure democracy," in the form of a full tribal council, only four people hold elective office on Crow. Therefore, Crow officials who run programs are not accountable directly to tribal members and do not even face re-election. Decisions and tribal operations often occur in the back room. Proposals to streamline and reform such tribal administrative operations are stalled in general council meetings and never see the light of day.

Another illustrative example of the present inertia in Crow tribal government is that there have been several attempts over the last few years by various factions within the Crow tribe to remove the tribe's elected tribal chairman. In the spring of 1985 one faction brought a vote of 419 to 401 to remove the current chairman from office. Although impeachment with a two-thirds vote is the only way to remove a tribal chairman, this action paralyzed the tribe for months. Eventually the situation required that the Bureau of Indian Affairs state who was the real tribal chairman and clarify who had the authority to continue to implement tribal programs and budgets. The issue was not resolved until the next council meeting, when the existing

Blasting overburden at Westmoreland Coal Mine, on the so-called ceded strip. Michael Crummett

chairman's constituents attended in full force and he clearly won a vote of confidence.

In a sense, the tribe has a general election every three months with the chairman having to make sure his faction has enough votes at council meetings to prevent impeachment or other attempts to remove him from office, which creates a great deal of chaos and uncertainty in all aspects of tribal functions. This is particularly true when the tribe is looking for large outside corporate interests to help them with their economic development plans. Such corporations need continuity and predictability in their work with tribal government and they presently cannot find that at Crow. That is why several tribal leaders and outside observers believe no significant economic development will take place on the reservation until there is structural reform of the tribe's constitution.

If the tribe does not make major changes in its government, the question arises as to whether the BIA should exercise its trust responsibility and force the tribe to do so. Some believe that the BIA should put the tribe in receivership; others think the BIA should take its name off the Crows' constitution and let them govern completely on their own.

Per-Capita Payments

Like the Confederated Salish-Kootenai Tribes, the Crows make a mandated per-capita payment three times per year to enrolled tribal members. These payments cause a huge drain on annual tribal revenues and capital that could be used in a variety of economic development projects. This necessitates joint economic-development ventures in which a cooperating party puts up the needed capital for a Crow project. Furthermore, per-capita payments greatly reduce the potential for a substantial land-purchase program on the reservation.

The 107th Meridian Issue

In 1947 the federal government made an error in surveying the eastern boundary of the Crow reservation. About 36,000 acres that should have been included within the reservation were not. Today, the Crow tribe has hired the law firm of former Secretary of Interior James Watt to pursue compensation from the federal government for the 36,000 acres. The surface rights are not valuable, but underneath each acre is almost 100,000 tons of coal. The tribe anticipates a settlement of at least $60 to $100 million and hopes that this will come before President Reagan leaves office. Then the big issue will be how to use the money. The current tribal administration wants to use it for land purchases and a capital development fund. Others in the tribe want the majority of it to be used for per-capita payments.

Coal Severance Tax Case

The Crow tribe is currently in federal court over Montana's coal severance tax and its application to the Westmoreland Resources mine on the ceded strip. At present, the state of Montana believes that it can tax the coal, but the Crow tribe does not agree and therefore has taken the issue to court. More than $20 million plus interest has been put into an escrow account while the legal proceedings take place: The case's disposition will create another opportunity for the tribe to forge ahead with economic development.

Coal Markets

In the 1980s, coal markets have been substantially reduced as a result of nationwide energy-conservation practices and an abundance of oil and gas. This has delayed the opening of many new coal mines such as the Shell mine and has postponed the tribe's plans for mine mouth conversion facilities. The tribe has sought markets for its coal overseas, and consultants have been hired to look into the possibility of developing a market for Crow coal in the Orient. The tribe also is looking into innovative ways of getting the coal to the Orient at the lowest possible cost. This includes having their own terminal island near Seattle.

Concluding Comment

The Crow Tribe, rich in tradition and resources, faces many dilemmas. There is little question that its present form of government needs restructuring. There is also little question that the Crows have the potential to generate large amounts of revenue from their reservation's rich natural-resource base. If and when such development comes, the tribe will have to confront a dramatic rise in the non-Indian population, perhaps even a situation in which the Crow would become a minority on their own land. Such development could seriously compromise the natural environmental integrity of the reservation and erode dramatically the maintenance of the Crow culture. It is even conceivable that a pure per-capita payment economy could develop, in which annual payments could be large enough that tribal members could live without working. (Something like this happens today on the Wind River reservation in Wyoming.) Or the tribe could see this as short-sighted and instead want to use thse financial resources to develop long-term employment opportunities on the reservation. Although mineral supplies are immense, they are limited and their value depends on unpredictable demands and markets. Obviously, Crow leaders face some hard, long-term thinking in handling this difficult issue.

The Battle of the Bighorn

On March 24, 1981 the U.S. Supreme Court, with a 6-3 decision, effectively transferred the ownership of 52 miles of the Bighorn River to the state of Montana. An issue that had been brewing for 15 years had been decided with far-reaching implications, not only for the Crow tribe, but also for Indian people in general.

The issue started with the construction of the Yellowtail Dam in the early 1960s, which dramatically changed the Bighorn River below it from a warm, muddy catfish stream to a clear, cool trout river with excellent prospects for the production of large fish. Yellowtail Dam also created a river that never froze, thus providing new habitat for ducks and geese that could rest and eat in the river during the winter and feed on nearby wheat and cornfields.

The Crow tribe, believing it owned this haven for fishermen and duck hunters because of the Fort Laramie Treaties of 1851 and 1868, began in the 1960s to require fishing and hunting permits. The $4 permit was a minor irritant to non-Indians using the river and no major issue arose as a result of the fee. Then, in the fall of 1973, the tribe voted to close the reservation to all hunting and fishing by non-Indians as of the first of May, 1974.

A few days later, a person by the name of James J. Finch fished the Bighorn River, was arrested by the Bureau of Indian Affairs Law Enforcement Officials and charged with trespassing. The Battle of the Bighorn River began.

To the Crows, the issue seemed simple. The Fort Laramie Treaties had given the Bighorn River and the tribal lands to them, along with exclusive use and occupancy including hunting and fishing. They assumed that they owned the river, and the lands around it. In the 1920s, the tribe had sold some of the land along the river to non-Indians, but the tribe still viewed the river and the fish within it as belonging to the Crows and under their jurisdiction. The state of Montana argued that the United States never granted navigable streams in these treaties, unless they made specific mention of it. Montana claimed that the treaties did not specifically deny rights to non-Indians on the Bighorn River and, therefore, when Montana became a state in 1889, it assumed jurisdiction over the river. Furthermore, the state of Montana maintained that an Indian tribe could not prohibit hunting and fishing on non-Indian lands within its reservation boundaries.

The court fight lasted seven years. The Federal District Court in Billings ruled against the tribe, but the Ninth

Bighorn Canyon from Devil's Canyon Overlook, a national recreation area bordering the Crow Reservation. Tom Dietrich

Circuit Court of Appeals ruled in favor of the tribe. The full Court of Appeals ruled against the tribe and finally, the Supreme Court upheld the Appeals Court.

After the decision, protests took place at the Supreme Court, the United Nations, the White House, in Helena, and on the Crow Reservation. After several delays, the river was opened in August 1981. Today the river is regulated by the Montana Department of Fish, Wildlife and Parks.

Leaders from most Indian tribes today view the Bighorn decision as one of their greatest losses in recent memory. They believe that this decision showed that the U.S. Supreme Court is not as serious about treaties as it once was and that tribes now are in the position of having to prove to the Federal Court what treaty rights they have. The case also has drastically changed legal strategies for tribes with mineral, energy and water resources, and for tribes having significant non-tribal lands within reservation boundaries. Reservations like Fort Peck and the Flathead now are more likely to try to negotiate a settlement before proceeding with litigation. The Bighorn case influenced the Fort Peck Reservation tribes to negotiate a settlement with the Montana Water Compact Commission in 1984. Unfortunately, this agreement too was overturned only to be re-negotiated and settled in May 1985. To many, the battle of the Bighorn was just as important, if not more so, than the Battle of the Little Bighorn just 15 miles to the east some 100 years before.

Indian Languages

Nothing is more important to one's culture than language. Language forms Indians' identity and it's the key ingredient to their survival as a culturally distinct people. Before European fur-traders and trappers came to the northern plains and the territory of Montana, each tribe living on the plains had its own language. Tribes communicated with one another with a highly-sophisticated form of sign language. Such sign language was used by the Europeans during their early contacts with Indians.

When the reservation system was established by the federal government, an essential ingredient of assimilation policy was to eliminate tribal languages as the primary language of Indian people. As early as 1868, a federal report concluded that "English only must be taught in all schools that the federal government supports." This also applied to private religious schools operating on reservations, because the federal government provided financial support to these missionary efforts. Missionaries and religious organizations at that time advocated bilingualism, but when the federal government threatened to cut their aid, they quickly relinquished their support.

The federal government's policy to force English on Indian people quickly ran into trouble with day schools in that Indian children went home to speak only their native tongue. In 1879 a policy shift occurred in Indian education when the federal government began to establish boarding schools. Carlisle in Pennsylvania was the first such school. The premise behind this change was to get Indian children

Top left: *At Crow Fair.* Michael Crummett
Top: *Night light.* Bill Yellowtail
Bottom: *Heywood and Mary Lou Big Day's 25th wedding anniversary.* Michael Crummett

to attend boarding schools so that they would learn English and speak it all the time. This would encourage them to forget their native tongue. By 1886 English was being taught to Indian youth in all formal education that the government supported. Even the Allotment Act of 1887 tried to help downplay tribal language. The act stated that when surplus lands were sold the money would be used to further educate the Indian (in English).

By the turn of the century, the federal policy of eradication of native languages was apparent everywhere. Even though it met with little real success in terms of making Indians speak English, it was devastating to an already destitute people's self-esteem. Finally the Merriam Report of 1928 supported bilingualism as a way of trying to strengthen the Indian social structure that the government had been trying to destroy for so long. When John Collier became commissioner of the Bureau of Indian Affairs in 1933, he re-introduced the concept of bilingualism into federal law and Indian policy. Consequently, during his tenure as commissioner, bilingualism enjoyed a brief renaissance. But when the era of termination emerged after World War II, bilingualism was no longer a preferred policy of the government. This coincided with substantial reductions in federal monies for Indian education as well.

During the Great Society era, bilingualism returned to prominence. It was promoted in the Elementary and Secondary Education Act of 1965. President Johnson's statement in 1968 on Indian affairs went even further as it strongly stressed the importance of using Indian language as the language of instruction for Indians in various Indian schools.

In Montana, there are four distinct Indian language families — Kootenai, Salishan, Siouan and Algonquian. The Crow, Assiniboine and Yanktonai all have a language stemming from the Siouan family. The Gros Ventre, Northern Cheyenne, Blackfeet, Chippewa and Cree languages all originate from Algonquian.

Over the last two to three generations there has been an incredible loss of native language within Indian tribes in the west and in Montana. While there is no one reason for this, the various assimilation policies over the years no doubt have taken their toll. Furthermore, until recently, bilingual education has not been a very sophisticated educational endeavor. Despite the resurgence in bilingual programs in Montana and elsewhere, there has been a problem as to how bilingualism should be taught. Specifically, one school of thought advocates learning by numbers and through the use of books and writing; another learning approach is that one best learns to speak his native language before learning the written forms. The thought behind the oral approach is that this is the way we all learn our language.

Today there are strong bilingual training programs at Eastern Montana College, Montana State University and the University of Montana. There is even a bilingual education office within the state Office of Public Instruction. As for the present status of native languages in Montana, the Crow have been far and away the most successful at retention. It is estimated that between 85 and 89 percent of Crow children entering school know Crow. This is one of the the highest rates of native language retention in the country. Reasons the Crows have been so successful are they never had boarding schools on their reservation; the clan system remains a very strong part of their culture, and they still practice the cultural tradition that a Crow never speaks English to another Crow.

The Northern Cheyenne, Assiniboine and Cree are next in standing with language retention in Montana. A recent study at Busby School on Northern Cheyenne showed that 56 percent of the parents of children could speak Cheyenne, but only 23 percent of their children could.

The tribe with the greatest language retention problem is the Gros Ventre, with allegedly only seven people living on Fort Belknap who know the complex Gros Ventre language. There are not that many more who know Kootenai, and there are only a few Salish-speaking people left on Flathead. Perhaps only 10 percent of Piegan on the Blackfeet Reservation can still speak Blackfeet, with only four percent capable of teaching it to others. Unfortunately for the Little Shell, their language has long since been lost.

A major reason for the loss of language on some reservations like Fort Belknap and Flathead, is that two tribes with two different languages reside within one boundary. Thus, the common language for Gros Ventre and Assiniboine is English. Another major reason for the disappearance of language within Indian tribes has to do with tribes that have been greatly assimilated into the white culture through allotment policies and the proximity to large non-Indian populations. This is particularly true of the Kootenai and Salish on Flathead who are a small minority on their own reservation. Not only do they have to speak English to one another, but also to the majority of people around them in daily life.

Although there are now disparate attempts to try to retain and promote the various Indian languages on reservations, much of this has been done in the immediate past with federal monies. The large cutbacks in education programs, including bilingualism, raise the serious question as to whether the recent resurgence of Indian languages will succeed. It appears that the Gros Ventre, the Kootenai, the Salish and the Piegan may well lose their languages, which casts a dark cloud on the long-term survival of their respective cultures.

Indian Beadwork

Beads and their facsimiles have been used for ornamentation since the beginning of time. Indian people in Montana first used seeds, shells, porcupine quills, claws, bones and even stones for ornamentation. The porcupine quill was perhaps the most prevalent material for decoration until beads were introduced into the plains and Plateau Indian cultures sometime in the late 18th century. The first beads probably came to Montana Indians from Spaniards through the tribes of the Great Basin country to the south of Montana.

In 1805, French fur trader Francois Laroque first documented Montana beadwork. He observed Crows using porcupine quills and blue beads for the ornamentation of clothes, riding gear and various containers.

The first beads to reach Montana tribes were made in Murano and Venice, Italy. Beads later came from Czechoslovakia and France. These first beads were put to

Top left: *Blackfeet beading.*
Top right: *Elk's tooth dress, Crow.*
Bottom: *Crow beading.* Michael Crummett photos

use only as secondary decorations. By about 1835 they became a major medium of ornamentation. Cut beads were preferred to bugle beads, because cut beads reflected light better. Despite the disappearance of porcupine quills in decorating during the latter part of the 19th century, quill design styles continued to influence the geometric shapes in plains Indian beadwork. Beads were sewn with sinew and the loom was not used as it was by tribes elsewhere in the country.

When the Cree came into Montana in the late 1800s, they brought a floral beadwork design with them. Before long many plains tribes were using a floral design as well as geometric ones, but geometric designs continued to predominate. These include the Sioux designs of the Sioux star, the four winds, turtle, rainbow, mountains and lakes. However, by the 20th century, the floral design had become very prevalent.

Today beadwork is a major art form and a source of pride on all reservations in Montana. A wide variety of designs are used to decorate jewelry, belt buckles, clothing, containers, moccasins and bolo ties.

Donald Stewart

Donald Stewart is one of many from the Stewart family who have served in leadership positions for the Crow tribe. Born in 1932 at home in the little community of Dunsmore on the Crow Reservation, Donald is from a family of seven. In speaking of his ethnicity, Stewart says, "I'm mostly Crow with just a little bit of Scotch." Fluent in Crow and a member of the Ties a Bundle clan, Stewart was raised on a small cattle and horse ranch until he was nine, when the family moved to Crow Agency because of his father's deteriorating heart condition.

Stewart never received a high school diploma. His work life began with the Northern Pacific Railroad, and then he worked 11 years for the Bureau of Reclamation doing land classification work as part of the Missouri River Basin project on land near the Bighorn River. He was transferred to their engineering division during the construction of Yellowtail Dam.

Upon leaving the Bureau of Reclamation, Stewart was involved in jobs that eventually led to elected tribal politics. He first started working for the Public Health Service as a community health worker, the liaison between tribal members and the medical community. From there he worked for three years in the tribe's law and order program. After that he returned to community work, spending 11

years working in Senior Citizens (Elders) programs on the reservation.

In 1978, when Stewart became tribal judge, he was the third generation Stewart to hold this position. In 1981 he ran successfully for vice-chairman of the tribe, which forced him to give up his tribal judgeship. Stewart claims that he had no intention of becoming a tribal political leader, but that his clan members had persuaded him otherwise. After serving a short while as vice-chair, Stewart became the Crow Tribal Chairman when his predecessor was removed from office. Now in his second term as the elected tribal leader, he has been beleaguered by tribal politics throughout his service. This has been particularly frustrating because he believes it is preventing the tribe from moving ahead in a coherent direction.

Stewart sees tribal politics and economic development as the two major issues facing the tribe. As for politics, he said he is frustrated with the current general council structure on Crow, which he believes kills most good ideas because of political in-fighting. The one advantage Stewart sees in the present structure is that it allows every person the freedom to say what he or she wants at a council meeting. He also believes that it doesn't allow "breeds," or mixed bloods, to control the tribe, as they often do on other reservations.

On the other hand, Donald feels that if the council were reorganized to a democratically-elected 12-person body, good ideas on the future direction of the tribe would be regularly considered and acted upon. Another problem Stewart sees with the present structure is that it does not allow some of the best educated and thoughtful Crows to get into tribal leadership. Therefore, he believes many of these people leave the reservation or ignore tribal policies and refuse to get involved.

In terms of economic development, Stewart wants to change somehow the incredible unemployment situation. This could happen, he thinks, with more coal and energy-related development on the reservation.

As of this writing, Donald Stewart is faced with a highly-organized campaign to try to oust him from office. Sadly, whether Stewart wins or loses this internal political fight, the tribe as a whole takes a back seat to such inter-factional conflicts. All this goes against the grain of what Stewart feels is essential for Crows to recognize in the future: that the Crows, like so many other Indian tribes, have to realize they are a tiny minority, powerless to move unless they unite on issues. It's clear to Stewart that the non-Indian world still wants the Crows' land and water and that they will get it if the tribe continues to allow itself to be divided and conquered. That's why he wants more than anything else of

his time as tribal chairman, to have the Crows come together and work as a group on the long-term future of the tribe. He knows this won't happen until the governing structure of the tribe is changed and Crow people see that their long-term strength can come only from within.

Angela Russell

One of the most respected women on Crow, Angela Russell in recent years has been involved in education, natural resource protection, social work and mental health work for her tribe. Born in 1943, she grew up in Lodge Grass and graduated from Hardin High School in 1961. She went to Montana State University before going on to graduate from the University of Montana, majoring in anthropology and sociology.

Russell is a strong traditionalist who can speak fluent Crow. Her father, William Russell, has been the leader of the Native American Church on Crow for decades. Angela is a member of the Big Lodge Clan.

After graduating from college, she worked in Denver for the United Scholarship Service, helping Indians and Hispanic people get scholarships to college. She then returned to the reservation as a Head Start teacher before going to Billings for four years to work as a social worker and later as a counselor for low-income and minority students at a local college.

In 1974, Russell received a master's degree in social work from Tulane and returned to the reservation to work as Director of Community Education in the Office of Coal Research. She became quite active in trying to halt coal development on the reservation because of her firm belief that the tribe did not have control over what was proposed.

Because of a change in tribal policy direction, Russell left the Office of Coal Research to work for the tribal newspaper and to teach school. She then worked as project director with the Denver Research Institute at the University of Denver on a feasibility study concerning social services legislation for tribal governments. In 1978, she returned to the reservation as a social worker for the Indian Health Service. Presently Russell works on issues of child and spouse abuse and has developed a children's survival skills program which is considered a model program in the region.

She is particularly proud of her political efforts on the reservation. She still believes that she was right in regard to coal development on the reservation. She also is proud of her work with Crows United, which was a grassroots

Donald Stewart, Jr.

Angela Russell

Janine Pease Windy Boy

Ellis Knows Gun

Michael Crummett photos

organization with support from the Montana Inter-Tribal Policy Board. Crows United was involved in the Bighorn River controversy, which Russell feels resulted in a devastating defeat for her people and for Indians in general. The organization also took on as a priority trying to change the tribe's constitution to a more representative form of government.

Russell today avoids the limelight in Crow political matters. She continues her role with the Montana State Advisory Committee to the U.S. Civil Rights Commission. She thinks that she is fulfilling an important function as a support person and role model for Indian women on the reservation.

Janine Pease Windy Boy

One of the more controversial and influential Crow women, Pease-Windy Boy has been active in education and politics. Approximately one-half Crow, she was born in 1949 on the Colville Reservation in Washington. Although she didn't go to school on Crow because her father and mother were teachers elsewhere, she spent her childhood summers there.

She graduated from Central Washington University in 1970 with a double major in sociology and anthropology. After working for a short while for Governor Dan Evans of Washington, Pease-Windy Boy spent the next several years working for community colleges in Washington and Arizona. In Arizona she worked for the Navajo Community College, which showed her the potential of tribally owned colleges.

She returned to the reservation in 1975 to become adult education director, not only for the Crow tribe, but also for the Northern Cheyenne and Fort Peck Reservations, funded by a Title IV grant from the U.S. Office of Indian Education. This was one of the first high school equivalent diploma programs on an Indian reservation in the state. She then worked on the establishment of the Crow Indian vocational education program before moving to Rocky Boy's Reservation with her husband and two children in 1979. However, it wasn't long before Janine found her way via Billings back to Crow, where in 1982 she became Executive Director and is now President of Little Bighorn Community College, chartered in 1980 by the tribal council.

Since returning to the reservation, she has been very active in Democratic politics and is chairperson of the Big Horn County Democratic Central Committee. Although many college presidents are known for staying clear of politics, Janine believes strongly that one must be active politically if the college graduates (as well as the tribe) are to have a good future.

Operating out of an abandoned building at Crow Agency, Little Bighorn Community College is a source of pride to this educator. Today there are more than 300 Crow Indian students and the school has achieved candidacy for accreditation. Pease-Windy Boy thinks that the future of the Crow tribe, and other Indian tribes, depends on education. She believes that tribal colleges are essential not only in helping Indian people achieve skills and knowledge, but also in providing them the necessary bridge to four-year colleges off the reservation. As the result of her active leadership at Little Bighorn College, she is the national president of the American Indian Higher Education Consortium, an organization of 21 tribal colleges.

Ellis Knows Gun

"Rabbit", to everyone, Ellis Knows Gun is the Assistant Director of the Office of Coal Reclamation on the Crow reservation. Another example of an Indian in his mid-30s who has returned to the reservation to help in the tribe's quest for self-sufficiency, he grew up in Crow Agency and went to high school at St. Labre in Ashland. He served in the Army for three years (1968-71) and entered the University of Montana in 1972. He was greatly influenced by historian K. Ross Toole, who helped make him keenly aware of what mining could do to his people.

In 1974, Knows Gun began work as a researcher for the Office of Coal Research. Two years later, he ran for one of the four elected positions in the tribe and was elected vice-secretary of the tribe for one term.

Knows Gun is married and has four children. He is most proud to be a direct descendant of Chip Rock, Goes Ahead and Pretty Shield, famous Crow leaders and medicine people.

Knows Gun's job today is funded primarily through the federal Office of Surface Mining. He is concerned with making sure that the tailings from '30s and '40s coal mining are reclaimed, and seeing that Westmoreland Resources abides by contract stipulations on reclamation at their present mine on the ceded strip just east of the reservation.

Ellis believes that some form of coal development is essential for the tribe's future, but the big issue for him is the need for the tribe to develop capital that can be invested for a good return.

LITTLE SHELL

Although they have no reservation and the federal government has never formally recognized them, the Little Shell people are a part of one of the largest tribes in the state of Montana. These people have contributed significantly to the history of Montana and to the local histories of many towns in this state, including Lewistown, Augusta, Frenchtown, Simms, Great Falls and Choteau.

Louis Riel, a political and military leader of the Metis, people of French-Chippewa blood. Courtesy, Montana State University Archives

Tribal Histories

To provide a historical perspective to the Little Shell, it is important to point out that the so-called landless Indians in Montana primarily have two different origins, the Metis heritage and the Little Shell Band of Chippewa. Bob Van Guten, the Little Shell's tribal historian and a faculty member at Salish Kootenai Community College makes it clear that "Most Little Shell, if not all, are Metis, and we don't really work at making a distinction."

Metis

The Metis are part Chippewa and French. Originally from the Red River and Assiniboine River country of North Dakota and the Prairie Provinces, these people were originally Chippewa who established close relations in the mid-17th century with French fur traders. Since the French and their Catholic religion strongly espoused the idea that all men were created equal in the eyes of God, and since the King of France didn't allow women to cross the ocean with the French fur traders and trappers, there was general encouragement for the French to marry Indian women. Therefore, with somewhat similar religions and a mutual respect, the Chippewa and French developed a half-breed culture of their own: the Metis or Mitchif. Most of these people lived in the area called Assiniboina in the prairie provinces of Canada. The Treaty of Ghent in 1818 divided Assiniboina into two countries at the 49th Parallel, the U.S.-Canadian border. At the time, it is estimated that there were 10-12,000 Metis.

In 1868, Mitchif Louis Riel, Sr., declared that he had established his own province called Rupert's Land. Riel made himself president until the English took over the area in 1870 in the so-called first Riel Rebellion of 1870. Even until today, this action provides a rallying cry for the Quebec Separatist Movement. Because Riel was French, separatists view the quashing of Riel in 1870 by the English as a classic example of English racism and prejudice toward people of French ancestry.

After the Rebellion of 1870, many Metis moved to Turtle Mountain Reservation in North Dakota and continued to the Milk River and Spring Creek country (Lewistown) of Montana, searching for their "Paradise Land." However, most of the Metis stayed north and went with Gabriel Dumont to the Saskatchewan River country.

Louis Riel, still dreaming of a native state in the west, spent several years in the east seeking support, but to no avail. He too moved west to the Spring Creek area of Montana where 150 Metis families lived. In June of 1884, he was asked by Gabriel Dumont to return to Canada and to help the Metis with their grievances against the Canadian government. Riel accepted the invitation and came north.

Canadians by this time were not at all sympathetic to the Metis interests and began to direct more and more Mounted Police into the Saskatchewan River area. In March 1885, the Metis attacked and routed the Mounties at Duck Lake, near Batoche, Saskatchewan. There was an immediate clamor from both sides. Metis sought help from the Blackfeet and other plains tribes. Canada sought help from the United States in making sure that no other Indians came across the border.

Nevertheless, the Cree pushed into the Saskatchewan country to help. Poundmaker and Big Bear, two Cree leaders, had several confrontations with the Mounted Police and white Canadians. The most famous involved Big Bear and Wandering Spirit at Frog Lake in eastern Alberta, where nine people were killed. The betrayal of the Metis by several Catholic priests enabled the Mounted Police and their government to defeat the Indians in the Battle of Batouch. Gabriel Dumont was able to escape to the United States and was granted political asylum. Louis Riel, on the other hand, gave himself up and was hanged in November of that year despite Dumont's elaborate plans for his escape to Lewistown, Montana.

Realizing that the dream of having their own homeland had disappeared with the various Riel rebellions, the Metis began to wander throughout Montana with Little Shell's band of Chippewas.

The Little Shell

The Little Shell are descendents of the Pimbina Chippewa from the Turtle Mountain Reservation in North Dakota. These people, with some mixed blood of Metis and Cree, left the reservation in 1892 to hunt in Montana under their Chief, Thomas Little Shell. While these 112 families were away, the United States Indian agent at the reservation seized upon an idea to shrink the size of the reservation to accommodate non-Indian pressure to homestead the agricultural land within the reservation's boundary.

Left: *Some of the Hill's residents, Julius Kennedy and family, probably Cree, no date.* Courtesy, Montana State University Archives

Above: *The infamous Hill 57 in Great Falls, which has been home to many landless Indians, circa 1930s.* Courtesy, Montana State University Archives

The agent picked 32 new full-blooded Chippewas as leaders and asked them to determine who was legally enrolled. The new tribal leaders' first decision was to strike from the rolls all of those Indians who had temporarily left the reservation, disenfranchising Little Shell's band from the Turtle Mountain Reservation. The "new leaders" at the reservation immediately negotiated a settlement with the U.S. government, giving up one million acres of land for approximately $90,000 in the infamous Ten-Cent Treaty.

After Little Shell and his people returned and found themselves no longer enrolled members of the reservation, they returned to Montana to find a new home. Soon the Little Shell-Chippewa and the Cree and Metis under Little Bear roamed from town to town and reservation to reservation, looking primarily for food and making their plea whenever possible for their own home.

In 1896, yielding to pressure from Montana citizens and the Governor, Congress allocated $5,000 to deport the landless Cree, Chippewa and Metis to Canada. First Lieutenant John J. Pershing — later to be the famous World War I general — was given charge of the deportation. His troops surrounded the landless Indians in Great Falls and told them a reserve awaited them in Canada. In August 1896, 537 Indians were delivered by Lieutenant Pershing and Montana government officials to Canadian authorities. They had been transported like cattle by box car or forced to walk the 258 miles to the Canadian border. As soon as the "deported" Indians were across the border, Little Bear was arrested for his role in the Frog Lake murders in the Riel Rebellion. Because there were no witnesses, he was later released. He and the rest of the "deported" Indians quickly made their way back from Canada realizing that the promise of a reserve was a fraud. By winter both the government and the press had labeled the deportation a failure since all the Little Shell were back and living on the outskirts of communities in north central and central Montana and near Fort Assiniboine.

Over the next few years these landless Metis, Cree and Chippewa were an embarrassment to Montana and the United States government.

Only a few voices could be heard in their support. The most prominent in this matter were Great Falls founder Paris Gibson, *Great Falls Tribune* editor William Bole, author Frank Bird Linderman and artist Charles M. Russell. Russell was quoted as saying,

> It doesn't look good for the people of Montana that they will sit and see a lot of women and children starve to death in this kind of weather. Lots of people seem to think that Indians are not human beings at all and have no feelings. These kind of people would be the first to yell if their grub pile was running short and they didn't have enough coal to keep out the cold. Yet because it is Rocky Boy and this bunch of Indians, they are perfectly willing to let them die of hunger and cold without lifting a hand.

As was mentioned under the history of Rocky Boy's Reservation, many years passed before some of these landless Indians received a home on part of what used to be Fort Assiniboine Military Reservation. Nevertheless, when Rocky Boy's Reservation was created, only 452 of 658 applicants were granted enrollment, and most of the non-enrolled were Little Shell and the Metis. They went back to their life as "garbage-can" Indians, wandering from town to town and living off of refuse from slaughterhouses and homes.

The ensuing decades brought many efforts to get the rest of these people onto Rocky Boy's Reservation, but leaders there, knowing that they had such a limited land base,

Left: *Joe McGuilless, a Little Shell resident of Hill 57, showing photo of his Chippewa-French grandfather and full-blood Chippewa grandmother.* Michael Crummett

Above: ***Little Shell Flag.*** *In 1978, this flag was adopted by the Little Shell tribe at their annual meeting in Zortman, Montana. It is much like the one that Louis Riel flew in Canada over his Prince Rupert's land, representing Indian, Irish, Scottish and French blood.* Frank Tyro

didn't want more people. The reservations didn't want these people, nor did the communities of Great Falls, Helena and Butte where so many landless people resided.

Joseph Dussone began to organize some of these landless Indians to try to get federal recognition in the 1920s, but no one really noticed them until the Great Depression. When welfare lines were created, many of the Metis and Little Shell were there, feared by so many non-Indians as carrying communicable diseases.

Nothing much happened and the landless Indians continued to live out of car bodies, dugouts in the sides of hills and cardboard houses. In 1941, five children died of malnutrition on Hill 57, a famous Indian community in Great Falls. In the mid-1950s a group of civic-minded leaders in Great Falls donated land to the Bureau of Indian Affairs at Hill 57, so that the BIA and the Indian Public Health Service could construct facilities there. The federal government refused the land, citing its position at that time of supporting termination of reservations, and stating that recognizing Hill 57's landless Indians would be inconsistent with long-range federal objectives for "taking care of" Indian people.

The Little Shell Today

The Little Shell today are very much a part of the Montana community. Thanks to the Montana Committee for the Humanities, a large Metis Centennial Celebration was conducted in Lewistown in 1979. Historians of the Little Shell like Lodge Grass Superintendent Larry La Counte, MSU professor Patrick Morris and Salish-Kootenai College staff member Bob Van Guten, are working hard at documenting their past.

Presently there are a little over 2,000 official members of the Little Shell in Montana. Membership is not easy to document and therefore, many who could be members have not been counted.

A Little Shell tribal council meets quarterly at various places throughout the state. Council members are elected every two years, with a tribal chairman elected every four years. At present, council members reflect very much the situation of the Little Shell band, because they live in various towns around the state.

Many of the issues that face the Little Shell today are focused on their request for formal recognition by the federal government. Although the government has not recognized a new tribe since 1927, Little Shell leaders have hope their petition will be approved through the Branch of Federal Acknowledgments in the Department of the Interior, which will make a recommendation to the Secretary of the Interior regarding recognition, with the Secretary making the final decision. A valid petition must show that the tribe meets a variety of criteria, including a common culture, a sense of community and descendency from the Pimbina-Chippewa through the Treaty of 1863.

Among the reasons for the tribe's wanting to be formally recognized by the federal government is access to certain tribal privileges such as health care, education and housing, through the Bureau of Indian Affairs. The Little Shell also want their 1978 settlement from the Ten-Cent Treaty to be paid in part to the tribe as well as to members, which will not happen without recognition of tribal status.

Because the Ten-Cent Treaty of 1892 was such a travesty of justice, and because many members of the reservation did not receive a share, the federal government in 1978 awarded $52 million to the descendants of the victims of this treaty. There was a small settlement made in December of 1984 of about $43 for each person who could prove their descendancy from the Pimbina band of Chippewa.

A much larger settlement will be made once the petition issue of the Little Shell has been resolved. If the petition is decided in their favor, 20 percent of the settlement, which, with interest, is closer to $100 million, would be divided among recognized groups such as the Little Shell for social services. The other 80 percent would be divided among the estimated 28,000 people who are descendants of the Pimbina-Chippewas.

Even more important than this eventual settlement, federal recognition would help the Little Shell to more effectively confront the debilitating problem of poor self-esteem that has plagued them for generations. Little Shell people are not accepted by Indians or by whites, and not having land or federal recognition has exacerbated the issue and made the Little Shell highly susceptible to many of this society's debilitating social diseases.

It is a testimony to the Little Shells' survival instincts that they are still here today and have kept fighting. In the early 1970s, only a few of the landless Indians in Great Falls graduated from high school. Today this statistic is beginning to change. In 1984-85, 955 Indian students were enrolled in the Great Falls schools. Outside of Browning's schools, this is the highest number of Indians in any school system in the state. Although not all are Little Shell, many are from landless origins.

Fortunately, urban Indian programs in Montana today assist landless Indians and others in coping with their situation. Great Falls has a Native American Center, which provides a health program and a job-training program for Indians in that community. Similar centers also exist in Havre, Helena and Billings.

Little Shell Culture

Little Shell celebrations today feature fiddling and dancing versions of the jig. This dates back to the French influence that started some 300 years ago. Their language has virtually disappeared, despite attempts to retrieve it. There is hope among younger members of the Little Shell that annual celebrations will revive the culture of their ancestors, and that the Red River Jig will be known by all members, as will some of their unique foods such as Rubabo and Bullets and Son-of-a-Bitch in a Sack.

A striking characteristic of Metis culture is a great sense of practicality. An old story illustrates the point: A steamboat captain was talking with an old man who owned a Red River Cart.

"You know," he said, "those carts wear out pretty fast. Why don't you take a piece of iron and put that underneath to reinforce the axle? You take two strips of iron and run them around the rims of the wheels so that they don't wear out so fast. Then you'll have a really heavy-duty cart."

The old man answered, "What are you going to get to pull it if you have all that iron on it, and what do you do to fix it when it breaks down? There are all of those cottonwoods all the way up the Milk River and all the way up Spring Creek and all across the prairie. If you break an axle, you knock that axle out and if you put a new cottonwood in you're on the road again. Now, if you have a piece of iron to replace and you break down, where the hell do get another one? Hold up an iron horse and melt down the axle? Or tear up a few tracks to make some stripping?" Such is the defense for one of the most ingenious vehicles ever to be used on the Great Plains!

So, in spite of the lack of land and recognition, the Little Shell people are still very much with us. If their current council and tribal leaders have their way, the Little Shell will continue to be an important community in the state of Montana.

Hill 57 today. Michael Crummett

The Red River Cart

No one is quite sure when Red River carts first came into existence —maybe as early as the late 1700s in the Red River area in Canada. The Red River cart is identified with the Little Shell and Metis of the early 1800s. These carts were made of log or pole frames and had huge wheels formed from rounds sawed off from logs. Because everything was wood, they were cheaply built and easily repaired in forested country.

The cart was used primarily to carry buffalo meat and robes. They were drawn by ox or pony and could carry 500 to 900 pounds. The Little Shell and Metis often removed the wheels to float a river. Their ungreased wooden axles made a characteristic screeching, so when 350 or more carts went on a major hunting party, the noise was heard for miles around. The carts were kept in the background when the actual hunt took place and were brought in for loading.

Above: *Red River cart.* Courtesy, Montana Historical Society
Below: *A Hill 57 residence.* Michael Crummett

Hill 57

Located on the northwest side of Great Falls, Hill 57 is synonymous with urban Indian poverty. In the late 1920s a salesman for Heinz Corporation, Art Hinch, built a large "57" of whitewashed rock on the hill as a promotional gimmick. It was some 80 feet long and 30 feet wide on what was then called Mount Royal. Below this sign, many landless Indians lived.

It is hard to say how many Indians lived there at any one time, but as recently as 1957, between 300 and 400 Indians called Hill 57 their home, mostly living in rag tents, cardboard houses or converted car bodies.

In 1957, there was an attempt to get the Bureau of Indian Affairs to set up a Hill 57 office, and for the Indian Health Service to have a clinic there. Some Great Falls residents donated title to some of the land to the federal government, but the government refused since it was trying to terminate reservations at the time.

During the winter of 1985, about a dozen landless Indian families still resided on Hill 57, with shacks and old campers as homes. Although many have left for low-income housing in Great Falls, Hill 57 continues as a symbol of the plight of landless Indians.

Great Falls Indian leader James Parker Shields, a Chippewa-Cree, states that "the hill is still a spiritual retreat for the Little Shell." Sweats and other traditional ceremonies are conducted there. No matter how bad the area may look, Hill 57 is an important link to the past for Montana's landless Indians and it is a solemn reminder to all of the result of neglecting the landless Indian.

Sweat ceremonies still are performed on the hill.

The hill represents urban Indian poverty to many.

Lance Brockie, 10, shooting baskets.

Michael Crummett photos

Art LaPier hauling water from the only well on the hill.

Don Bishop

Chairman of the Little Shell since June of 1984, Don Bishop is one-half Chippewa. Born in 1938 in Phillips County, he attended Malta High School and received his high school equivalent diploma in 1958. He served in the Marines for almost 2½ years, then returned to the Malta area, where he worked at various jobs before enrolling in a plumbers' apprenticeship program in 1965.

In 1973, Bishop became a plumbing instructor for the Indian Action Program in Lame Deer. This program evolved into Dull Knife Memorial College, where Don served as Dean of Students and taught plumbing in the vocational-technician program. While at Dull Knife, he married a member of the Northern Cheyenne tribe. The couple participated in the NAES College program and received bachelor's degrees while holding down full-time jobs.

Today, Bishop is facilities manager at Dull Knife. Now with a family of five children, he looks forward to the future of his tribe and people. "My education at NAES has really served me well. It helped me in writing skills, self-confidence and self-worth — that's what we Little Shell need most of all."

Bishop hopes that not only will federal recognition be in the Little Shell tribe's future, but also formal recognition by the state. That is why he has been active with the Montana Intertribal Policy Board as a Little Shell delegate since 1976, and sees this as one way of working towards the fulfillment of government-to-government relations with state and federal agencies for the Little Shell.

Don Bishop, Chairman of the Little Shell.

103

NORTHERN CHEYENNE

Tribal History

The Cheyenne, like the Blackfeet, the Assiniboine, Arapaho and Gros Ventre are of Algonquian language ancestry. It is believed that they originally lived in the Great Lakes Region, south of the Hudson Bay and James Bay areas, and began to move west into northern Minnesota sometime in the 15th century. Originally thought to be primarily fish eaters, they began to farm when living on the Upper Mississippi country. Like many tribes that were to become plains Indians, the Cheyennes began to move out of Minnesota into the Missouri River country of North Dakota when colonists settled on the east coast. While living in the Dakotas in the 1700s, they were still primarily farmers, growing corn and other grains but also doing some buffalo hunting. About 1750 they obtained horses and suddenly shifted from farming to a culture based entirely on the buffalo. Some historians believe that this shift from farming to full-time hunting occurred in just one generation.

By the early 1800s, moving just behind the Arapahos, the Cheyenne had migrated westward to the Black Hills country. It was at this time that the Cheyennes began to ally themselves with the Ogalala Sioux with whom they hunted buffalo and fought their common enemy, the Crow tribe.

Around 1830, the Cheyennes separated into two groups, the Northern and Southern Cheyennes, because smaller nations better fit their continuous nomadic searches for food. The Southern Cheyennes, who were more numerous, moved south and settled along the Arkansas River in Colorado. The Northern Cheyenne continued to roam the area of the Black Hills north of the Yellowstone and the Bighorn Mountains, their southern boundary being the North Platte River. The tribal groups, each numbering from 300 to 400 families, gathered on a regular basis for ceremonies and hunts. Moreover, all of the Cheyennes, in about ten bands, were governed by 44 chiefs who made overall decisions for the Northern and Southern Cheyenne groups. Their common religion was important to all Cheyennes, who viewed the earth as their grandmother and respected it as a living being. According to Cheyenne belief, all creation is alive and has supernatural powers. Sacred covenants are the Sacred Arrows and the Sacred Hat.

The Sacred Arrows are with the Southern Cheyenne and the Sacred Hat is kept by the Northern Cheyenne.

The Cheyennes first participated in treaty-making as early as 1825 when the chiefs of one of the ten Cheyenne bands participated in the Friendship Treaty with the U.S. government. The Fort Laramie Treaty of 1851 again involved Cheyennes, but the federal government viewed them as one people and did not acknowledge the split they had made some 20 years earlier. In 1861 a specific treaty was established with the Southern Cheyennes in southeastern Colorado. However, a few years later the Southern Cheyennes were the victims of one of the worst atrocities of the Indian war era. Popularly known as the Sand Creek Massacre, it involved 500 Southern Cheyennes and Arapahos, two-thirds of them women and children, who were in an encampment under an American flag and a white peace flag at Sand Creek, Colorado, when 1,000 troops under Colonel Chivington marched on the camp, killing all but the few who escaped. This resulted in terrific animosity by the Cheyenne and Arapaho peoples toward the government.

It was only after several years of skirmishes that a new treaty was signed at Fort Laramie in 1868 with the Northern Cheyenne, Arapaho and Sioux. This was the first time that Northern Cheyennes were formally recognized in a treaty with the United States government. The treaty acknowledged that the Indians would withdraw opposition to the construction of the railroad in their country and that, in return, the federal government would close the Bozeman Trail and would set aside most of the Northern Cheyenne hunting grounds as Indian territory. Unfortunately for the Northern Cheyenne and other Indian tribes who signed this treaty, almost immediately gold was discovered in the Black Hills. Non-Indians totally disregarded the treaty and flocked into the reserved country, searching for gold.

In 1875 all western tribes were ordered onto reservations, and many tribes, such as the Northern Cheyenne, refused. In the following spring, Lieutenant Colonel George A. Custer set forth to force the recalcitrant tribes onto reservations. On June 25, 1876, with the Northern Cheyennes allied with the Ogalala Sioux, the Battle of the Little Bighorn took place. Although the Indians won, it was the beginning of the end for the Northern Cheyennes' buffalo and open plains lifestyle.

The Northern Cheyenne remained on the plains in scattered bands, but they began slowly to come under the U.S. Army's control. One band, under Two Moons, was convinced by General Miles to surrender at Fort Keogh near Miles City in April 1877. A larger band under Dull Knife and Little Wolf had surrendered in Nebraska a short while earlier and were sent to live with the Southern Cheyenne and Arapaho in Oklahoma.

A little more than a year later, in September 1878, one of the most famous, yet tragic, chapters of Cheyenne history began to unfold. Approximately 300 Cheyennes, led by Dull Knife, Little Wolf, Wild Hog and Old Crow, left Oklahoma, determined to join with Two Moons' band and live in the Tongue River area of Montana. Along the way, Dull Knife decided to surrender at Fort Robinson in Nebraska, hoping to live with the Sioux at Pine Ridge in South Dakota. Little Wolf continued north and finally made it to Fort Keogh and surrendered in March 1879. But both Dull Knife and Little Wolf had met stiff resistance along their separate ways. In the end only a few Northern Cheyennes, numbering fewer than 100, survived and united with Two Moons. The long tragic march was over and those who remained of the Northern Cheyenne were back in their country.

Starting in 1880, various Cheyennes began to settle in the Lame Deer area. They tried to become self-sufficient farmers along the Tongue River, Muddy Creek, Otter Creek and Hanging Woman Creek. Government officials at Fort Keogh encouraged the tribe despite the protests of local homesteaders, and the Northern Cheyennes began to slowly carve out a de facto reservation. Finally, on November 26, 1884, the Tongue River Reservation was formally established. In 1900 its boundaries were enlarged to their present size. At long last, the Northern Cheyennes had their own reservation and a home.

Over the next several decades the Northern Cheyennes were pretty much ignored by the federal government. They attempted farming and harvested some of the timber on the reservation. During this time the government was more interested in trying to assimilate Northern Cheyenne with the neighboring non-Indian pioneers and then with the Crows — their old enemies and now neighbors. Predictably, this met with little success. Although the Cheyennes consented to allotment, no surplus lands were auctioned off to non-Indians. Therefore, when other reservations during the 1900s gradually came under the control of non-Indians, Northern Cheyenne never did. Even today more than 90 percent of the land within the reservation boundaries is controlled by tribal members or by tribal government.

Shortly after the Indian Reorganization Act was passed in 1934, the Northern Cheyennes organized themselves into a council form of government. At the same time, many New Deal programs were carried out on the reservation, bringing relative prosperity for the first time since the reservation had been established, but during World War II, Cheyennes once again became an impoverished people with little or no attention given to them. After the war, the government attempted to merge the Northern Cheyenne Reservation with the Crow Reservation and, at one point, it operated the office of the Bureau of Indian Affairs Superintendent for the Northern Cheyenne out of Crow Agency. Even the medical clinic that had been in Lame Deer was transferred to the Crow. All of this created tension between the tribes as the Northern Cheyennes wanted no part of living and working with the Crow people.

In the late 1960s, the issue of coal development became a major issue for the Northern Cheyenne; the reservation is in the heart of the Fort Union coal field. Every square foot of the reservation is known to have coal beneath it. With the consent of the Bureau of Indian Affairs, the tribal council signed leases with six different coal companies between 1966 and 1971. Many of these leases were exploratory permits that held an outright option-to-lease clause that could be exercised by the coal company. Promises, including a new health facility on the reservation and large per-capita payments, made these lease arrangements initially look inviting. Before long, leases covered more than 56 percent of the reservation.

In the fall of 1972, CONSOL, Inc., made a proposal to the tribe that would have placed over 70 percent of the reservation under the control of outside energy companies. Many tribal members were suspicious of this proposal and decided to protest. Soon, a full-scale grassroots organizing effort was under way, headed primarily by traditional people and allottees. In the winter of 1973, after a large feast that focused on the economic and environmental concerns posed by the leases, the tribal council, with the help of their Native American Rights Fund, decided to petition the federal government to cancel the leases. They argued that the Bureau of Indian Affairs did not follow their own regulations and procedures in lease promulgation.

The Cheyennes once again were fighting desperately for their reservation. Tribal council members elected on anti-coal lease platforms dominated the council. Many legal and political actions were occurring: the Hollowbreast case, which was to determine who owned the allottee's sub-surface coal rights, adjudication of water rights of the Tongue River, an appeal against Colstrip Power Plants 3 and 4, and the petition for air quality redesignation on the reservation (to Class I).

A major catalyst for this aggressive posture was a tribal entity called the Northern Cheyenne Research Project. Established in 1973, with money from the Office of Native

Top: *Cheyenne tipis, no date.* Courtesy, Montana State University Archives
Bottom: *Lumbering on the Northern Cheyenne Reservation.* Courtesy, Montana State University Archives

American Programs and from the Environmental Protection Agency, this research project inventoried tribal resources, including social, economic, cultural, water, mineral, land, vegetative, wildlife and air. It also developed and helped implement a variety of management plans for the tribe's resources. It prepared the tribe's Class I air redesignation request, and provided a great deal of factual information for various tribal legal strategies and position statements.

In 1975 the tribe's petition to cancel leases was acknowledged by Rogers Morton, then Secretary of the Interior, when he ruled that the leases could not be developed further unless both sides agreed. In 1978, legislation was introduced and passed in Congress to cancel the leases. Another Northern Cheyenne battle for survival had been won.

With the reservation literally ringed by coal development projects and with Colstrip a few miles to the north, the Cheyennes realized that their fight for survival was not about to end. Still insisting on no development of their own coal, the Cheyennes did enter into an agreement for a reservation-wide leasing arrangement with the Atlantic Richfield Company (ARCO) for oil and gas. It was hoped that this particular agreement would help the incredibly poor economic conditions on the reservation. Although controversial, the ARCO agreement injected a large sum of money onto the reservation, but after drilling seven wells, ARCO pulled out of its agreement during the summer of 1984. This has meant a loss of revenues amounting to one-third of their budget in 1984.

Today, the Cheyenne have control of almost the entire reservation. Yet, faced with severe unemployment, their future is uncertain.

The Northern Cheyenne Today

Population

As of October 1984, 5,250 members were enrolled in the Northern Cheyenne tribe. 3,600 of these are 28 years old and younger and approximately 3,200 live on the reservation.

The Northern Cheyenne claim all the discharge of the Tongue River, an assertion that soon will be adjudicated in the state water court system.   Bill Bryan

Unlike other tribes, the Cheyenne have very much stayed to themselves, with more than 52 percent of the enrolled members having one-half or more Northern Cheyenne blood. Enrollment is decided by blood quantum, with one-eighth Northern Cheyenne generally being the minimum.

Reservation Lands

Reservation boundaries enclose 444,679 acres. 287,697 acres are owned by the tribe, with 146,723 acres being individually allotted. There are 10,259 acres that are either owned by the state or federal government or are under fee title. Therefore, the tribe controls approximately 98 percent of the reservation. The reservation is divided by Rosebud and Bighorn Counties. The topographical extremes range from a high of 4,733' to a low of 2,920'. Its average annual rainfall is approximately 16", with a growing season of fewer than 120 days. It is open ponderosa pine plateau and valley country.

Tribal Government

The Northern Cheyenne Tribe was organized in 1936, under the 1934 Reorganization Act. The constitution calls for 15 council members and a tribally-elected chairman. The council members are elected every two years from five political districts on the reservation: Muddy, Ashland, Birney, Lame Deer and Busby. Each district's representation is pro-rated with regard to the total population of the reservation. Every four years the tribal chairman is elected at large. With a minimum number of signatures on a petition, anyone can run for tribal council or tribal chairman, creating the potential for large numbers of candidates. In the 1984 tribal chairman election, 13 names were on the ballot.

Tribal Budget

Tribal expenditures over the past three years have been greatly curtailed as a result of substantial reductions in revenue. In 1983, tribal expenditures were $6.17 million; in 1984, $3.92 million and in 1985 they are estimated to be $2.62 million. Revenues have decreased similarly from $7.77 million in 1983 to an estimated $3.67 million in 1985, which includes $2.2 million that was in the tribe's account at the beginning of the year. The huge decrease in revenue is the result of ARCO's oil and gas lease cancellation in August 1984. One lease-cancellation settlement by Chevron remains and accounts for almost 46 percent of the tribe's estimated 1985 income. When the Chevron settlement is completed, the Northern Cheyenne may well have annual revenues of fewer than $600,000 unless new sources of revenue are found.

Rosebud Creek is the second major water source on the reservation, although it often issues no flow in dry times.
Michael Crummett

Natural Resources

Unlike some Montana reservations, the Northern Cheyenne is rich in natural resources. Its fairly large timber resource, excellent grazing lands and the potential for adequate water provide the tribe with important resources that could be parlayed into economic development, but all of these resources pale in comparison to its huge coal resource that is yet to be mined.

Timber Resources. Approximately 30 percent of the reservation, or 148,755 acres, is timbered. Of this number approximately 104,380 acres — almost all in ponderosa pine —are classified as commercial. In the mid-1960s

Douglas fir was introduced but has not done well. The total timber inventory is estimated at approximately 371 million board feet.

Logging on the Northern Cheyenne reservation began just before the establishment of the reservation, with logs cut on the Ashland-Lame Deer Divide and floated down the Tongue River to a small sawmill at Fort Keogh in Miles City. Shortly thereafter, some timber was cut for railroad ties. Other than that, very little timber was cut except for reservation use until well after the Depression. Because of the timber potential, a large active Indian division of the Civil Conservation Corps operated on the Northern Cheyenne during the Depression on a variety of forest-management projects.

After World War II, timber was sold despite the marginal quality of the ponderosa. In 1955 the Tongue River Lumber Company was established in Lame Deer with up to 55 Cheyennes working there. An accelerated public program in 1964 had a substantial impact on the Northern Cheyenne timber resource as there was a concerted effort to improve the timber stand on the reservation. From 1969 to 1980, timber was the largest source of non-government income to the tribe accounting for as much as 23 percent of the tribal budget.

Today two sawmills operate sporadically on the reservation, one in Lame Deer and one in Ashland. Both are small and have been hampered by low demand for the marginal ponderosa. Furthermore, the tribe's forest has been hit hard in recent years by insects and fire. The current forest-management plan suggests an annual cut of 8 to 12 million board feet which is consistent with a sawmill's need for at least 10 million board feet annually. Market conditions and better transportation still dictate the allowable cut and, so far, the 50 to 60 Cheyennes who work in the mills or for the tribal logging associations have little job stability.

Agriculture. Only 3 percent of the reservation is presently being used for crop land; 93 percent of this is in hay. Range land covers 66 percent of the reservation, with most grazed by herds owned by tribal members. There is no tribal herd.

Along the Tongue River up to 18,000 acres have potential as irrigated crop lands. Approximately 3,900 acres are currently irrigated, which leaves a healthy potential for irrigated farms. The tribe has attempted to develop its own irrigated wheat and barley farms; the most recent effort was from 1976 to 1978 with the Tipi Ranch along the Tongue River. Poor wheat prices and poor management caused the Tipi Ranch to be taken over and managed by individual allottees.

Water Resources. With an average annual precipitation of only 12" to 16", the Northern Cheyenne seek substantial water rights on streams in and along the reservation. The major water systems are Rosebud Creek and the Tongue River. The Rosebud has not had a discharge record except for one off the reservation at Forsyth, which has averaged 17,000 acre-feet of water per year. The Tongue River at the Tongue River Dam south of the reservation has registered an average flow of 317,000 acre-feet per year. However, both have had a history of no-flow during dry times. The Northern Cheyenne claim all water in both the Rosebud and the Tongue. Adjudication proceedings with the state of Montana will ultimately decide the extent of this right.

Wildlife Resources. Located in excellent deer country, the Northern Cheyenne Reservation has populations of

Top: *The town of Colstrip north of the reservation, and its power generating facilities, which employ some Northern Cheyenne.*
Bottom: *The Ashland Sawmill, one of two small sawmills on the reservation.*
Michael Crummett photos

a.

whitetail and mule deer, antelope and some elk that come from the Little Wolf Mountains. Unfortunately, the tribe performs little management of these herds, so all ungulates are extremely over-hunted and are quite scarce. Only 250 head of deer occupy the entire reservation.

The tribe has an elk herd that lives in an enclosure along the Tongue River. Their antlers are harvested and sold, mainly in the Orient as aphrodisiacs. The tribe also has a herd of approximately 80 buffalo in a 1,200-acre enclosure and plans to sell these buffalo commercially, but at the present time they are used primarily for ceremonial purposes.

The tribe has an active trout-stocking program for some of the small impoundments on the reservation, but this has been only for recreational purposes.

Coal Resources. The Northern Cheyenne have one of the largest coal reserves of any tribe in the country. Recent estimates show 23 billion tons of mineable, low-sulfur, sub-bituminous coal. At $9 per ton, this adds up to $200 billion worth of coal.

Although the Cheyenne developed in the mid-1970s a small mine (Midway Coal Company) for their own heating needs, they have strongly resisted major coal development. The reasons are several. One is their cultural and religious tradition that all things in the environment are alive, so in a sense, coal development would be like murder.

Another reason for their resistance is that the Cheyenne have historically not wanted large influxes of non-Indian populations on the reservation. They assume that large-scale coal development would bring a new element of people, to them, an undesirable prospect. Thirdly, coal development schemes that have been proposed have been exploitive. In the first lease arrangements, royalties were 12½ percent. The Cheyennes now know what their coal is

b.

c.

d.

Wesley Spotted Elk and *Jason Whiteman* are two young Cheyennes with degrees from junior colleges who have benefitted from natural resource training programs through the Northern Cheyenne Research Project over the last decade. Spotted Elk was a technician in water-quality monitoring and now is the air-quality administrator for the tribe, checking air quality with a mind to enforce the tribal ordinance on air-quality as soon as it's approved.

Whiteman has been monitoring surface and ground water on the reservation for more than six years. EPA monies have provided six surface-water gauging stations on the reservation, four for measuring precipitation and 40 wells for this work. All the information is computerized and will be essential in developing water-quality standards for the reservation as well as helping the Cheyennes in their adjudication proceedings with the state of Montana. Jason also is working on water-quality codes and safe drinking-water standards for the tribe.

a. *Thomas Rock Roads, tipple operator, Colstrip*
b. *Clara Spotted Elk, Western Energy, Colstrip*
c. *Wesley Spotted Elk, tribal air-quality administrator.*
d. *Jason Whiteman monitoring water.*
Michael Crummett photos

a.

b.

c.

d.

a. Wild turkeys crossing Highway 212 at Busby.
b. Lloyd Little Bird and Scott Russell deliver coal to home of Ella Tall Bull
c. Northern Cheyenne youngsters take in powwow.
d. Northern Cheyenne girl in hides and beads
a., b.—Michael Crummett; c., d.—Bill Woessner

worth, and if future development is to occur, the terms will be far more generous and equitable.

The Cheyennes realize that their grave unemployment situation may eventually be resolved only through some form of mineral resource development. However, with a soft coal market, coal development on the Northern Cheyenne seems to be a long way into the future. If and when it occurs, it will be done on their own terms with maximum environmental protection.

Oil and Gas Resources. The Cheyennes have felt for some time that oil and gas could be found under the reservation. The geology seemed right, particularly in the Muddy Creek drainage. Therefore, the tribe decided to pursue a leasing arrangement with the Atlantic Richfield Company in the late 1970s. The tribe signed in 1980 an oil and gas lease with ARCO, covering the entire reservation. The agreement was very controversial with tribal members; some felt that the tribe could have gotten more money and retained more control over the drilling and should not have agreed to such a long-term arrangement.

However, the agreement did provide for tribal participation in all management decisions surrounding the ARCO operations. It provided funding for a tribal oil and gas office, a training program for tribal members, a scholarship program, good and clear accounting procedures, a stringent permit system regarding land use and water quality, and it took into consideration environmental and cultural impacts during all phases of the drilling.

The agreement provided for an up-front payment of $6 million to the tribe. If any oil and gas were found, approximately 25 percent of its worth would go to the tribe. Most, including the Council of Energy Resource Tribes, felt that it was a relatively good contract. The Cheyenne leadership liked it because it brought immediate financial relief and did not involve huge disturbances of the land.

Until the summer of 1984, a third of the tribe's budget, $1.3 million, came from the ARCO agreement. However, after seven wells were drilled at an investment of $28 million, ARCO exercised a provision in its lease whereby they could cancel the program. They did. Today ARCO is no longer on the reservation and the tribe has a much more conservative view of whether there is oil and gas beneath their land. The tribe has all the raw data that ARCO developed from their seismic activity and geological mapping.

Education

Outside of the economic development issues, the biggest problem facing the Northern Cheyenne tribe is education. This is ironic in that the St. Labre Mission has operated a school on Northern Cheyenne for generations, and Dull Knife Community College was one of the first community colleges on an Indian reservation in the state. But today the Cheyennes have the only reservation in Montana without a contract or public high school. As a result, in the winter of 1985, approximately 25 percent of high-school-age students were not in school. This statistic is most discouraging considering that the high schools operating near the reservation are quite healthy and haven't been able to recruit Cheyennes. The Colstrip High School District is one of the wealthiest in the state and approximately 60 percent of the Cheyennes who are in high school go there. Hundreds have chosen not to, partly because of poor transportation, racism, irrelevant programs and other cultural issues.

St. Labre has also allowed a BIA contract high school to operate since 1979 in its facilities, but this was recently reconverted to a private Catholic school. Almost 40 percent of the Cheyennes attending high school in 1984-85 went to St. Labre, with a few going to boarding school or to Hardin High School. There was another high school in Busby, but insufficient funds forced the school board to close the facility in 1982 because it was not up to state standards. However, at the beginning of the 1985-86 school year Busby tried to reopen its high school for more than 70 students. Its future is uncertain and all realize that this action is only a stop-gap measure.

The tribe has adopted as its highest priority a plan to locate a high school on the reservation as soon as possible. In the meantime, unless the Bureau of Indian Affairs provides short-term relief, even more Cheyenne young people may fail to complete high school.

Economic Development

In March of 1984, the unemployment rate on Northern Cheyenne was approximately 60 percent. With the cancellation of the ARCO lease and the continued reduction of federal funding, unemployment has grown worse. With the timber market and the cattle market in poor condition, no coal market, no oil and gas, and tourism being non-existent, the future looks bleak. The tribe's Economic Development Committee is seeking to attract light industry, like a manufacturer of automobile hood covers or an electronics firm. A railroad may be built from Miles City up the Tongue River to the MontCo Mine just off the eastern edge of the reservation south of Ashland, which might solve some transportation problems for the tribe's timber industry.

The St. Labre Mission provided and manages a $2.5 million tribal economic trust fund whose interest income is used for new economic enterprises. The tribe also is looking into the beleaguered Tongue River Dam south of the reservation, which has been declared unsafe, and the Montana Department of Natural Resources is not sure if it wants to fix it. The tribe believes that with the capital to fix the dam, a small hydroelectric plant could be developed to provide subsidized electricity for the reservation. The probability of that project seems low because of the high cost to repair the dam and build a generating facility.

Many Northern Cheyenne believe their future is in coal. The Cheyenne leadership believes that eventually the market for coal will improve and that the tribe should carefully enter that market. Although it is true that coal development on the reservation cannot take place without a reservation-wide referendum, some leaders believe that if it is planned in an environmentally-sound manner and controlled by the tribe, coal development would be accepted.

Above: *Northern Cheyenne powwow.*
Bill Bryan
Left: *Alice Kinzell, 94, thought to be the oldest living Northern Cheyenne, to whom more than 400 Northern Cheyenne can claim their lineage.*
Michael Crummett

111

The Northern Cheyennes' Future

The Northern Cheyenne are a nation with great potential, resulting in part from their long struggle for their own reservation. The recent battles over coal development have resulted in a much greater sense of pride and self-esteem within the tribe. Because of their accomplishments the tribe has more outright control over their resources than ever before.

But the Cheyennes' short-term future is extremely bleak. Having been suddenly cut off from the ARCO payments, as well as having to deal with the severe federal financial cutbacks, they face an abysmal economic situation. With no present large-scale economic development activities, the Cheyenne suddenly may be pressured into developing a resource in a way that is not best for them in the long term. Furthermore, the pitiful high school situation is a real obstacle because it prevents the tribe from moving beyond serious social problems originating from lack of self-esteem and confidence. It is particularly bad for the prospect of tribal management of economic development on the reservation.

On the one hand, the Cheyennes can be optimistic about their long-term future, thanks to their tenacity for control of their resource base. Yet, what is happening today is most discouraging. Most Northern Cheyenne observers believe that the tribal leadership is faced with perhaps its biggest challenge since Dull Knife and Little Wolf began the trek from Oklahoma back to the Tongue River country.

Top: *The chapel at St. Labre Mission.*
Bottom: *Giveaway during a Northern Cheyenne powwow.*
Bill Bryan photos

St. Labre Indian Mission

St. Labre, at Ashland, is known to hundreds of thousands of people throughout the United States as a charitable mission helping poor Indian people, particularly Northern Cheyennes, in the west. To Northern Cheyennes, it is known as the "Mission," a sometimes controversial endeavor that has helped people with schooling, provided jobs and met other social needs.

The Mission was established in three log cabins in 1884, after a Catholic soldier, stationed at Fort Keogh near Miles City, told stories to his church of the plight of the Cheyenne. The name, Labre, is derived from the "Begger's Saint," Joseph Labre, who was the patron of the poorest of God's poor children.

Today it is run by the Capuchin Order. In the mid-1920s, one of the fathers compiled the first Cheyenne dictionary. In the early 1950s, a major effort was made to help the Cheyennes become economically self-sufficient. A craft factory was built in 1959, which employed as many as 200 people. These crafts were sold on a direct mail appeal and brought in millions of dollars to the mission. In 1977 the factory was closed for a variety of reasons, including poor sales and the thought that the crafts and the mission were really taking an unfair advantage of the Cheyennes.

Today the mission operates an alcoholism program, Headstart, the Cheyenne home for orphans, and a health clinic. It also has an extensive school program. In the late 1970s, this school program was turned over to a community-elected school board that contracted with the mission for $1 per year for the facilities and contracted the educational program through the Bureau of Indian Affairs. In July 1985, the mission took control over the school once again and plans to continue it as a private Catholic school, for Cheyennes, Crows and other Indian students.

In spite of its occasional controversiality, the mission has played an important role in helping Northern Cheyennes and Crows who are interested in the Catholic faith and benefit from important educational and social services.

The Giveaway

Giveaways are a traditional custom of all Montana Indian tribes. They are derived from the Indian belief that people should share with relatives and friends who have done good deeds for them or whom they respect. It is also customary for surviving family members to give away the material possessions of the deceased to his or her friends.

Usually the items given away are greatly prized by the owner and the ones receiving them are greatly honored. Even today, giveaways frequently involve cattle and horses, although it is more common to give blankets, beadwork and quilts. Sometimes a giveaway culminates in cooking and serving a meal for the entire tribe.

Giveaways usually take place during celebrations in the summer, and almost all Indians participate regardless of their financial situations. The giveaway is an expression of Indians' attitude toward the accumulation of material goods and their emphasis on the communal spirit and tribal good will.

Moonrise over the Rosebud Hills. Michael Crummett

Class I Air Quality

The 1974 federal air quality amendments dictated a classification system for airsheds throughout the United States, primarily to control sulphur dioxide and suspended particulates. The three categories of air quality included Class I, which was for wilderness areas and national parks.

The rest of the country would be designated Class II, unless local governing bodies wanted to reclassify their airsheds to the more stringent Class I or the less stringent Class III.

The Northern Cheyenne, as a local governing body, decided to place their reservation's airshed in Class I and the tribal council passed a resolution in May 1976 to ask the EPA for this change. The Cheyenne believed that air pollution would disrupt the tribe's ability to continue a unique lifestyle, and that Class I status would further the goal of increasing the tribe's control of its future.

Some threats just off their reservation provided catalysts for tribal action. One was the beginning of construction of a huge 2100-megawatt coal-fired generating plant at Colstrip, and another, the Crow tribe's proposals for gasification and power facilities on the Northern Cheyenne-Crow boundaries. The Cheyennes saw Class I airshed redesignation as essential to control such off-reservation growth and to protect future economic development projects that might occur on the Cheyenne reservation. In August 1977, EPA granted the Northern Cheyennes' request.

Two years later the Confederated Salish-Kootenai Tribes also requested the Environmental Protection Agency to reclassify their air resources to Class I. The tribes sought to protect the productivity of their huge forestry resource and their agricultural land, as well as to help protect the health of tribal members. They also worried about wildlife resources, the scenic quality of the reservation and the possible impact if a large, polluting, industrial facility were located on the reservation, attracting many non-Indian people. This concern is particularly appropriate on Flathead, because so much of the land within the reservation's boundaries is controlled by non-Indian interests. The tribes' petition for redesignation was granted in 1981.

With two tribal governments' successes at redesignation, the Assiniboine and Sioux tribes on Fort Peck began to pursue Class I designation for their air resources as well, prompted by the construction of a major coal-fired power plant on the Poplar River just north of the Canadian border, and 12 miles north of the reservation boundary line. Fort Peck had begun an orderly process to develop small, clean industries on the reservation and did not want a major polluting industrial enterprise within or around its boundaries. In March 1983 the Assiniboine and Sioux tribes formally asked for redesignation and a year later became the third tribe in Montana, and in the United States, to obtain Class I air-quality status.

Today these three reservations are all in the process of developing air-quality control programs and enforcement ordinances so that their Class I designations can be upheld.

Busby School

The story of Busby School on the Northern Cheyenne Reservation exemplifies a growing problem caused by federal cutbacks in education on Indian reservations. Busby originally was a Bureau of Indian Affairs boarding school, called the Tongue River Boarding School. In the early 1970s, the facility included an elementary school and a high school, two dormitories and 26 homes for faculty members.

After Public Law 638 was enacted, Busby received approval in 1972 to become a contract school. At the time it enrolled 263 students in elementary school and 207 in its high school.

A community-elected school board oversees and operates the school program under a financial contract with the BIA. The facilities remained government property and were to be maintained by the bureau. So when Busby went to contract status, the BIA employed 14 people for upkeep of the plant. In 1977, despite the need for a new high school facility, the Bureau of Indian Affairs gradually began a reduction of its maintenance support. By 1982 the bureau employed only two maintenance people. Conditions at the school became deplorable with both the Montana Department of Public Instruction and the Indian Health Service reporting that the facility violated several building and health codes and suffered from a gross lack of maintenance. By then there were only about 100 elementary students and 45 high school students. Most parents simply did not want their children in the bad conditions at Busby.

It seemed apparent to everyone that the Bureau of Indian Affairs had decided to close the school through attrition and did not want to build a new facility. Cheyenne leaders point out that Busby was being allowed to deteriorate at the same time the Bureau was remodeling its local agency building in Lame Deer at a cost of more than $500,000. Immediately after the 1982-83 school year ended, the Busby School Board suspended operation of the high school. The Bureau then decided to spend $880,000 to repair the elementary school, but it steadfastly refused to do anything with the high school. As of now, estimates for refurbishing and rebuilding the dorms and the high school facility are between $10 and $14 million. However, the current administration in Washington has recommended no federal construction money for Indian schools for the

Left: *Boarded up dormitory, Busby School.*
Below: *Loading up for bus ride from Lame Deer to Colstrip.*
Michael Crummett photos

1986 fiscal year. Even if there were monies available, both Harlem High School, near the Fort Belknap reservation, and Rocky Boy's High School on Rocky Boy's Reservation, have the No. 1 and No. 2 priorities nationally and Busby isn't even on the list.

What this means is that Northern Cheyenne is now the only reservation without a public or contract high school. High school students can go the private Catholic school at St. Labre Mission in Ashland or to Colstrip and Hardin off the reservation. Because of the distance involved and the insensitivity in public high schools to Northern Cheyenne needs, very few students have gone on to high school. In the 1984-85 school year approximately 25 percent of high-school-age students on the reservation were not in school. If one considers a high school education essential in helping the tribe deal with critical issues in the coming decades, this devastating statistic paints a bleak picture for the future of the Northern Cheyennes.

The Busby school board is still desperately trying to re-open the high school. It has filed a $7 million contract claim against the BIA but the bureau refuses to consider it. The school board now has taken the BIA to court. In the meantime, the school board has initiated with the tribal council a reservation-wide planning commission to look into a reservation-wide high school. The tribe now has taken this on as a major project of their own. The need is obvious, but major obstacles lie ahead with regard to

funding an adequate facility and maintaining its year-to-year operation.

Does the federal government have the responsibility to make sure that Northern Cheyennes, as well as other Indians, get an adequate education? In the Northern Cheyenne case explicit language in the 1868 and 1877 treaties stipulates that the federal government will accept responsibility for educating Northern Cheyennes. The Treaty of 1877 specifically states that the government will furnish the Cheyennes schools and instruction in vocational education. Besides treaties, there is the Indian Education Act of 1972, and a variety of Title IV programs that make it clear the federal government accepts the responsibility of helping to educate Indian people. Furthermore, Public Law 638, the Indian Self-Determination and Educational Assistance Act, includes policy language that states, "The Congress declares that a major goal of the United States is to provide the quantity and quality of educational services and opportunities which will permit Indian children to compete and excel in the life areas of their choice, and to achieve the measure of self-determination essential to their social and economic well-being."

Because of these treaty obligations and policy statements about Indian education, the Northern Cheyenne tribe has bitter feelings about the federal government's present attitude toward educating Northern Cheyennes.

Mr. and Mrs. Allen Rowland. Michael Crummett

Allen Rowland

The powerful Northern Cheyenne tribal chairman for 16 years, Allen "Chuggie" Rowland finally retired in September 1984, after taking the tribe through one of the most difficult periods in its history — the controversial coal leases, the ARCO oil and gas lease and the decline of so many of the Great Society programs.

Born in Lame Deer in 1926, he lived both in Lame Deer and in Muddy Creek in his early years. As soon as he was old enough, he went into the service in World War II and was wounded in action on Okinawa. Upon leaving the service he went to Haskell and earned a high school diploma in May 1947.

Rowland's sense of humor and blunt talk have always been his trademarks. When asked if he has a high school diploma, he often may say no, if the assumption behind the question seems to be that Indians can't learn. When asked if he speaks Cheyenne, he often replies that he used to talk Sioux when he was young, because he thinks has some Sioux blood, but that he doesn't know any Cheyenne. Specifically, Allen is three-eighths Cheyenne and about one-quarter Chippewa of the Leech Lake band.

He trained as a plumber in Kansas and went to the west coast to work. He returned to the reservation in 1948 and tried cattle ranching, helped by the tribe's replacement-herd program with the Bureau of Indian Affairs. Unsuccessful at this, he worked for St. Labre Mission, the tribe and then the mission again until 1968. He was the only Indian employed at the mission and his jobs included watchman, truck driver and janitor.

In 1962 Rowland was elected to the tribal council from the Muddy district. In 1964 he was elected from the Ashland district and, at that time, ran for tribal chairman. He lost by three votes.

It wasn't until 1968 that he ran for chairman again, winning by a landslide. Rowland believes the U.S. Supreme Court case known as the Hollowbreast decision was the high point in his 16-year term as chairman, because it gave the tribe ownership of all the coal on the reservation. He also believes cancellation of the coal leases has important implications for the tribe's future. He is proud of the very extensive housing program undertaken during his tenure.

His greatest disappointment was that ARCO's $6 million up-front payment on oil and gas leases was made in per-capita payments. If it had been put into a trust account, today "we'd be one of the richest tribes in the west," he said, with a pool of capital for long-term economic development. The day the per-capita payment was made, Allen said it made him sick to see more than 15 abandoned cars alongside the road when he drove over to Hardin — all had been bought in Lame Deer at a temporary used car lot with per-capita money and had broken down on the road.

Today Rowland suffers with diabetes and must make three trips a week to a dialysis machine. Nevertheless, from his home on Muddy Creek he ponders the future of the tribe. The new chairman is his hand-picked successor, but the tribe sees no income from timber and ranching and no major coal development is on the horizon. He thinks that perhaps the only salvation is water. "We need to get as much as we deserve through the state adjudication process, and then intensely develop irrigated lands along the Tongue River," he said.

Although Rowland is quick to say that there are no more chiefs — that they disappeared from tribal life years ago — it's hard to believe when looking at his record and talking with him that Rowland himself hasn't been a modern-day Dull Knife or Little Wolf to the Northern Cheyenne. Despite controversy and turmoil, it was under Allen Rowland's leadership that the tribe was able to maintain control of its reservation so that today its options are greater than ever before.

Windy Shoulderblade. Michael Crummett

Windy Shoulderblade

Windy is young (born in 1951), extremely capable, and totally dedicated to helping the tribe better itself. He was elected tribal chairman in the fall of 1984.

Born in Miles City, Windy was raised in Lame Deer as well as in Seattle. After his schooling he entered the U.S. Special Forces and served in Vietnam; today he is active in the Army National Guard as a First Lieutenant. Windy, as were so many of his ancestors, is proud of his military background and acknowledges that it influences his way of operating as the new tribal chairman. Efficiency, dress code, punctuality, planning and strategy are all part of Windy's new regime, all qualities learned from his military experience.

Broadcasting in Billings and worked in a variety of radio positions. He returned to the reservation in 1978 to be public relations specialist for the tribal council. He then was elected to the council and became vice president, and

the council he was also chairman of the Land Committee and the Law and Justice Committee. All of this helped groom Windy for the tribal leadership position.

Although backed by the past chairman, Allen Rowland, in the 1984 election, Windy had to beat 12 other people. This meant that he won with a minority of votes cast, which did not smooth the early going. Nevertheless, faced with the need to make extensive cutbacks in the tribal budget, Windy has worked hard at a major reorganization effort. He is trying to make sure that the council is the policy-maker, with the chairman's office leading and the administration implementing policy.

As he looks at the tough tasks ahead, Windy sees the issues of education, economic development and more management training of tribal members as key priorities for his administration and for the tribe. He knows he has four difficult years ahead of him and he knows he can't play politics if he thinks he is going to get the upper hand in directing the tribe toward a viable future. So almost every night Windy is out in one community after another, or is traveling to Washington to seek what federal support he can count on. He readily admits that the first few months have not been easy on his wife and two children, but he hopes that life will settle down once his administration is fully oriented, reorganized and moving forward.

Joe Little Coyote

One of the best educated Cheyennes living on the reservation, Joe was raised in the Ashland area, went to St. Labre School, joined the U.S. Marines and served in Vietnam. After seven years in the service, he went to the University of Utah and Eastern Montana College. In 1976 he earned his master's degree in Education from Harvard University. After two years of further study, he received a certificate of advanced study in Administrative Planning and Social Policy from Harvard as well.

After graduate work Joe returned to the reservation and was elected to the tribal council. Cheyenne, with Cree in his ancestry, Joe speaks fluent Cheyenne. He and his wife, Brenda, have five children, the oldest of whom is now attending Montana State University. Joe is active in the traditional ways of the Cheyenne people, being one of the leaders of the Sun Dance.

Joe strongly feels that the overall goal of the tribe must be relative social and economic self-sufficiency. Working toward this end, he was the principal negotiator which produced the multimillion dollar ARCO/Northern

Joe Little Coyote at the 212 Diner in Ashland. Michael Crummett

Cheyenne exploration and drilling agreement in 1980. After the contract had been approved, Joe became the contract administrator for the tribe, whereby he oversaw all operations under the agreement. This included monitoring and accounting of seismic activity, drilling, data gathering, reclamation, rentals and damage payments. This work continued for four years until ARCO halted all activity in August 1984.

Because of Joe's educational background and farsighted thinking, he has been controversial on Northern Cheyenne. But Joe Little Coyote has clear visions for social and economic development, resolving health problems, and the need to better utilize the tribe's human resources for self-sufficiency. Like many in similar positions, he has had problems in fitting into tribal leadership, because of his outspoken ideas for the betterment of his people. Today the tribe has him actively involved in economic development, but he no longer is a member of the tribal council. Instead, he is in charge of the tribe's Business Development Endowment Fund, which he helped to establish. Little Coyote continues to help the tribe pursue self-sufficiency in whatever ways he can.

Dennis Limberhand

Dennis Limberhand was born in Forsyth in January 1947. His family moved often between the reservation and Forsyth during his early years and he attended Colstrip and St. Labre schools. After graduating from high school in

1965, he went to Eastern Montana College and then to a technical engineering school in California.

Upon returning to the reservation in 1970 he served on the tribal council during the critical coal leasing years from 1971 to 1980. Dennis found himself one of the key tribal spokesmen on the coal development issue, knowing that, on one hand, the tribe needed economic development, but that, on the other hand, the energy companies were not offering a fair deal for the tribe's resources.

With coal development stagnant on the Northern Cheyenne Reservation, Limberhand was hired by the Montana Power Company in 1979 as a liaison between Indian employees at Colstrip and the company. Montana Power Company was operating under strict Indian preference guidelines, yet the Cheyennes were largely unskilled and apprehensive about the off-reservation development. Limberhand undertook the huge task of helping recruit, train and employ Cheyennes at Colstrip. He also has helped Cheyennes get contract work there, ranging from janitorial to transportation and reclamation responsibilities.

In the fall of 1984, Montana Power Company was the largest non-government employer of Cheyennes, with between 120 and 130 tribal members working at the Colstrip generating facility. At least 90 of these jobs are permanent; the rest, in construction. Although he is satisfied with his progress regarding Cheyenne employment there, Limberhand hopes to have Cheyennes permanently holding at least 100 of the 600 to 700 jobs at the power facility. That's roughly the ratio of Indians to non-Indians in Rosebud County, the proportion he believes should pertain at Colstrip.

Another big issue for Limberhand has been trying to get Cheyennes into skilled and management jobs at Colstrip. Cheyennes could easily fill many instrument and control operater positions with the proper training. "That's an uphill battle," he said.

Dennis has now moved on to a new management position within Montana Power. He is pleased with the company's progress in employing, retaining and promoting Indian people. "Let's face it, Colstrip is an excellent training ground for our tribal labor force. Some day we also may have a major development around coal of our own, so why not employ people here now as it only is in the best interest of the tribe's long-term future."

In spite of the 20-mile commute, Dennis, his wife and three children still live in Lame Deer. He is on the Board of Directors of the Cheyenne Western Bank in Ashland and is a member of the Montana Human Rights Commission. Although not actively involved now in tribal politics, Dennis is still viewed as one of the key people of the tribe's future.

FLATHEAD RESERVATION
SALISH & KOOTENAI

The Flathead Reservation is occupied by the Salish and Kootenai tribes. Unlike the rest of the tribes living in Montana, these Indians migrated from the Columbia Plateau. They were the first of the present-day Montana tribes to call this area their home.

Chief Charlo and family on Flathead Reservation, circa 1900, from Forsyth stereograph, Butte. Photo courtesy of Museum of the Rockies

Salish

Historically, the term Salish refers to the linguistic character of many tribes that occupied the Columbia plateau of northwestern North America. This language family included the Flathead, the Pend d'Oreille, Kalispell, Coeur d'Alene, Spokane and others, tribes that occupied what we now know as the plateau area of Washington, Oregon, Idaho, western Montana and north to the Fraser River in Canada. It is generally believed that these tribes originally came from the north, moving into the Columbia Plateau and up the rivers of the Columbia system. Most Salish-speaking people stayed near the Pacific Coast, but the Flathead and Pend d'Oreille tribes gradually moved eastward into Montana. They may have begun to trickle into the western part of the state as long ago as 5,000 B.C., which would make them the first of the present-day Montana tribes to arrive here.

Salish moving into Montana had to make a cultural change from a lifestyle based on salmon fishery to one more dependent on plants and small game because Montana waterfalls in the Columbia River system blocked fish coming from the ocean.

Eventually the Salish came in contact with some of the early plains Indians who hunted buffalo on the plains of Montana, probably the Kiowa, the Plains Apache and the Shoshone. In short order the buffalo became important to the Salish as well. The Salish aboriginal range gradually extended to the Sweetgrass Hills in the north and the Bighorn Mountains in the east. The Salish apparently had six main centers of activity east of the Continental Divide, all focal points for buffalo hunting. These included the Helena Valley, the Three Forks area, the Big Hole country, the Jefferson Valley, and probably areas along the upper Yellowstone and Sun Rivers.

The Salish living east of the Divide were Flatheads, while the Pend d'Oreille, a larger tribe, held most of the valleys of western Montana.

The Pend d'Oreille lived mostly from what is now Paradise, Montana, upstream perhaps as far as Butte. Most of them settled in the Bitterroot, the Missoula and the Flathead Valleys. It was not until the early 1800s that the Pend d'Oreille, under Chief Alexander, ventured onto the eastern plains with their newly-acquired horses to hunt buffalo. They found this rough going, because so many other tribes already were there. Therefore, the Pend d'Oreille decided to concentrate their hunting interests in the safer confines of western Montana. Around 1830 the Pend d'Oreille began to focus most of their activity near what is now called St. Ignatius. This allowed them good access to all three major western valleys as well as to buffalo hunting routes to the east.

Kootenai Indians telling stories, 1929. Montana State University Archives.

The Confederated Salish-Kootenai Tribes

In 1855, Isaac Stevens, who was Governor and Superintendent of Indian Affairs for the Territory of Washington, met with representatives of the Kootenai, Flathead and Pend d'Oreille at Council Grove near Missoula, to persuade the three tribes to live together on one reservation. At the time there were approximately 450 Flatheads, 1,000 Pend d'Oreille and 800 Kootenai. Victor was the leader of the Flatheads; Alexander, leader of the Pend d'Oreille; and Michael, head of the Kootenai. Alexander and Michael signed an agreement that became known as the Hellgate Treaty. They agreed to a reservation that encompassed the southern half of Flathead Lake down through the Jocko Valley. Although Stevens preferred that they all live north of the Missoula Valley, he reluctantly agreed to establish a reservation in the Bitterroot Valley for the Flatheads as well. The terms of the agreement also called for a payment of $120,000 per year for 20 years to the tribes.

Because of intense pressure from white settlers, in 1872 the government negotiated an agreement with the Flathead band in the Bitterroot to open up their land for white settlement and to move to the Jocko Reservation. Two sub-chiefs, Arlee and Joseph Nine Pipes, agreed to the move, but Charlo, who was Victor's son, refused to sign the agreement because he didn't want to move from the Bitterroot. Despite the fact that in November 1871 President Grant signed an executive order to remove Charlo and his band from the Bitterroot and to put them on the Jocko Reservation, they spent 20 more years in the Bitterroot. Thus Flatheads were still in the Bitterroot in 1877 when Chief Joseph of the Nez Perce came over Lolo Pass and pleaded with Charlo and his 390 followers to assist him in his flight through Montana. Charlo refused to take sides, and Chief Joseph moved on.

Finally, on October 10, 1891 Charlo and his remaining band of 157 hungry and destitute people declared that the time had come to move to the Jocko Reservation. So with federal promises of housing and annuities, they quietly left the Bitterroot for the Jocko Reservation (to be known thereafter as the Flathead Reservation). Although the Kootenai, Pend d'Oreille and Flatheads were all on the reservation, their fight to exercise their own rights to the reservation had just begun. As a result of the passage of the Allotment Act in 1887, reservation lands could be allotted, meaning that each tribal member could receive ownership of a certain number of acres. Allotment quickly became a major issue on the Flathead. Agent Peter Ronan saw

In the early 1700s the Flatheads returned west of the Divide because they had been decimated by a smallpox epidemic. Then, about 1730, they were introduced to horses by the Shoshone. Flathead horses eventually found their way to the Pend d'Orielle, and (most likely, finally) to the Blackfeet and Kootenai. Even though they loved their plains hunting forays, the Flatheads' smaller numbers made them more vulnerable, and they reduced their dependency on the buffalo and obtained at least half their food and materials from plants such as camas and bitterroot as well as small game animals.

Christianity in the form of Catholicism came early to the Flathead and Pend d'Oreille. Some Iroquois under Big Ignace came from the east and settled with the Montana Salish in the early 1830s; they fascinated the Salish with descriptions of the basic principles of Christianity. From 1836 to 1841, four delegations from the Salish were sent to St. Louis to persuade the Catholics to send a priest. Finally, Jesuit Father Pierre Jean DeSmet came to the Bitterroot Valley in 1841 and established St. Mary's Mission in Stevensville. Later moved to St. Ignatius, it still exists. The church played a major role in keeping western Montana relatively peaceful during the Indian wars. The mission's priest kept open communication between Indian people and the white settlers who were migrating into the area. The mission also spearheaded an attempt to change the life of the Salish from a subsistence-gathering culture to a more agricultural one.

Kootenai

The Kootenai were originally called the Ksunka, meaning "People of the Standing Arrow."

To them standing arrow has meant strength, unity and dexterity. However, when the French first met the Ksunka, they called them Kootenai, meaning "water people," because they were so adept at canoeing the Columbia River and its tributaries.

Around 1500, the Kootenai are presumed to have been located in southeastern British Columbia, northwestern Montana and southwestern Alberta. It is thought that they were divided into at least three major bands. One inhabited the area along the Kootenai River; another was located near Lake Windemere, British Columbia; and another, near McLeod, Alberta. Most historians believe that the three bands were actually two distinct groups of Kootenai, with those living in Alberta having a culture and lifestyle built on hunting the bison. They were called the Plains Kootenai. The other bands were called the Plateau Kootenai. They lived in the mountains of the Columbia Plateau and their lifestyle was focused on rivers and lakes. All three groups were nomadic.

Eventually the Plains Kootenai, who had ventured as far south as Havre, were forced over the mountains into northwestern Montana by the plains tribes advancing from the east. They then merged with the Plateau Kootenai.

When the Pend d'Oreille moved south of Flathead Lake to St. Ignatius, the Kootenai moved into the Flathead Lake country. By the 1850s the Salish tribes and the Kootenai were close allies living in the mountain valleys of western Montana and making regular forays east of the Divide to hunt buffalo. Catholicism by this time had made major inroads on the lives of both the Salish and the Kootenai. And they all had the Blackfeet as their common enemy.

allotment as a pending disaster for the tribe and he was able to prevent it from happening until his death in 1893. Charlo took up where Ronan left off and continued to fight allotment. Finally, Congress passed a law in 1904 to allow Flathead lands to be allotted. Chief Charlo and his aide, Antoine Moiese, still resisted. They did not want the white settlers it would bring onto the reservation and they did not want to reduce further the amount of land that the tribes controlled.

In 1908 the Jocko Reservation was surveyed and allotted, with each member receiving 80 acres of agricultural land or 160 acres of grazing land. The rest of the reservation was to be opened for homesteading. Charlo successfully fought this until his death on January 10, 1910. Sadly, 15 days later the government announced that on April 1, approximately one million acres of the Flathead would be opened to homesteading. This, coupled with a later law allowing Indians with allotted lands to sell to non-Indians, destroyed the integrity of the reservation's land base. It was fortunate, however, that in 1919 the filing for homestead land on the reservation was suspended so that a new allotment act could be implemented. This was to give allotments to eligible Indians and their children who had not received allotments earlier. It should be noted, though, that from 1916 to 1919 some 20,000 acres of reservation land was set aside for the Moiese National Buffalo Range and several thousand more acres were set aside for two wildlife refuges.

After the new allotment act, selling of allotted lands and surplus lands continued sporadically until allotment was eliminated by the Indian Reorganization Act of 1934. By then just over half of the lands within the reservation boundaries had been sold to homesteaders, most of which were the rich agricultural lands of the Flathead Valley.

In 1928, a small power company negotiated a lease with the tribes for construction of Kerr Dam on the Flathead River. This proved to be a historic event in terms of tribal economic development because it allowed for annual rental payments to the tribe, which have continued to the present.

In line with the Indian Reorganization Act of 1934, the Salish and Kootenai tribes reorganized with a tribally-approved constitution in 1935. Much activity then focused on various Indian New Deal programs, including an Indian Conservation Corps. The Corps was responsible for building many roads, trails, and lookout towers along with developing fire protection measures throughout the forested portions of the reservation. This was particularly important because most of the land that the tribes and their members still owned was forested and located on the perimeter of the reservation.

Woman on log. Flathead Lake, no date. Photo courtesy of Montana State University Archives

From the mid-1930s to the mid-1960s, times were relatively quiet on the Flathead. Unlike many other Montana reservations, the Flathead Reservation had a large white population coupled with extremely valuable agricultural and timber lands. Therefore, it is not surprising that during the termination era in the late 1940s and 1950s, the Flathead Reservation was a prime target for termination. In 1953 House Concurrent Resolution 108 selected the Confederated Salish and Kootenai tribes for termination of federal services. Fortunately the tribal council decided that the uncertainties of maintaining a timber program after termination were so great that they had to oppose the idea. The tribes then worked hard to prevent termination of their reservation.

In 1951 the tribes sued the federal government for unfair payments for approximately 12 million acres of land that had been ceded to the government in the Hellgate Treaty of 1855, and for unfair compensation payments for the loss of lands following allotment in 1908. This began a long series of offensive moves by the Salish-Kootenai in asserting their rights. It wasn't until 1971 that the suit was settled and a judgment of $22 million was awarded. The Confederated Tribes then initiated other land and rights-related suits and began pushing for clarification on the access rights of non-members to tribal lands. A controversy arose over

whether the tribes could control the shore of Flathead Lake and docks being built on non-Indian shorelands. The tribe eventually won such rights in the Damen Case decision. With this, they won the right to control fishing over their portion of Flathead Lake and non-members now need a permit to fish in tribal waters.

The Confederated Salish-Kootenai tribes are viewed today as one of the more prosperous and self-reliant tribes in Montana. They operate most of the government programs existing on the reservation from road construction and credit to welfare, housing and education. They also have become the recognized leaders among Indian tribes in defining areas of jurisdiction within their reservation. This not only includes treaty and agreement clarification with the federal government, but also jurisdiction issues with the state of Montana in areas such as taxes, law and order and recreational management. Their aggressiveness, as well as their strong resource base, have given the Confederated Tribes confidence in their push toward self-reliance.

The Present Status of the Confederated Salish-Kootenai Tribes

Factual Information

As of December 1984, tribal enrollment was 6,180 members with 3,271 living on the reservation.

Tribal enrollment doesn't make a distinction between Kootenai and Salish, but it is commonly held that more than twice as many Salish as Flathead are enrolled members. Approximately 23 percent of the total enrollment figures are members with one-half or more Indian blood. Before 1960 tribal members could have as little as one-sixteenth Salish or Kootenai blood and still be enrolled members. In 1960, the tribes changed the blood quantum level to one-fourth Indian blood for members born after that year. This change was made under the specter of termination and pressure by the federal government. Fewer Salish and Kootenai meet the minimum blood requirement, and more than likely, the rolls of the reservation will become smaller with time. But it should be noted that the council can make changes in the eligibility requirements.

An important population statistic for the reservation is that approximately 19,750 people live within the Flathead Reservation boundaries, so only 16.6 percent of the reservation's population are enrolled tribal members. As a minority within their own reservation, the tribes encounter many more conflicts than are found on other reservations, such as Northern Cheyenne and Fort Belknap, where almost the entire population within the reservation is Indian.

Reservation Lands

The reservation is in a beautiful setting with the Cabinet Mountains on the west and the Mission Mountains on the east. Flathead Lake, the largest natural freshwater lake west of the Great Lakes, is found on the northern portion of the reservation, and the Rattlesnake Mountain Wilderness is found on the southeastern border. The Flathead River flows south out of Flathead Lake through the center of the reservation, as it makes its way toward the Clark's Fork of the Columbia River.

There are 1,242,969 acres within the reservation, of which 622,615 acres are owned by the tribe (92 percent) and by tribal members. Almost 52,000 acres on the reservation are set aside as refuges and public parks. These include Nine Pipes and Pablo Wildlife Refuges and the National Bison Range. Most of the Salish live in and around the communities of St. Ignatius and Arlee. The Kootenai live primarily in the northwestern part of the reservation near Elmo.

As on so many reservations, many jurisdictions criss-cross the boundaries of the Flathead Reservation. Four counties overlap portions of the reservation: Lake, Flathead, Sanders and Missoula. Most of the land owned by tribal members and the tribe is forested and most of the non-tribal land is in agricultural land in the valley.

Precipitation varies from 30 to 40 inches a year in the valley to 100 inches or more a year along the Mission Divide. Topographical extremes vary from just below 4,000' to more than 9,000'.

Tribal Government

Before the 1934 Indian Reorganization Act, the Confederated Salish-Kootenai tribes were governed by a loose association of chieftainships. In 1935, soon after the Indian Reorganization Act was passed, the tribes reorganized as a charter corporation with a constitution. Today there are 10 tribal council members serving staggered four-year terms. The council elects its own chairman, vice-chairman, secretary and treasurer to two-year terms. Council members are elected from eight districts with Arlee and St. Ignatius districts having two council members each.

The council recently has undertaken a major overhaul of tribal government for greater efficiency, reducing the

Top: *Moving cows under Chief Cliff, an ancient vision-quest site of the Kootenai Indians.*
Bottom: *St. Ignatius Mission. Jesuit priests had a strong influence on the Salish and Kootenai peoples by 1850.*
Michael Crummett photos

121

number of departments within tribal government from 33 to 10. This centralization process is intended to clear away much of the red tape that at times has been a nightmare for tribal members.

A unique aspect of the Flathead Reservation is that it is presently under the Bureau of Indian Affairs Area Office in Portland, Oregon rather than the Billings office that serves Montana's other tribes. Tribal leadership made the change several years ago, believing that services would be better provided from an office that dealt primarily with tribes from the Columbia Plateau and the Pacific Northwest. This has been found to be generally unsatisfactory; the jurisdiction of the Billings area office is being sought again.

Tribal Budget

In 1984, the tribal operations budget was $1.95 million. However, the total tribal and federal program budget was closer to $5 million. Actually, the tribes took in $12 million in revenue but much of this went directly to members in per-capita payments that are made by law two times a year. Much of these revenues come from the Kerr Dam lease and forestry revenues.

Flathead Reservation Natural Resources

No other reservation in Montana has the wealth of natural resources the Flathead Reservation has. Its abundant water, timber and rich soils have given the Confederated Salish-Kootenai tribes a critical asset in charting their future.

Agricultural Lands. Unfortunately, most of the prime agricultural lands are not the tribes'. There are approximately 20,000 trust acres that are in crop land with 14,000 acres irrigated. Although some wheat and barley are grown, much of this is in hay production. The famous Flathead cherry orchards are primarily north of the reservation boundary or on non-Indian lands within the reservation.

The tribe does not have a cattle herd nor are there many cattle within the reservation boundaries except for leases on the forested lands in the summer. The tribes attempted to develop a bison herd, but found it to be too expensive.

Wildlife and Fisheries. The reservation's forested and wilderness areas on the reservation perimeters and the wet lands and lakes throughout the valley provide abundant wildlife habitat. But, as on most reservations, wildlife regulations are insufficient; therefore, game populations are not what they could be. This is slowly changing despite cultural traditions regarding the role of wildlife in subsistence living. For example, to increase deer population there is now a doe season.

Top left: *The Jesuits attempted to work with the Flatheads from St. Mary Church in the Bitterroot Valley before their removal to the current or "Jocko" reservation in the 1890s.* Tom Dietrich
Top right: *The Flathead Reservation contains the National Bison Range at Moiese.* Michael Crummett
Bottom: *Ninepipes National Wildlife Refuge near Ronan.* Michael Crummett

Elk are found all along the perimeter of the reservaton, and mule and white tail deer are locally abundant. The reservation also has bighorn sheep, mountain goats, black and grizzly bears. The herd of approximately 80 bighorn sheep that reside on Flathead Lake's Wildhorse Island may be the most famous of the reservation's wildlife. These sheep for years have been the subject of wildlife management and biology studies. There are substantial trout and Kokanee salmon fisheries on the reservation. The tribes, whose fishing rights on lower Flathead Lake have been upheld in the Supreme Court, are turning their attention to building up the Flathead Lake Kokanee salmon fishery.

Forest Resources. The Flathead Reservation has approximately 480,000 acres of forest with 80 percent in tribal ownership. Douglas fir, ponderosa pine and western larch make up approximately 75 percent of the annual harvest. Besides logging, a healthy Christmas-tree industry exists. Tribal members are allowed to cut trees and sell them on the retail or wholesale markets.

Historically the reservation's forest resources have played an important role in the development of the tribe. The Hellgate Treaty provided for the government to construct a sawmill on the reservation. In 1883 when the Northern Pacific came through the southern part of the reservation, it opened a market for the timber as well as a means to transport it to other markets. Until 1909 tribal forests were managed by the Forest Service in the Department of Agriculture. After gross mismanagement and as a result of a major blowdown on the reservation in 1906, the government transferred timber management to the Department of the Interior. Fortunately the Indian Reorganization Act of 1934 advocated a sustained yield policy for reservation timber management. The first forest management plan on the Flathead wasn't complete until 1945 when the suggestion was made that approximately 10 million board feet of lumber could be cut. During the ensuing years, the timber plan was largely ignored, with market conditions dictating the cut. The 1966 and 1972 timber plans promoted intensive forest management on Flathead, suggesting that as much as 58 million board feet of timber could be cut each year. The most recent plan has gone even further and set an allowable cut of 71 million board feet annually. Such cuts have not been realized partially because of a depressed timber market. Furthermore, tribal council objectives regarding the employment of tribal members in logging, as well as their conservation resource objectives, have kept the cut much lower. In 1980 the cut was less than 10 million and in 1984 it was approximately 33 million board feet.

The forest industry will be a critical employer of tribal members in the future. As recently as September of 1983,

Salish-Kootenai College in Pablo enrolls 170 students in vocational and occupation training, Indian culture, history and community service classes. Michael Crummett

more than 55 tribal members were employed in one aspect or another in the timber industry, and more than 250 had employment on a seasonal basis.

Mineral Resources. Mining exploration has occurred on the reservation, but no sizeable discoveries have been made. The possibility of oil and gas has attracted ARCO and Mobil Oil to do seismic testing. In 1984 Mobil covered the reservation with seismic activities but no finds have been reported as of this writing.

Flathead Lake and Other Water Resources. The Flathead Reservation contains approximately 65,000 acres of surface water, most of it in the southern half of Flathead Lake. Many of the other lakes on the reservation are also connected to the Flathead Irrigation and Power Project, which provides irrigation water to many of the reservation farming interests. Flathead Lake is clearly the most important water source on the reservation, thanks in part to the Damen Supreme Court case decided in 1982. This asserted the right of the tribes to claim ownership of the beds and banks of Flathead Lake to nine feet above the high water mark. The Confederated Tribes have a seven-member shoreline protection board which is composed of four tribal members and three non-Indians. This board has as its main concerns the beauty and quality of the lake. It administers a dock tax for structures that go out into the water. The

money collected is used to monitor water hazards and water quality throughout the year. The Board has a cooperative agreement with the University of Montana's Yellow Bay Biology Station to work on water-quality issues, including stringent phosphorus standards. Although Flathead Lake provides for hydroelectric power at Kerr Dam, lakes are viewed by the tribe primarily as a recreational resource. The other lakes and rivers within the reservation such as Lake McDonald, the Jocko River, the Little Bitterroot and the main Flathead River provide boating, excellent fishing and other water-related recreational opportunities.

Economic Development

A generous natural resource base and years of effective tribal planning have created a relatively good economic environment for the Confederated Salish-Kootenai. Unemployment is still more than three times higher than non-Indian unemployment. It was estimated at approximately 31 percent during the winter of 1984-1985. However, this "guesstimate" does not include underemployment, the segment of the tribes not looking for work, nor those who have had to leave the reservation to find jobs. Nonetheless, the unemployment rate is half of that on many other reservations in Montana.

Top: *Mount Harding and the Mission Mountains.*
Michael Crummett
Bottom: *Pablo division of Plum Creek Timber, a major employer on the reservation.* Michael Crummett

Economic development goals on the reservation are similar to the goals of the counties within which the reservation lies. For example, the reservation wants clean industry that doesn't ruin its natural resources. It also wants to follow tribal values in developing businesses on the reservation. Another goal is to actively assist tribal members who are trying to establish business ventures. Furthermore, its current economic strategy is to create enterprises based on the tribes' natural resources, including post and pole, ranching, logging and hydroelectric power operations.

The second tribal economic strategy is to produce, as much as possible, the goods and services that tribal members consume. The tribal credit program, forest management enterprise, the Community College, Patcore (the Flathead building program) and the CharKoosta Print Shop reflect this plan. The third strategy is to develop as much labor-intensive, clean industry as possible. This is one of the reasons that the Kicking Horse Job Corps Center, which employs 70 tribal members, is a high priority of the tribes. Another is S&K Electronics, which recently received $3 million in defense contracts for building heaters in military tanks and preparing electronic circuit boards. Tribal members hope that some day this new enterprise will rival the size of A&S Industries on Fort Peck.

With the federal government over the last five years cutting tribal programs as much as 25 to 40 percent, the tribes are all the more determined to develop their own economic bases as quickly as possible. Although a timber products industry and agriculture are important in the tribes' economic plans, they know how much these industries are controlled by outside events. That is why these three economic strategies are so critical, and why the Confederated Salish-Kootenai believe their ownership and control of Kerr Dam will play such an important role in their future; it already provides $9 million per year through rental agreements.

The tribes have been involved in another hydroelectric project with the recent completion of a small-head hydro facility on Boulder Creek in the Mission Mountains. This prototype has a generating capacity of 350 kilowatts and an annual energy production of 1 million kilowatt hours. This energy is currently being sold to the Montana Power Company. The possibility exists that the Boulder Creek project can be replicated on 10 to 20 other sites over the next couple of decades.

Salish-Kootenai Culture and Celebrations

The culture of the Confederated Salish and Kootenai tribes is far different in origin from that of the plains tribes to the east. For example, the Salish never had a sun dance or military society. Rather, their major religious rites have been spirit ceremonies. The Kootenai also have winter sports ceremonies, except for the Plains Kootenai who had adopted the sun dance in their plains years.

Because of the importance of water to the Salish and the Kootenai, the canoe and the fish played an important role in their cultures. Salish canoes were made of bark, much like their eastern counterparts. However, these canoes peaked under the water, instead of on top, which gave them a "sturgeon" nose. The Salish also were expert in making baskets and mats. Today, beadwork and tanning hides are additional parts of the craft lore of the Salish and Kootenai.

The ancient Salish house was a subterranean pit house, with floor level below the ground, covered with a structure of logs which formed a peak at the center where the entrance and smoke hole were located. A later Salish house was located on the surface of the ground and was constructed of a framework of poles, resembling two large lean-to's facing each other. This was covered on all sides with overlapping mats to seal out the weather, leaving only the length of the top open for a smoke hole and an entrance on each end.

Along with a cultural committee that is a part of tribal government, there are two major cultural centers on the reservation. One is the Salish Cultural Center in St. Ignatius and the other is the Kootenai Cultural Center in Elmo. The major annual festivities are the Arlee PowWow during the first weekend in July and the War Dance Championships on the third weekend of November in St. Ignatius. A buffalo feast and Hand Game Championships occur on the third weekend in May in St. Ignatius.

Education

School-age children of most tribal members go to public schools in Arlee, St. Ignatius, Ronan and Polson. A BIA contract school in Dixon called Two Eagle River enrolls approximately 70 Indian students. The Salish-Kootenai College in Pablo is the only Indian community college in the state that is accredited. Established in 1977 as a non-profit institution after being affiliated as a satellite center of Flathead Valley Community College, the college has programs in vocational training, occupational training, community service, Indian culture and history, and a wide variety of college transfer programs. The fall 1984 enrollment was 170 students.

a.

b.

c.

a. *Stretching buckskin in hide-tanning class at Salish-Kootenai College*
b. *Vic Charlo, Agnes Vanderburg baking camas*

c. *Hanging hides in Elmo, Flathead Lake in background*
Michael Crummett photos

Major Issues Facing the Tribes

Environmental Protection

In recent years the Confederated Salish-Kootenai tribes have been very concerned about environmental protection measures. The tribes spent several years seeking air-quality redesignation for the reservation and the federal government granted Class I air status in May 1982. This made the Flathead the second reservation in the country to obtain the highest air quality standard available.

Why did they do it? Their request says: "To maintain the existing high-quality air and to preserve the scenic beauty and natural resources of the area; and to control industrial development on the reservation which otherwise might contribute significantly to a reduction of air quality."

The tribes recognize the uniqueness of their wilderness resource in the Mission Mountains and its 89,500-acre wilderness, established in 1982, is the only wilderness of its kind on any Indian reservation in the country.

The tribes also have fought successfully over the last 10 years against the use of their lands as corridors of high-voltage transmission lines from eastern Montana to the Pacific Northwest. The tribes' opposition to utility corridors also included the proposed Northern Tier Pipeline, which was opposed until an agreement was finally struck in 1981 that insured a large annual rental payment and extra environmental protection. The pipeline never was built because the state of Washington did not allow it.

The Damen Case, which determined jurisdiction of the shores of the Flathead River, interested the tribes primarily in terms of environmental preservation. The tribes have followed up with their water quality monitoring program under their Shoreline Protection Board.

Despite tribal concern for the quality of its environment, environmental issues continue to confront the Salish-Kootenai. One of the tribes' best fisheries, the Crow Creek Reservoir, is now suspected of contamination from pesticides and herbicides flowing into the reservoir from surrounding non-Indian agricultural lands. So the tribes are concerned about the possibility of Crow Creek and others on the reservation being toxic sinks. In the meantime, tribal leadership is seeking remedial and preventive measures regarding the use of toxic chemicals on the reservation.

The Confederated Salish-Kootenai are the only tribes in the country who have declared their reservation a nuclear-free zone. This was done in July 1984. Since then the tribes have actively supported anti-nuclear efforts throughout the west. One tribal leader summed up the tribes' rationale for this stand by saying, "So what if we're doing all of these other things in our quest for self-determination and a quality environment? If there is a nuclear war or a nuclear accident of some kind, our efforts will go for naught."

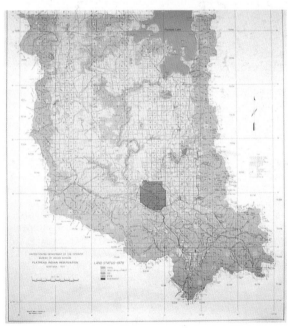

The Flathead Reservation probably suffers the most from mixed tribal/non-tribal ownership. Green is tribal, pink is non-tribal. Michael Crummett

125

Land Reacquisition

Since half the land on the reservation is not owned or controlled by the Salish-Kootenai, attempts are being made to reacquire non-Indian lands. Unfortunately, the land not in Indian ownership is prime agricultural land worth hundreds of millions of dollars. While the tribes entertain no serious thoughts of acquiring all the lands within their boundary, they do want to reacquire as much as possible for a variety of economic and jurisdictional reasons. The lack of capital restricts them from doing more as the tribal land reacquisition budget is only $500,000 per year, which allows them to acquire approximately 200 acres annually. However, this could change in the future if tribal revenues increase.

The Flathead Irrigation and Power Project

The Flathead Irrigation and Power Project is under the control of the Bureau of Indian Affairs, but is managed and operated entirely by non-Indians. It services more than 125,000 acres on the reservation and uses more than 100,000 acre-feet of water annually. It is estimated that the annual value of the crops grown on this land is close to $20 million. The project also owns and maintains most of the power lines on the reservation, and therefore provides the electrical power to tribal members.

The Irrigation Project has supported a dam proposed at Kootenai Falls; it is also an integral part of the Kerr Dam program. The recent Kerr Dam agreement has been opposed by the Flathead Irrigation and Power Project because the power it receives from the dam is not necessarily guaranteed when the tribes take over in 30 years.

A major future issue is control over the irrigation project. The tribes believe that the project and the tribes' interests have conflicted, not only over Kerr Dam and Kootenai Falls, but also on basic water rights issues, and the tribes would like some, if not all, control over the project.

Water Rights

Many tribal leaders see the single most important issue facing the tribes as the adjudication of their water rights, because water is such a critical resource on the reservation and there is so much of it.

In August 1984, the tribes formed a negotiations team to adjudicate the reservation's rights with the Water Compact Commission. Little progress was made during the first year of negotiations.

From Wildhorse Island, looking south across Flathead Lake to the Mission Mountains. Bill Bryan

Per-Capita Payments

Per-capita payments are legislated on the Flathead Reservation. Tribal members receive per-capita payments at the discretion of the tribal council. Payments are drawn from tribal timber sales, the leasing of tribal land for grazing or farming, and rent from Kerr Dam. Some of the total payments are distributed as per-capita payments, and the remainder is used for the operation of tribal affairs. A major question for the tribes is whether this large per-capita schedule is practical. If such payments were reduced, a sizeable capital base could result so that industry, land acquisition and other economic development programs to help with chronic unemployment could be undertaken. The volatile nature of this issue makes choices difficult, but the potential capital is there to lay a good foundation for economic self-sufficiency.

Discrimination

The tribes are a small minority within their own reservation controlling vast natural resources, so serious disagreements have occurred between Indians and non-Indians on Flathead. Property-rights groups such as Montanans Opposed to Discrimination and All Citizens Equal have been active within the valley trying to curtail tribal authority on certain issues. These issues historically have been jurisdictional as to administration of lands and political processes within reservation boundaries and judgmental as to whether the tribes are an overall liability to the economic and social environment in the valley. Recently the tribes have launched an aggressive campaign to promote the idea that they lead the way in protecting the valley's environment as well as contributing to its economic growth. The tribes believe that it is good for the local economy to have the reservation there. They also believe that the more tribal rights are protected and exercised, the better it will be in the long run for the economic, social and natural environments of the reservation.

Wildhorse Island

This is a beautiful 3,200-acre island that lies in the southwest corner of Flathead Lake within the boundaries of the Flathead Reservation. Although it has not been under Indian ownership since shortly after the turn of the century, it is an important historical place for both the Salish and the Kootenai. As Salish elders tell the story, when threatened by Blackfeet horse-stealing parties, the Salish would take their most valuable horses, swim them to the island and hide them there until the raiders left the valley. Rounding up the horses was not easy because of the island's huge size, and some old horses were never retrieved and became wild — thus the name, Wildhorse Island.

In 1939 two young bighorn sheep were brought to the island by private interests. Eight years later the Montana Fish and Game Department brought in six more, bringing the population at that time to 12. As a result, for the next several decades, the island became known for its bighorn sheep population, which expanded to more than 300 before dropping to fewer than 100. This made the island a haven for wildlife biologists studying the population dynamics and behavior of the animals.

In 1978, with help from The Nature Conservancy and federal land and water funds, the Montana Department of Fish, Wildlife and Parks acquired the island and created a state park.

Today there are no more wild horses but there are still plenty of mule deer, coyotes and black bears, alongside the herd of about 80 bighorns. One cannot stay overnight, but for the day visitor Wildhorse Island provides an opportunity for an unforgettable experience. The Salish-Kootenai tribes are working in cooperation with the state to provide public boat-docking facilities and a possible transportation system.

Mission Mountains Tribal Wilderness

Running counter to most stereotypes of reservation lands and Indian management of land is the Mission Mountains Tribal Wilderness, an 89,500-acre tract on the eastern boundary of the Flathead Reservation.

With more than 100 mountain lakes, snow-covered peaks that rise to 10,000 feet, and indigenous populations of wolverines, grizzlies, lynx, elk and mountain lion, this wilderness area is one of the most spectacular in the United States.

The Mission Mountains have always been a wilderness homeland to the Flathead, Pend d'Oreille and Kootenai tribes. The Flathead Cultural Committee described the mountains as having "served as a guide, passage-way, fortification, and vision-seeking grounds as well a place to gather medicinal herbs, roots and a place to hunt for food

Cliff Lake in the 90,000-acre Mission Mountains Tribal Wilderness, the first tribally-established wilderness area in the country. Bill Bryan

for the Pend d'Oreilles and Salish Indians since they have lived at the foothills of the Missions."

In 1936 the Tribal Council voted unanimously to set aside 100,000 acres of the mountains as an Indian-maintained and managed national park. Nothing came of this resolution, but a year later, Bob Marshall, then chief forester for the Office of Indian Affairs, drafted an order to establish the Missions on the Flathead Reservation as a wilderness area. BIA Commissioner John Collier signed the order, which differed from U.S. Forest Service wilderness regulations and the Wilderness Act of 1964 on at least one major point: "If there are reservations where the Indians desire privacy, sizeable areas are uninvaded by roads, then it will be possible for the Indians of these tribes to maintain a retreat where they may escape from constant contact with white men." (CFR 1937)

In the 1950s, when the U.S. Congress was considering establishing a wilderness preservation system, the tribal portion of the Mission Mountains was included. The tribes objected mainly because they weren't involved in establishing or managing this wilderness. Not until 1979 did the Tribal Council decide to establish a tribal wilderness. Their ordinance uses much of the same language as the 1964 Wilderness Act, but still provides its own definition of wilderness. For example, the ordinance says, "Wilderness has played a paramount role in shaping the character of the people and the culture of the Salish and Kootenai tribes. It is the essence of traditional Indian religion and has served the Indian people of these tribes ... in countless ways for thousands of years. Because maintaining an enduring resource of wilderness is vitally important to the people of the Salish and Kootenai tribes and the perpetuation of their culture, there is hereby established a Mission Mountains Tribal Wilderness Area, and this area shall be administered to protect and preserve wilderness values." In June 1980 the tribes established a tribal wildland recreation department that developed a wilderness management plan now in force.

The tribes have taken a particular interest in the small grizzly bear population within the wilderness area. Each year since 1982, a sizeable portion of the wilderness is closed to all human use for two and a half months because the grizzlies concentrate in the Cliff Lake-McDonald Peak area to feed on ladybugs and army moth larvae. As many as 10 to 12 bears have been observed at one time in this area. The grizzly has been significant in the history of the Salish and Kootenai tribes, who see maintaining its population as important not only from an ecological perspective but also for spiritual and traditional reasons.

Today the wilderness is a symbolic statement of the tribes' long-held spiritual beliefs regarding environmental values and the concept of wildland preservation.

Kerr Dam, an important source of revenue to the tribes, who eventually will assume its operation. Michael Crummett

Kerr Dam

Built by the federal government more than 50 years ago, Kerr Dam is a 204-foot high, 180-megawatt hydroelectric dam within reservation boundaries on the Flathead River. Its operating license, approved by the Federal Power Administration, has always been awarded to the Montana Power Company. The dam now produces approximately 11.5 percent of Montana Power's electricity, with annual future revenues estimated from $20 to $50 million.

Recently, when the Montana Power Company went through a relicensing procedure for the dam, the Confederated Tribes decided also to apply to the federal government for an operating license, because the dam was located on their reservation. After a long negotiating process, an agreement was reached in the fall of 1984 that allowed the Montana Power Company to operate the dam for the next 30 years with the tribe operating it over the remaining 20 years of the licensing agreement. During the next 30 years, the tribes also will receive $9 million per year for rent, adjusted annually according to the cost of living index.

The Kerr Dam issue has presented a classic tribal-sovereignty issue involving the control of reservation resources. A great deal of off-reservation interest has been generated during relicensing negotiations because the Montana Power Company said that the cost of electricity in the state of Montana would increase significantly if the tribes were to control the license. Both sides acknowledged this to be the case but the tribes did not believe the increase would be great.

Although some tribal members believe that the tribes lost the Kerr Dam fight, most believe that it was a victory because it will provide long-term security for the tribes. The agreement was finalized in summer 1985 by the Federal Energy Resource Commission. The Flathead Irrigation and Power Project still contends that its rights have been largely ignored in the agreement, but the consensus speculation is that the agreement will be approved and that it will be a significant long-term economic asset for the tribes.

Kootenai Falls

Certainly the largest and most spectacular waterfall in Montana is Kootenai Falls, a sacred site for the Kootenai tribe. The people view the falls as the center of their world, a place where tribal members can commune with spiritual forces that give direction to the tribe and to individual members. It is a vision-quest site and a sacred site for meditation.

In recent years a consortium of rural electric cooperatives and utility companies have looked into the possibility of damming the falls and creating a 144-megawatt hydropower plant. Curiously, approximately $400,000 in Bureau of Indian Affairs funds was spent in planning the dam and trying to get the facility approved and constructed. Even though the Salish-Kootenai tribes, environmentalists and others have vehemently opposed the project, Kootenai Falls is a classic case of the conflict of interest within the Bureau of Indian Affairs and its parent agency, the Department of Interior.

In 1931, the BIA's Flathead Irrigation and Power Project acquired control of a bankrupt utility company supplying electricity to the reservation. Today the irrigation project is directed by non Indians, and up to 90 percent of its irrigation resources are used to irrigate non-Indian lands. The power supplied by the project goes to 13,000 electrical customers, and approximately 2,600 farmers and ranchers who work more than 127,000 acres of land on the reservation. With 90 percent of its water and 80 percent of its electricity going to non-Indians, the Flathead Irrigation Power Project is hardly an Indian entity.

Nevertheless, when seven electric cooperatives wanted to build a $226 million dam and power plant at Kootenai Falls, the Bureau of Indian Affairs lent support. Many believe that the $400,000 used by the Bureau of Indian Affairs in promoting the dam was money illegally spent. Today the dam project has been stopped because of "no demonstrated need for the power," and the potential environmental damage.

Kootenai Falls, not on the reservation, is a site sacred to the Kootenai tribe. Lance Schelvan

Kicking Horse
Job Corps Center

Nestled beneath the Mission Mountains on the Flathead Reservation is the only Job Corps center in the country that is designed for and operated primarily by Indian people. Kicking Horse is operated under contract with the Confederated Salish and Kootenai tribes and staffed by 46 tribal members or approximately 70 percent of the workforce. Like other Job Corps centers run under the auspices of the U.S. Department of Labor, Kicking Horse exists to help low-income and disadvantaged youth gain job skills and social experiences so that they have a better chance of being gainfully employed. It is an occupational training program that also prepares students for high school equivalency diplomas. Potential students apply through their tribes' career development or employment assistance programs. If accepted they are given tuition, room and board and other living expenses.

Kicking Horse's enrollment of men and women between 16 and 21 years of age varies from 200 to 235 people, all of whom live on campus. Approximately 10 to 15 percent of the students come from Montana reservations. Students attend for one to two years. Kicking Horse's heavy

equipment operator program is popular with people from both the Crow and Northern Cheyenne Reservations, because mining jobs are available on or close to their respective reservations.

Kicking Horse has a group-life program for all its students based on a holistic approach derived from the Medicine Wheel concept. The group-life program's components include physical, intellectual, emotional and spiritual aspects. While students at this Job Corps center learn a specific skill, they also participate in a variety of activities in these four areas.

Joe "Dog" Felsman

Joe "Dog" Felsman is currently chairman of the Salish-Kootenai tribes, presiding over one of the more progressive tribal councils in the state. Born in 1932 in St. Ignatius, he grew up as an orphan, and had just started high school before being sent by his foster family to Chemawa Indian School in Salem, Oregon. Known as "Joe Dog" by

Joe Felsman. Michael Crummett

almost everyone, he says that his nickname was given by friends in his early years; his namesake was an elder on the reservation, Joe Little Dog.

In 1949 Felsman entered the Navy and served in the Korean War. He said the Navy gave direction to his life, and he spent 12 years in the service. He has continued his service ties by participating in the Veterans of Foreign Wars (VFW). In 1963 he moved to the east coast where he worked 10 years in a steel mill.

Felsman's ancestry is Salish and Pend d'Orielle but he also is one-quarter German. He is 11/32nds Indian, so only one of his children is a tribal member because of minimum blood-quantum limits.

In the spring of 1974, he returned to the reservation for good, delighted with the quality of the environment and with being among his people. He did a variety of odd jobs before becoming an environmental health technician for six years, collecting water samples throughout the reservation.

In 1981 he ran for tribal council and was elected from the St. Ignatius district. It was a surprise to him that during his tenure as councilman his fellow members wanted him to be tribal chairman. In 1983 he was elected by unanimous vote and has presided effectively during a time of great change. The successful negotiations regarding Kerr Dam during his short tenure as leader have been a great personal victory. Felsman knows well that the future of the combined tribes depends almost completely on what the tribes do with their natural resources. He's very proud of the wilderness designation as well as of the post-and-pole operation and the new hydro-development on Boulder Creek. "Our future depends on how we use resources such as these," Felsman said.

Teresa Wall

Teresa Wall is a member of a new group of young tribal council members in Montana active in the area of natural resource protection and development who believe that this area of the tribes' affairs is crucial to their future. Born in January 1954 in St. Ignatius, Wall is the youngest council member for the Salish-Kootenai tribes. Of both Salish and Kootenai ancestry, she grew up in the reservation's largest

Teresa Wall. Michael Crummett

Thomas Swaney. Michael Crummett

town, Polson. She graduated from Polson High School and went to Montana State University part-time for four years. After transferring to the College of Great Falls in the Indian teacher's training program, she graduated with a B.S. in elementary education in 1980.

She returned to the reservation to direct the youth employment program, helping design the apprenticeship program for carpenters, electricians and plumbers in the tribes' Community Planning and Development Division. Seven people graduated from the program while she was there. In 1982 she came to the Natural Resources Department to do research work on three controversial environmental issues on the reservation: Flathead Irrigation Project, Kerr Dam and Crow Creek Reservoir. Wall quickly became known as the natural resources specialist on Kerr Dam, its history and present status with the tribe.

In March 1984, Wall was appointed to the council to fill a vacancy. Her first reaction was that this would give her a chance to work in the most effective way for the combined tribes. However, she didn't anticipate the fact that many non-Indians in Polson suddenly saw her as "one of them," which she feels is a small price to pay for being a tribal leader.

Despite problems of being young, female and Indian on a reservation where Indians are in the minority, Wall finds the job most challenging. "I want to protect tribal rights," she said. She is pleased with the recent settlement of the Kerr Dam issue and hopes that this is just one of many issues that can be resolved in ways that enhance the tribes' future.

Thomas "Bearhead" Swaney

Bearhead Swaney is known within his tribe and throughout national Indian circles as one of the most forceful and articulate of all Indian environmental leaders. To that description we would add colorful. His lectures regarding the misuse of herbicides and pesticides are well known, as is his fight to get Class-I air-quality redesignation for the reservation. Class I is the category applied to wilderness areas and national parks.

Swaney was born in St. Ignatius in 1931. Of Salish descent, he lived in Dixon and graduated from high school in 1950. After military service, Swaney returned to the reservation in 1954 and worked in the Ravalli sawmill. He went to Western Montana College before transferring to the University of Montana. In 1960 he left the university and went on to spend the next two years as treasurer of the tribes.

In 1963 he was the Bureau of Indian Affairs Employment Assistance Officer. "This was a dark phase of my life," Swaney says, because he worked for five years as a BIA relocation person. "I didn't know what I was doing until I finally moved to the city myself." On moving to Riverside, California, he soon believed that relocation really meant adding another skid row to Los Angeles.

He returned to Flathead to help prevent termination of the reservation. In 1969 he became director of the Ranger program. This Citizen Action Program (CAP) project focused on wildlife management and the use of gamebirds and fish to help tribal members economically. It was during this period that Swaney's environmental ethics became well articulated. He soon was elected to the tribal council, where he served for four years ending in 1976. He returned as tribal chairman from 1978 to 1979 and remained on the council until 1981.

Although quick to be critical of people who are not working toward the best interests of the Salish-Kootenai tribes, Swaney also can be critical of himself. He said of his last few years on the council, "they went to my head. I wasn't in touch with the people. I thought that I was more important than I should have been." And for those reasons, Swaney believes, he was voted off the council. This hasn't made him bitter, only wiser.

He believes that his greatest accomplishment while on the tribal council was securing Class I air designation for the reservation. Swaney today is Director of Air Quality, a program that is three-fourths funded by the Environmental Protection Agency, and one-fourth funded by the tribe. Besides air quality, his duties include water quality work and monitoring the use of herbicides and pesticides on the reservation. His steadfast determination in working toward protecting the environmental quality of the reservation has earned him the prestigious American Motors Conservation Award and, more importantly, a great deal of respect among Indians and non-Indians alike.

131

MONTANA'S INDIANS IN THE FUTURE

There Will Be Change

Youth in the driver's seat, Crow Fair. Michael Crummett

This is a time of uncertainty and change among Indian tribes in Montana and throughout the United States. As a minority of 1.5 million people, Indians believe they are still in a survival situation in this country. The biggest political issue they see is the changing role of the federal government. With the social experiments and the "easy" money of the Great Society gone, they wonder if the pendulum of government policy is swinging completely the other way toward extreme social and fiscal conservatism. In short, might the federal government be getting out of the "Indian business" altogether?

One of the many reasons why the question is being raised is that Indian leaders point with concern to administration proposals in 1985 to eliminate funding for the Johnson-O'Malley education program and the educational facility construction program (815 monies), along with the reduction in money for federal higher-education scholarships, and conclude that the government wants to accept less responsibility for education —an essential need of Indian people. Indian leaders also worry about the future status of treaties between the government and various Indian nations. Many believe that treaty rights are not something they can count on in the future. Those who are concerned about this in Montana point to the Northern Cheyenne and their treaty rights with regard to education, and compare what is happening to Busby School and the lack of a high school on the reservation. The Big Horn River fishing rights issue is another example, as is the recent U.S. Supreme Court ruling that tribes must negotiate with the State of Montana regarding adjudication

of their water rights. And the Blackfeet point to their treaty rights in Glacier National Park and Lewis and Clark National Forest and see little if any federal recognition. This is also why there is so much concern among Indian people about groups like the Wisconsin-based "Equal Rights for Everyone," the Minnesota group called "Totally Equal Americans" and the Montana-based "All Citizens Equal." All have organizational goals that are concerned with limiting Indian treaty rights and opposing tribal sovereignty.

This then raises the issue of what might be the role of the government's historic policy of trust responsibility, as well as the role of the Bureau of Indian Affairs. Its long-standing negative image has made it extremely difficult for the BIA to recruit bright, young Indian people, which is exacerbating a long and difficult relationship between the bureau and the tribes. Another question about the bureau is whether it is too politicized to act effectively. Many, both inside and outside the bureau, believe that Congress has used the BIA as a political whipping boy, which does not have a consolidated constituency to defend it. Legislators often attack it in ways that make it almost impossible to develop coherent and consistent long-term programs. Also the bureau's budget appropriations have not kept up with inflation. In Montana, the bureau's weakened positon becomes evident in its handling of the almost constant crises of the Crow government. Finally, many observers wonder if the BIA will be abolished altogether, as recommended by the Presidential Commission on Indian Reservation Economics in 1984.

The issue of federal participation in Indian affairs is so important because of the grave social and economic situation on most reservatons. This is easily illustrated by the fact that 30 percent unemployment is considered good and 40 to 50 percent is passable; but most reservations have between 60 and 80 percent unemployment. The social consequences of such long-term, high unemployment rates are devastating.

Social instability, of which unemployment is one measure, touches almost every family on Montana reservations in the form of alcoholism. Racism continues to be an issue around the reservation borders (examples are Cut Bank and Hardin), and within reservations (examples: Polson and Wolf Point). A leadership-drain is drawing the brightest and best educated Indians from the reservation. The disappearance of languages, namely the Gros Ventre,

Kootenai and Salish, are significant cultural losses. This only aids and abets the cultural homogeneity of the Indian and is disastrous for the long-term survival of Indian nations and cultures. Tribal political issues are stalling the drive for self-determination. Some tribes could enhance continuity with staggered council terms. Others allow a huge slate of candidates to run, instead of two or three viable ones. And still others have unwieldy governing structures.

Being confronted with this list of political, economic and social dilemmas, it would be easy to envision only a grim future for Indian people. But what if we looked at the future differently and concentrated on the strengths of Indian culture with hope rather than despair? And what if we promoted the idea that Indians have a right to survive in tomorrow's world, rather than merely reacting to today's bad news: Let's look at the future of Indians in just such a constructive way.

There are more Indians today than at any other time in this century. They're healthier, they live longer, they're actually more prosperous and even more confident than ever before. Many Montana tribes have a lot going for them: A & S Industries on Fort Peck, the oil and gas development on Fort Peck and on Blackfeet, and the oil and gas exploration on all other reservations are positive economic developments. The Northern Cheyenne and Crow tribes have enormous coal resources. The new Kerr Dam agreement on the Flathead Reservation gives the Confederated Salish-Kootenai tribes a long-term capital resource. New leadership is emerging on reservations in the Dan Deckers, Joe McKays, Gail Smalls and Bill Yellowtails. All of this points to how far Indians have progressed over the past few decades. Earl Old Person, chief and tribal chairman of the Blackfeet Nation said, "We used to be directed and then followed after orders had been given. Now, we are walking alongside." He is suggesting that a new partnership is emerging between the Indian and non-Indian world.

In pursuit of this partnership and a viable future, Montana tribes are focusing on what Alvin Josephy in *Now That the Buffalo's Gone* calls quests. One is the quest for sovereignty; another is for self-sufficiency; and the third is for cultural preservation. All three comprise the overall goal of self-determination. The quest for sovereignty involves the clarification of the rights of tribes, and the pursuit of legal and political control of what takes place on the reservations. This quest originates from the government-to-government relationship that each tribe has with the federal government and its trust responsibility. The search for sovereignty explains why Montana tribes have engaged in so many legal efforts and why the American Indian Movement has gained headlines for its political actions focusing on Indian treaty rights. Recent legal actions and court decisions in Montana about the role of tribal courts, the ability of tribes to tax energy industries on the reservation, and whether the state has the right to tax royalties from oil and gas on reservations reflect various examples of the sovereignty quest undertaken by Montana tribes.

Another part of the sovereignty agenda is the tribes' desire to know the potential of their resource base and how it can best be protected, managed and developed. The sovereignty quest in Montana and other western states is being greatly aided by the Council of Energy Resource Tribes, which is providing technical and legal assistance on legal and ownership rights for tribes that have energy resources. Another important organizational resource for tribes in the west is the Tribal Sovereignty Project, now called the Seventh Generation Fund, which helps tribes understand their treaty rights and helps them build their tribal economies. The Native American Rights Fund in Boulder, Colorado, is another important national organization that is assisting Montana tribes in clarifying and asserting their legal rights.

Clarification of tribal sovereignty is essential to developing an economic agenda and therefore essential to the quest for self-sufficiency. This quest means that tribes would like to be less dependent on the federal government, or any other governing body. To many, this runs counter to the stereotypical belief that Indians are totally dependent on the federal government and want to continue indefinitely in this dependency relationship. In interview after interview, tribal leaders made it clear that nothing could be further from the truth. And tribal economic development plans are good testimonials to commitments to becoming economically independent.

Unfortunately, economic self-sufficiency on each Montana Indian reservation is years away from reality. One reason is that in trying to develop viable economies, tribes are wrestling with deciding what types of economy they should have. For example, on Fort Peck, the success of A and S Industries shows that the tribes there have made the decision for an employment economy. However, others following the employment economy bias are promoting individual businesses rather than tribal businesses. For example, some Montana tribes are supporting businesses such as Morningstar Construction on the Northern Cheyenne Reservation and Old Elk Construction on the Crow Reservation, which are run by individual tribal members. Most tribes, believe, however, they should be supporting both individual and tribal economic projects.

Another important aspect of the economic self-sufficiency quest is whether tribes can develop their own venture capital for new businesses. Unfortunately, Montana

tribes have a long way to go in this area because the per-capita payment philosophy is still so dominant. However, the federal Mineral Development Act of 1982 has been very helpful in side-stepping this issue, as it has allowed tribes to make joint venture agreements with oil and gas companies, whereby the outside company puts up the capital but the tribal business partner maintains control. Despite this development, tribes are trying to figure out other ways to begin to amass and make effective use of capital resources. The economic development trust fund set up on Northern Cheyenne with assistance from St. Labre Mission is one positive example.

A critical ingredient in the quest for economic self-sufficiency is leadership continuity on the reservation. One reason economic development programs have progressed so well on Fort Peck is that their tribal chairman, Norman Hollow, has been able to provide continuous leadership. Another ingredient is training individual Indian entrepreneurs to develop and run businesses and inducing such people to remain on the reservation.

On a cautionary note, it is tempting to think that by simply turning tribal resources over to private industry, on a lease or fee basis, that economic development and self-sufficiency could be accelerated. However, experience has shown that too often private sector developers move quickly with their own managers and their own business cultures, and the financial returns to Indians is dissipated by per-capita payments. This is partly because there is no long-term plan with a goal of self-sufficiency. Practically speaking, economic self-sufficiency most likely will come in the long run from an economic base that is owned, controlled and managed by the tribe.

Another dimension of the tribes' quest for self-sufficiency directly involves the Bureau of Indian Affairs. Public Law 93-638, passed in 1975, allows tribes to take over many services the bureau historically provided by contract. This has had mixed reviews. The Confederated Salish and Kootenai have been particularly successful at contract services, but reductions in contract funds on the Northern Cheyenne Reservation, which has no supplemental funds, make the continuation of contracts there doubtful.

Conflicts exist within the Interior Department's various agencies that hinder the drive for self-sufficiency. For example, the BIA is bound by law to implement the government's trust responsibility, but at the same time another agency in Interior, the Bureau of Reclamation, sometimes promotes resource development on public lands in conflict with Indian interests. The Kootenai Falls issue is a classic example. Here, former Interior Solicitor and ex-Montana Power Company executive William Coldiron stated recently, "There is a conflict here that is almost irreconcilable. We have a situation where the

Indians, to whom we owe a special obligation, take a position that opposes a position taken by say, the Bureau of Reclamation. To be a lawyer representing both sides is very difficult to live with."

The quest for cultural preservation recently has been pursued as a very high priority by all tribes in Montana. Many know that if they are or become a minority on their own reservations, their cultures are in serious trouble. The Salish and Kootenai languages are almost gone for that very reason, and it is also one of the reasons why both tribes have placed such a high priority on developing their own reservation cultural centers and why reversing the loss of tribal languages is the single most important cultural preservation issue on Montana reservations.

Indian community colleges in Montana are playing an important part in the tribes' pursuit of cultural preservation. All Montana reservations have some form of college or branch campus and all have integrated tribal languages and cultural traditions into their curricula. But federal funding of these colleges is most precarious and internal management has caused problems that let one believe that despite good intentions tribal colleges face an uncertain future.

Religious and cultural traditions such as the sun dance, the Native American Church, the sweat ceremony and other traditional rituals are enjoying a revival, with tribal elders passing to younger members various rituals, songs and dances. This is happening especially successfully on Rocky Boy's Reservation. Community colleges, federal entitlement programs in education and tribal resource-development programs, as on Blackfeet, also are helping in this process by employing elders to advise and educate on appropriate cultural matters. Furthermore, private institutions such as the American Indian Institute in Bozeman are hard at work maintaining the circle of elders within the Indian community. They continually promote in a most impressive manner the importance of the elder circle as well as the need for cross-cultural communications between the Indian and non-Indian cultures.

Behind this quest for cultural preservation is the important issue of developing self-esteem and confidence among Indian people. Indians have suffered for generations from federal policies that have made them feel less than worthy in this society. Past policies outlawed Indian ceremonies and customs, and forbade Indians to speak their native tongue in schools. And the continuing stigma of social problems and economic malaise on reservations only adds to the problem of little self-worth among young Indians.

One way of helping Indians develop a better sense of self-worth and assist in cultural preservation is to promote

Indian cultural training programs among interested non-Indians. A positive example of such cultural training is found at A and S Industries on the Ft. Peck Reservation. The staff of Brunswick Corporation, the financial management and marketing consultants to A and S, participate in programs to learn about the Sioux and Assiniboine cultures. They have been able to integrate what they have learned into day-to-day plant operations, which has been very important in the overall success of the business. Western Energy at Colstrip also conducts similar programs about Northern Cheyenne culture, for their non-Indian employees. The State of Montana briefly required teachers on or near reservations to take Indian awareness courses, but today such courses are voluntary.

Despite the importance of the quest for cultural preservation, the non-Indian world continues to want to assimilate Indian people, which conflicts with cultural preservation. Another serious obstacle is that cultural preservation programs often are viewed as frivolous and are the first ones to be cut when monies are tight. Finally, cultural preservation programs do not bring immediate economic returns. Even though a viable cultural heritage is synonymous with the long-term economic and social well-being of tribes, cultural programs are hard to sustain when so many tribal members have to deal with the immediate reality of economic survival. In a sense, survival in its various forms is a serious foe to the pursuit for cultural preservation.

These then are the quests that the Montana Indian finds essential in pursuing his or her own destiny. But if all of this is to be successful, Indians and tribes need to have the ability to influence important sectors of the non-Indian society. This means that Indians need an adequate power base so they can mobilize enough power to make the dreams of sovereignty, self-sufficiency and cultural preservation into realities. Such power can come in five forms: through educaton and research, money, politics, promoting or playing on the moral and social consciousness of the non-Indian society, and the law. All of these ingredients, in various mixtures, are necessary if the Indian's overall goal of self-determination is to become a reality.

To amplify briefly on each one of these components of power and their importance to the vital quests of Indian people, let us first look at education and research. Many believe that education is the number one priority for Indian people. It is difficult to make headway in today's world with insufficient education. This is particularly true for ethnic minorities. Tribes need educators, managers, generalists, technicians, specialists and entrepreneurs with good educations. That is why so many tribes, like the Chippewa-Cree on Rocky Boy's Reservation, and the Assiniboine and

Gros Ventre on Ft. Belknap, have placed education as their top tribal priority. And that is why tribes are so concerned about the reduction of federal funding for Indian education. Uneducated people, whether they are Indian or white, are going to be far more socially and economically dependent than those who receive a good, relevant education.

Related to education is research. Tribes need basic information about the exact nature of their natural and human resource bases. The tribal research project approach has been such an important tool on Montana reservations over the past 12 years. Still, much research is needed in such areas as how to best codify and assess the strengths and weaknesses of tribal laws. Research into treaties is also necessary, because many tribes do not know the extent of their treaty rights. Research and data gathering is also needed in the practical and essential social and demographic areas of knowing exactly how many children are going to school, how many tribal members are unemployed, the status of language and traditions and Indian medical needs. It is appalling to realize how little accurate, base-line data is available regarding Indian tribes.

Another component of building a power base is having adequate financial resources and a strong reservation economy. Although much has been said about the importance of economic development and its relationship to self-sufficiency, one cannot overemphasize its importance. To put it bluntly, tribes need money — so the questions are: where does it come from, who controls it and how might it best be managed and utilized to enhance the long-term futures of the tribes? Answers to these questions are critical as tribes try to acquire wealth. While doing so, many Indian leaders believe tribes need to see the fallacy of economic decisions that meet only short-term needs. Instead, they believe tribal economic policies need to carefully follow the basic axiom of the Seventh Generation Fund and the great law of the Iroquois Confederacy, which states, "In every deliberation, we must consider the impact of our decisions on the next seven generations." Such long-range thinking is vital in developing the present and future economic wealth of tribes.

Also essential to power for Indian people are the people themselves. Often, in politics, people are viewed only in raw numbers: If one can organize the necessary number of people in a democratic society, one can enact laws, implement programs and elect candidates. But Indian people are such a small minority that their ability to influence via the voting booth is minimal. In Montana, however, if more Indians were registered and voted in local and state elections, they could strongly influence seven to ten legislative races. And in a state where the Democratic

and Republican parties are so closely divided, the Indian vote can make a significant difference. For example, in 1984, a state legislative race that encompassed much of the Flathead Reservation was decided by five votes. If more Indians had voted and/or the losing candidate had been supported by Indian interests, the results could have been changed, thus preventing the 50-50 split between parties in the state House of Representatives! Aside from looking at Indians in terms of raw numbers in the political process, one might also look at the people themselves. Indian people may not have the ability to influence their own future unless they have pride and self-confidence in who they are. We know that a quality education and the maintenance of one's culture helps this, but so do good health programs, a strong sense of family, women's rights, and other equity issues. Positive role models also can help. Young tribal leaders like Larry Wetsit, Teresa Wall and Joe McKay are proof that Indian people can lead, communicate effectively with non-Indians and manage tribal affairs.

Leadership development is crucial, then, in the Indian's quest for articulating and pursuing his own destiny. This means more Indians seeking elective offices in county, state and national government, more Indians controlling successful reservation businesses and good Indian teachers and administrators in reservation school systems.

Another dimension in Indians' effort to influence their future is making use of the social or moral dimension of power. One way is being able to communicate effectively with non-Indians, to create a higher priority on learning more about who Indians are, and how better to work together in creating a viable future. Indians can educate others on exactly what is meant by trust responsibility and a government-to-government relationship, present their perspective on the history of the United States' policies toward Indian cultures and religions over the last 200 years, and reiterate that only a little over 100 years ago the buffalo culture dominated Montana Indian tribes, who have since had to experience and adjust to abrupt and drastic changes in government Indian policy. Non-Indians can learn a lot from Indian people: views of the natural environment and on the importance of elders are but two examples. However, this will not come spontaneously, but in part, through more persuasive techniques of communication, whereby Indian interests utilize information that directly appeals to the values, moral standards and personal interests of the majority society.

And certainly, the utilization by Indian people of the law and the legal process needs to continue. Indians are finding that it is essential to know what exactly are all the laws that apply to them, how these laws are interpreted and how best to use them not only to articulate and protect their rights, but also to chart their future. Montana tribes already have utilized the legal process to help define their rights in areas of water, taxation, law and order, economic development and natural resource protection. And they are fully cognizant that a great deal more needs to be done in all these legal areas. Certainly no one ingredient of power can be relied upon solely as Indian tribes diligently pursue the vision of self-determination. All need to be pursued in a vigorous manner in order for the quests and dreams of Indians to have a chance some day of becoming a reality.

The Seventh Generation Fund

(Formerly the Tribal Sovereignty Project)

The Seventh Generation Fund is an excellent example of a national grassroots effort by Indian people to work with tribes and individuals on issues of self-sufficiency. Its name is derived from a basic law of the Six Nations Iroquois Confederacy, which states, "In our every deliberation we must consider the impact of our decisions on the next seven generations ... on those faces that are yet beneath the ground." Since 1977 the organization has been providing funding and technical assistance to local Indian communities. It has become the only national Indian-controlled community foundation. Its controlling premise is that Indians need to apply the concept of sovereignty to concrete efforts in rebuilding the economic and political infrastructures of native communities.

Over the years the fund has helped more than 75 grassroots Indian projects throughout the country. These have included protecting tribal- and treaty-guaranteed rights to land, life and water, rebuilding tribal economies in a traditional way and trying to prevent unnecessary exploitation of tribal natural resources. For example, on the Northern Cheyenne Reservation, the fund helped a group of Cheyennes who were concerned that the 1980 lease agreement with ARCO for oil and gas rights was unfair and not in the best interests of environmental protection. The fund also helped protect Bear Butte in South Dakota from commercialization promoted by the state of South Dakota. Bear Butte is an area sacred to the Sioux, Cheyenne, Arapaho and Kiowa peoples, and for generations has been a site for meditation and vision quests. Tribal members from the Fort Peck and Northern Cheyenne Reservations regularly visit this area.

As the Fund looks to the future in its home in Reno, Nevada, its total annual budget now exceeds a quarter of a million dollars. It publishes a quarterly magazine entitled *Native Self-Sufficiency.*

Three Montana Indians were elected to the 1985 Montana legislature (left to right): Roland Kennerly, Blackfeet Tribe; Ramona Howe, Crow Tribe; Bill Yellowtail, Jr., Crow Tribe.
Michael Crummett

The American Indian Movement

The American Indian Movement (AIM) officially started in 1968. Its birth was a direct result of the termination and relocation policies of the federal government during the late 1940s and the 1950s. Many Indians found themselves in urban areas, frustrated and angry about what the government had been doing to them over the years, and they saw other ethnic minorities exercising their rights. It seemed natural to them they begin to fight in a more visible and forceful way for Indian sovereignty and other basic human and civil rights.

AIM started in Minnesota, but quickly appeared almost everywhere in Indian country. AIM's original intent was peaceful but it became more militant, and at times was influenced by extreme points of view. Regardless, AIM has brought a great deal of pride to Indian people, particularly to young Indians. The culmination of its protest efforts occurred in 1972 with the Trail of Broken Treaties that originated from reservations throughout the country and made its way to Washington, D.C. The general purpose of this protest march was to bring national attention to the conditions of native peoples. A specific six-point agenda included (1) having the federal government fulfill its treaty obligations, (2) having the federal government carry out its trust responsibilities with regard to Indian lands and reservations and the rights of Indian people, (3) wanting Indian affairs to be placed directly under the President, (4) not allowing the federal government to terminate any kind of social service to Indian tribes without a referendum, (5) that appropriation funds be increased for Indian peoples, and (6) wanting the federal government to guarantee education at the highest level for all Indians who want it.

With Indians pouring into Washington, the Nixon Administration was in an uproar and instructed the Bureau of Indian Affairs not to give any credibility to the Trail of Broken Treaties and to AIM. Since they could not get the ear of the government and were labeled criminals and outlaws, some of AIM's leaders occupied the federal building housing the Bureau of Indian Affairs. Sadly, this action gave credibility to the administration's portrayal of AIM and it created serious tension on the reservations with those Indians who strongly adhered to the law.

After the Washington protest was disbanded, another AIM occupation occurred at Wounded Knee in South Dakota a few months later. This was at times violent and lasted for 71 days until federal agents regained control over the town.

Throughout the 1970s AIM continued to push the federal government to fulfill its trust, treaty and basic human rights obligations to Indians. It also pressured tribal governments and local BIA agencies to make sure exploitation of natural resources and tribal lands did not occur. For example, in late 1979 and 1980 the Northern Cheyenne tribe was considering a blanket oil and gas lease with the Atlantic Richfield Company. Although the tribal council eventually signed the lease, concerns raised by AIM people were important ones and were consistent with AIM's overriding beliefs about the rights of Indian people, natural resource protection and making sure the federal government and corporations would no longer take advantage of Indian people.

Although today AIM rarely employs physical confrontation, it is still involved in political action, particularly on the reservations. It still raises issues and brings tribal councils together. AIM also organizes tribal leaders from many reservations, because of the need for Indian people to act as a coherent group to effectively stand up for their rights.

Of course when tribal and other political leaders aren't sensitive to Indian needs, AIM still takes action. As an example, in December 1984 the Montana Highway Department increased the speed limit on Highway 2 in Poplar, where it passes a public elementary school on the Fort Peck reservation. The stated reason for this action was that truckers had to slow too much. AIM replaced the new speed limit signs with still newer ones posting the speed limit of 20 miles per hour, because it said the tribe was not consulted and Indian lives were in danger. (See p. 47.)

Another important activity of AIM today is the establishment of the Yellow Thunder Camp on National Park Service land outside of Rapid City, South Dakota. Historically, the ownership of the Black Hills has been questioned by Indian people. Seeing that the government hasn't moved on this issue, AIM leaders who are members of the Sioux bands in South Dakota have set up a spiritual center in the Black Hills. So far there has been no confrontation and Yellow Thunder Camp has become a mecca for Indians with traditional interests and concerns from the northern plains and the West.

Although AIM has been controversial over the years, Richard Whitesall, the BIA area director in Billings, admits that as a result of AIM's militancy in the '70s, the Bureau has become dramatically more responsive to and cooperative with Indians than it used to be.

As for the future, AIM leader and Ogalala Sioux Russell Means said, "If you believe in treaties you are AIM." With this creed AIM continues to be active, although perhaps not as visibly. On any reservation in Montana today are Indians from elected leaders to unemployed tribal members who

are proud to say they "are AIM." They believe that AIM has shown Indian people to stand up for what the Great Spirit has given them.

Montana Inter-Tribal Policy Board

Located in Billings, the Montana Inter-Tribal Policy Board is the coordinating body for Montana Indian tribes. It is governed by a board composed of tribal chairmen and their delegates from each reservation, and from the Little Shell. MITPB is funded through grants and contracts from state and federal governments. Its role is to be a networker, catalyst and resource provider on certain issues for tribes in the state. It does not have binding authority on reservations, and does not interfere or infringe in any way on the jurisdictions of individual tribal governments.

Merle Lucas, current executive director, and Tom Tailfeathers, the board chairman, have played critical roles in establishing the Inter-Tribal Policy Board as a meaningful agent within the Montana Indian community. Because MITPB actions are not binding on reservations, there is no vested interest; so it has not been easy to develop an appropriate niche for the organization in the Montana Indian community. Lucas and Tailfeathers have seen to it that MITPB has a three-year organizational plan and has clear goals.

Recently the policy board has operated programs in law and order, education, social services, natural resources and economic development, and has helped administer programs for senior citizens (elders) on the reservation.

Providing a variety of educational opportunities is important for MITPB. Annually it sponsors a major conference on an important Indian issue such as economic development and helps sponsor the Montana Inter-Tribal Youth Practicum. MITPB regularly holds seminars on such topics as tribal sovereignty, natural resource planning, child and sexual abuse and supervisory training and administration.

In recent years MITPB has been an important lobbying force at the state legislature for tribal interests. Promoting Indian voter registration was a priority in 1984. MITPB also helped set up a national task force on Indian agriculture and is now in the process of establishing an inter-tribal development corporation that could take over a variety of maintenance and construction contracts from the federal government.

Despite the cultural diversity and different needs that exist among Montana Indian tribes, an organization like the

Above: *Flanked by Caleb Shields (left) and Merle Lucas, Thomas Yellowtail smokes the pipe of peace at the opening ceremonies of the Montana Inter-Tribal Policy Board.* Michael Crummett

Montana Inter-Tribal Policy Board can lead to effective action on issues of common concern. So far, MITPB has proved this in areas like water, alcohol abuse, economic development, political action and education.

Who Owns What Water? Montana vs. The Indians

In 1979 the Montana State Legislature enacted Senate Bill 76, which created a comprehensive water adjudication system for the state of Montana. Despite protests from the Indian community, the law provided for a state Reserved Water Rights Compact Commission to negotiate water rights with Indian tribes. The commission's purpose was to negotiate an agreement with each reservation, to be submitted to the legislature and to the appropriate tribal government. When the state legislature and tribal council concurred on the agreement, the state Water Court would supervise implementation.

Montana Indian tribes lobbied against such legislation in 1979 to no avail. The issue was then taken to federal district court in Billings, which ruled in favor of the state. The Ninth Circuit Court of Appeals ruled against the state, but the U.S. Supreme Court reversed the Ninth Circuit Court's ruling. This ruling was based on the federal McClaren Amendment, which allowed any state that had established a comprehensive system for adjudicating water rights to adjudicate federal water reserves in the state. The Mary Aiken federal case ruling upheld the McClaren Amendment and established that it also covered Indian water rights. The state of Montana since has had to defend in court the validity of the adjudication system, and its consistency with the McClaren Amendment. The state also has argued that its comprehensive adjudication system includes the adjudication of water on Indian reservations as well.

Although Montana tribes believe that treaty and other legal rights allow them to litigate their claims on their own, all except the Blackfeet have decided to negotiate. This process is cheaper and avoids the chance that a federal ruling may go against the tribe. Most tribes believe they can get what they deserve through negotiations.

Some precedent-setting issues are involved. One is the role of the state in tribal concerns, since, historically, states have played a minor role in Indian resource issues. The second issue is the willingness of both sides to put negotiations ahead of litigation, an innovative form of conflict resolution that may benefit both sides. The third major issue is the quantity of water that reservations can claim, which will determine the types of development they can undertake. Tribes need to know how much water is available as they make major plans for agriculture and energy-related development and consider whether they could market their water for substantial, regular income.

Once most of the legal issues had been resolved, the Compact Commission decided that a model water-rights agreement should be drawn with one particular reservation. Working with the Fort Peck Reservation tribes, they made that agreement in late 1982. The state Attorney General's office spoke against the agreement, saying it contradicted the state's case before the U.S. Supreme Court, which defended Montana's water adjudication system. Furthermore, Montana's Department of Natural Resources privately felt that the Commission had given too much away. The Department agreed with the Attorney General that the state should have sole jurisdiction over water rights disputes and they rejected the idea of the administration being shared by both the state and the federal government.

Many members of Montana tribes believed that once again a non-Indian government was reversing itself after having made an agreement. Their distrust extended toward the Compact Commission and the state of Montana. Fortunately, the Compact Commission was able to meet again with the Fort Peck tribes and negotiate a new agreement, accepted by the state legislature and by the Fort Peck Tribal Business Council in the spring of 1985.

Using the Fort Peck model agreement, the Compact Commission now is negotiating with other tribes. The Commission was given a two-year extension by the 1985 legislature to prepare agreements that will be presented to the 1987 legislature. However, it is still assumed that the Blackfeet tribe will not negotiate and they eventually will have to resort to litigation to resolve their water rights issues.

Council of Energy Resource Tribes

The original idea behind CERT was to develop a parallel to OPEC. If Indian tribes with their huge energy resources could work together, they could increase their bargaining leverage in negotiating with major energy companies. In its early years CERT found itself frequently attacking the Bureau of Indian Affairs for not doing its job, but at the same time asking the government for huge sums of operating money. CERT's board was originally led by Peter McDonald, who was the outspoken tribal chairman of the Navajo Reservation until he was defeated by Peterson Zah in 1980.

Today, McDonald is gone and tribes face a whole new energy development situation so CERT plays a much different role. Its emphasis has expanded from energy resources to helping tribes on issues like severance taxes, water rights, and to offering a variety of technical assistance in developing baseline research to broad economic development strategies. Today CERT believes that its new priorities are cooperation, communication and helping tribes prepare for a more favorable marketplace for their vast energy resources. The council has tried to erase its image of promoting energy development on reservations. Rather, it would like to be seen as a technical resource in helping individual tribes develop and/or preserve their resources, and at the same time keeping the tribe's own concerns foremost in mind. Since the recent passage of the Indian Minerals Development Act, CERT has helped tribes develop and negotiate their own oil and gas or coal contracts that involve profit-sharing and shared management arrangements. At present it is working particularly hard in this area with the Crow and Fort Peck tribes.

The American Indian Institute

One of the most special cross-cultural efforts in the western hemisphere, the American Indian Institute was established in 1973 in Bozeman to develop better understanding and cooperation among native and non-native peoples in the Americas. Its basic premise is that, after 400 years of co-existence, Indian people remain as little understood by Europeans as when the latter first arrived in this hemisphere. The Institute believes that this lack of understanding has resulted in many problems that Indian people face today.

The Institute sees itself as a uniting agent, making sure that the voices of traditional Indian people are heard in the contemporary world.

A major effort each year is the sponsorship of the traditional circle of elders. These circles have involved as many as 600 people and have been held in New York, Alberta, New Mexico, Montana and other places. The circle helps to focus the four major objectives of the Institute: 1) to help Indians reconstruct themselves, to rebuild traditional values and to promote self-sufficiency; 2) to foster better communications where Indians and non-Indians confidently talk and share their points of view with each other; 3) to create opportunities where good minds from both points of view can sit down with no boundaries separating them and have a constructive dialogue; and 4) to promote education of younger Indians by traditional elders who help build a solid cultural base and teach traditional beliefs.

Aside from the Circle gatherings, the Institute also has launched a development program for an endowment that will allow the Elder's Circle to continue indefinitely.

The Institute is sponsoring a touring contemporary Indian art program, with a large exhibit, seminars and a variety of media presentations. It continues to sponsor a variety of cross-cultural activities such as the International Cross-Cultural Peace Council in the spring of 1985 on Northern Cheyenne. Held on the land of Northern Cheyenne tribal elder Austin Two Moons, this council was a good example of an Institute activity — bringing both Indian and non-Indian people together to participate in spiritual renewal and strengthening ceremonies in the name of world peace.

Larry Wetsit

One of the young tribal leaders on Fort Peck, Larry Wetsit is a member of the Assiniboine tribe. Born in 1953 in Oswego near the southwestern border of the reservation, he graduated from Frazer High School in 1971, and went to the University of Montana majoring in pre-pharmacy. He didn't finish college there but returned to the reservation and recently graduated from Native American Education Service college.

Wetsit worked for a while at Wolf Point High School as a counselor, then for the tribes' Employment Rights Office and eventually was hired in the tribes' oil and gas program as a field technician, and later as project supervisor. In February 1984 he was named Minerals Director, a position he welcomes as one of importance to Fort Peck.

Wetsit and his wife are raising two sons in a traditional manner. He is proud to be pipe-carrier in sweat ceremonies and in the sun dance. His work as Minerals Director for the tribe is consistent with his strong feelings about the land, and he says, "If we take something from the land, we must give in return." This belief guides him to make sure conservation practices are followed in oil and gas drilling and pipeline construction. He also makes sure a traditional religious ceremony is performed at the site before a well, like the tribes' successful Wenona well, is drilled.

He strongly believes his future is with the tribes and hopes for many years of helping the tribes chart a viable course that blends cultural concerns, natural resources development and economics for their general welfare.

Daniel Decker

Dan Decker is one of three Salish-Kootenai tribal members who have gone to law school and returned to practice law on behalf of the tribe. He is Salish and grew up in St. Ignatius. He received a bachelor's degree from the University of Montana in 1975 and entered the Educational Media Program at the University of South Dakota in 1976. He taught at Dawson Community College and worked for the Office of Public Instruction in Helena before enrolling in the University of Montana Law School in 1979. Three years later he received a law degree with an Indian law and natural resources emphasis. He specializes in water-related issues and is working on water adjudication between the Salish-Kootenai tribes and the state of Montana. Already well respected in the Indian legal community, Decker has a great future ahead of him in the Indian-rights arena as well as in tribal leadership.

Gail Small

Gail Small, a member of the Northern Cheyenne tribe, epitomizes, in many ways, Montana's future Indian leaders. Smart, tough, articulate and a fierce advocate of human rights and Indian self-determination, she was raised on Northern Cheyenne. After losing a bitter election fight for the Montana House of Representatives, Small today resides in Lame Deer and is a private attorney.

Born on a small ranch, she attended public schools on the reservation and then went to high school at Colstrip. She was an excellent athlete, but because major coal development was just beginning, with an accompanying influx of construction workers and miners, racial prejudice seemed to permeate the school. She tried to start an Indian club in Colstrip, but because the school didn't want it, she decided to finish high school at St. Labre.

Small received a scholarship to the University of Montana. Although she struggled the first year, she became very active in the Indian Studies Program. Because she majored in natural resources and sociology, she spent summers on the reservation doing youth counseling and working for the newspaper.

After graduating in 1978 she returned to Lame Deer to work full time for the Northern Cheyenne Research Project, helping with various environmental impact statements. She was also active on the Police, Communications and Natural Resource commissions, as well as playing an extremely active role in the petition for Class I air redesignation.

In 1980 Gail spent one month in Havana, Cuba, at an international youth festival and got an insight into the role that Indians could play in the international arena.

She chose to go to law school at the University of Oregon because she could get a combined Indian law and natural resource degree. While she was in school she became involved in the ARCO lease controversy, and she believed that the terms were not good enough and that the tribe didn't have much control in the arrangement, particularly in the areas of water and taxes.

After finishing law school she worked in California on Indian fishing rights issues, and then decided to return home "to work for my own people."

Small ran for the state legislature in 1984 and said that one reason for running was to provide a role model to help establish more self-confidence in young people on Northern Cheyenne.

Larry Wetsit by tribal oil well of Fort Peck Reservation.
Michael Crummett

The first task in the campaign was to register Northern Cheyenne voters. She and her friends increased by five times the amount of registered voters on the reservation. Although she won heavily on Northern Cheyenne and Crow, she did poorly in the non-Indian portions of her district, falling a couple of hundred votes short overall.

Small now looks to the future and is more determined than ever to live on the reservation and help her tribe. Being very respectful of her culture, she is an excellent traditional dancer, and wants to make sure that the essence of traditional life on the Northern Cheyenne is not lost. She believes that most members of her tribe don't realize the value of the Northern Cheyennes' traditional government and that it needs to be included in daily life.

The big issues before the tribe, from her viewpoint, are education, coal development and water rights. She also is pushing the tribe to get an air-quality code as soon as possible and make sure that it is enforced, to support the Class I air designation.

What made Gail Small come so far so quickly in her young life? She responds easily. "It was my family. I have five sisters and four brothers who have been extremely supportive of what I've done throughout my life. And besides, Uncle John Wooden Legs, the tribal chairman before Allen Rowland, was a great influence on me, pushing me to get my college degree. Uncle John kept saying to me over and over again that they'll never take this education from me." And, she says emphatically, "He's right!"

As for her future, besides practicing law, she may decide to run again for the state legislature, but may run for tribal council as well. For the moment, she has put electoral politics aside to concentrate on law work to ensure the tribe gets through these tough times.

Dan Decker

Gail Small

Sen. Bill Yellowtail Michael Crummett photos

Joe McKay

Serving his first term on the Blackfeet Business Council, Joe McKay is another example of the new style of Indian leadership in Montana. At 31, he has a degree in Business Administration from the University of Montana, and in 1983 received a law degree from the same institution. Married and the father of two children, he returned home to work on behalf of his tribe. He believes that if the tribe is to survive as a strong government and sovereign political entity, it must act like a government while being accountable in service to its members. At the same time, McKay feels that such accountability has to combine with both administrative efficiency and a sense of vision directing the Blackfeet Nation.

Bill Yellowtail

When one looks toward the future of Montana Indian people, one can't help but notice Bill Yellowtail, a first-term state senator from Wyola. Ever since he came into this world in 1948, he has lived up to his Indian name, Wings On Fire, and has accomplished much in little time. Raised on a ranch, Yellowtail went to school in Wyola and was voted outstanding citizen at Boy's State in 1964. Because his dad wanted Bill to have a good college education, he went to the family automobile dealer and their lawyer to ask for help in applications to the universities they had attended. The next thing Bill realized, there were two thick envelopes in the mail, one from Harvard and one from Dartmouth, both accepting him as a freshman. Bill chose Dartmouth because he was told that it was in rural northern New Hampshire, which was in an environment somewhat similar to the one in which he grew up.

Yellowtail was the first Indian to attend Dartmouth in more than 20 years. His time there was not easy. He left after two years and enrolled at Montana State University. A year and a half later he decided to return to Dartmouth, and this time he continued until his graduation in 1971. He continued to live in Hanover to run the Native American ABC Program that helped place Indians in educational institutions around the country.

Following his return to Montana he worked for four years at the Office of Public Instruction in Helena in Indian education. He then became Director of Education for the Crow tribe before becoming active with the Montana Inter-tribal Policy Board. After serving as the Crow delegate to the board for a few years, he became its Executive Director during a very trying time for that organization. If it wasn't for Yellowtail, the policy board would have died a sad death. Some way, somehow he was able to get it back on keel.

Bill is 13/32 Crow and is a member of the Greasy Mouth Clan. He was very close to his father, so when he passed away, Bill left Billings to return home to work on the ranch. Despite the tough financial times facing ranchers, Bill, his brother and sister and mother have been able to make a living on Lodge Grass Creek in the Big Horn Mountains on Crow Reservation.

Experiencing first-hand the problems of Indian people and ranchers, Yellowtail decided to run in 1984 for the state senate. His campaign wasn't easy because he had to convince not only a vast majority of Crows and Northern Cheyennes to vote for him, but also a good percentage of the non-Indian community living in Hardin and on the Crow Reservation. He did not make an issue of his heritage, but won by almost one thousand votes. His first term, during the 1985 legislative session, won him a great deal of respect on both sides of the aisle, many political observers believed that he was the best rookie legislator in years. He concentrated on the areas of education, judiciary and fish and game, and stood against the governor on the critical issue of temporarily reducing Montana's coal severance tax.

Yellowtail is not sure of his political future, but he said, "It's real important for Montana Indians to really take their place in the future of Montana. They've got to participate, they've got to be part of the process."

Murton McCluskey

One can't talk about the future of Montana Indians without mentioning Murton McCluskey. Born in Browning on the Blackfeet Reservation in 1936, he was raised in Babb by his grandparents. He graduated in 1955 from the BIA Fort Totten Indian School in North Dakota. After serving in the armed forces for four years, McCluskey returned to Browning and enrolled in the Bureau of Indian Affairs relocation program. Although he wanted to learn welding, he was talked into training as a teacher. After earning his Associate Teacher's Certificate at Northern Montana College in Havre, he taught at Rocky Boy's Reservation. Teaching by day and attending Northern Montana College night classes, McCluskey earned his bachelor's and master's degrees over the next 14 years. He went on to earn an education doctorate from the University of North Dakota. By then he had become a full-time advocate of Indian education.

Since 1975, he has served as Director of Indian Education for the Great Falls school system. The program, one of the most extensive Indian education programs in Montana public schools, is funded by both Title IV monies and school system funds. McCluskey is proud that there are 955 Indian students in Great Falls schools, the second highest Indian enrollment in the state. Ten years ago, he explains, there were only 12 Indian seniors in Great Falls high schools; today there are 50.

Perhaps one of the most impressive things that McCluskey has accomplished is establishing an Indian resource library for Great Falls teachers and students — one that is unequalled in the state public school system. Although McCluskey is Blackfeet, his major professional emphasis has been with the urban and landless Indian, who in Great Falls tends to be Chippewa-Cree. He is professionally dedicated to correcting not only the white's stereotypical images of Indian people, but also the Indian's negative self-image. He sees self-image as the most fundamental issue facing Indian people, particularly the urban and landless Indian. To him, the high Indian dropout rate and the many social-related problems that plague Indians are rooted in negative self-image. McCluskey believes that education can correct this, especially when what Indian people learn about themselves in school is interpreted positively.

NAES College

A highly experimental college, NAES (for Native American Educational Services) College, was started in 1974 in the Chicago Indian community as an affiliate of Antioch College in Ohio. NAES is now independent, with main offices in Chicago and satellite branches, created in 1980, on Northern Cheyenne and Fort Peck. NAES offers a Bachelor of Arts Degree in Community Studies for Indian people who are employed in American Indian programs and agencies. Students have to be at least 24, have a high-school diploma, a full-time job and a background in Indian affairs.

The purpose of NAES is to develop a professional, credentialed leadership on Indian reservations who are accountable to the community. It helps Indians who are already in leadership positions develop their administrative and leadership capabilities. The program relies heavily on individualized and independent study in which students are to integrate their coursework with community needs. Many students find the NAES program very rigorous because it is so difficult to work full-time and simultaneously attend college. Nevertheless, through July 1984 the Fort Peck site had graduated 21 students and the Northern Cheyenne site 15.

Although the programs on Northern Cheyenne and Fort Peck are small, their administrators believe that NAES currently exerts a positive influence on their tribes. They point to their graduates and what they are now doing in various positions of tribal leadership as a concrete measure of the effectiveness of NAES.

Some who question NAES wonder whether its graduates seeking advanced degrees will be recognized by other institutions. Such skeptics also worry that NAES doesn't teach basic skills as thoroughly as do four-year institutions. But NAES leaders counter by listing universities like Chicago, Berkeley, Nebraska, Montana State and Montana where graduates have gone to do advanced degree work and have done well.

NAES's program looks bright even though it doesn't rely on federal money. Its income must come from tuition, grants and general fund-raising. Over the last three years the Fort Peck tribes have provided up to three quarters of their campus's operating budget. The Northern Cheyenne tribe has helped their program as well. Administrators hope to expand the program to other Montana reservations and are considering creation of a satellite college somewhere in western Montana. But in spite of its good early record, NAES is a fledgling, experimental institution with an uncertain source of income at a time when monies, particularly for Indian education, are becoming more and more scarce.

Art instructor Chris Dixon helps Ted Brings Yellow at Two Eagle River School, Flathead Reservation. Michael Crummett

Montana Inter-Tribal Youth and Natural Resource Practicum

Over the past 12 years more than 1,300 Indian high school students in Montana have participated in a week-long educational event similar to Boys State and Girls State. The Inter-tribal Youth and Natural Resource Practicum has been sponsored primarily by the Montana Inter-Tribal Policy Board and the United States Forest Service, with help from the Bureau of Indian Affairs, the Montana Indian Community Colleges and various state universities and colleges. Each year it's held on a different Montana reservation.

The objectives for attendees are (1) developing an understanding of tribal government and how it functions, (2) learning about natural resource issues and related concerns of tribal governments, (3) being exposed to natural resource management activities and career opportunities, (4) becoming acquainted with the educational processes and academic requirements for degrees in natural resource discipline, (5) developing leadership, communication and problem-solving skills, and (6) experiencing different tribal cultures that exist in Montana.

Professionals from around the state teach sessions in range management, wildlife and fisheries management, geology, soil conservation, air quality, water resources and engineering. Accompanying the academic portion of the practicum are a variety of recreational activities that include a powwow, horsemanship, canoeing, camping, and stick games. The Practicum has been a success and is the highlight of the academic year for high-school age Indian participants.

Indian Community Colleges

Originating from the success of the Navajo Community College established in 1968 and the more recent Kennedy Report on the quality of education for Indian people, the Indian Community College Assistance Act was passed in 1978 to provide the opportunity for community colleges to be created and operated on Indian reservations. The act was passed because there is little or no tax base on reservations; therefore, Indian people did not have the opportunity to establish their own community college unless the federal government could help financially.

Soon after the act was passed, the Salish-Kootenai Community College was established in Pablo. Today there is an Indian community college operating on every reservation. Their 1984 fulltime-equivalent enrollments are as follows:

Salish-Kootenai Community College, Flathead Reservation, fully accredited in June 1984, 170

Dull Knife Memorial Community College (affiliated with Miles City Community College),180

Blackfeet Community College (affiliated with Flathead Valley Community College), 165

Little Bighorn Community College (affiliated with Miles City Community College), 82

Fort Belknap Community College (affiliated with the Salish-Kootenai Community College), 69

Rocky Boy's Community College (affiliated with Belknap Community College), enrollment counted under Fort Belknap

Fort Peck Community College (affiliated with Dawson Community College), 68

Indian community colleges offer a variety of degrees, including an Associate of Arts degree, Associate of Science degree, and vocational-education certificates and apprenticeships. Most, if not all, credits are transferable to universities and state colleges in Montana and elsewhere.

Indian community colleges are a bridge between the reservation and non-reservation institutions of higher learning. Indian students who wish to go on to a four-year institution often can best prepare by going first to a community college, and Indian community colleges can create a better match between education and economic manpower needs on and off the reservation. Indian community college administrators also believe that they can train students in elementary and secondary Indian education to help them administer such programs on the reservations.

The Indian community college is still an experiment. Those involved are pleased with the initial success, yet there are major obstacles ahead. One is the large attrition rate. Another problem is that community college graduates still do not seem to benefit when they go on to institutions like the state university system. Those who do still seem to struggle at the larger, four-year institutions.

Perhaps the most serious problem facing the Indian community college is the reliance on government monies. Authorization funding for community-college students was initially passed at the level of $5,000 per student. However, this level, since fiscal year 1981, has gone down to approximately $2,800 per student. As a result, community colleges are just barely scraping by. In 1985 most closed their doors for the summer. While it is true that tuition monies could be raised and tribal funding could help offset the costs of the community college, the fact remains that tribal monies are very scarce. Furthermore, when there is 50 to 70 percent unemployment on reservations, there is very little available income for sizeable tuitions.

Most Indian affairs experts believe that the Indian community college is a great step toward Indian self-determination. Unfortunately, federal cutbacks threaten to jeopardize this important educational experiment before it has had a chance to prove itself. So another innovative educational program operating on Montana reservations is faced with a precarious future.

Author's Epilogue

A final thought on the future of Indians in Montana and elsewhere, is that despite their visionary agendas and the need to develop a better power base, Indian people could be helped by a lot of contrary and innovative thinking. As Gerald Wilkinson, Executive Director of the National Indian Youth Council recently stated, "The next revolution for Indian people must be one of ideas." In other words, the future of Montana tribes might best be served by looking at the myriad issues facing Indians in creative and radically different kinds of ways. Some possible examples include seriously considering county redistricting so that Montana's reservations are in single counties instead of split into as many as four counties, as are Fort Peck and the Flathead Reservations. Perhaps public school redistricting also could take place in and around Indian reservations so that school districts are based more on Indian needs and involvement and not just on sports dynasties. Often, Indian star athletes attend non-reservation schools, where the school board, teachers and curriculum reflect little Indian representation or interest.

Another proposal that tribes might want to consider is the establishment of a tribal government review commission that convenes every 10 years and must come up with a proposed change in structure that is then voted on by the tribe's members. With its 1972 constitution, Montana presently has similar commissions for city and county governments. If tribal governments legislated themselves to review their governments periodically, basic restructuring might occur that would deal with such issues as staggered terms, primaries for tribal chairman races, efficiency in government, and changes that effectively separate policy and administration and politics and business at the tribal council level.

Another idea that might be worth pursuing is a tribal member service program where all members are asked to put in at least two years of service for the tribe, much like the Mormon missionary program, or the philosophy that all young able-bodied people provide two years of service to the federal government, whether it is in the military or community service like the Peace Corps or VISTA. Such a program might help alleviate the present issue of many educated Indians and potential tribal leaders leaving the reservation and not returning. A tribal service program could work on making the best use of all the skills of people on tribal roles. There would have to be a variety of economic incentives to make sure that such a service program could take place. Such incentives could include monetary compensation, tax breaks, educational loans and scholarships, job preference and certain forms of insurance.

New thinking also might address the future of the Bureau of Indian Affairs. While the government should *never* consider abdicating its treaty and trust responsibilities, the bureau could be restructured in a way that makes it more consistent with long-range federal Indian policy in this country. Right now the bureau lacks direction. There is little long-range planning within tribal government. Furthermore, changes in Indian policy that inevitably occur with every change in administration ridicule any attempts at long-range planning. If the federal government is to help in the areas of sovereignty, self-sufficiency and cultural preservation, long-range programs and policies are needed. Perhaps the government, in concert with tribes, needs to articulate a long-range plan over the next 20 to 50 years regarding Indian self-sufficiency and the role of the federal government and the Bureau of Indian Affairs. It could well mean that a 50-year plan may eventually phase out the Bureau of Indian Affairs. The end result may very

well be the establishment of an Indian Rights and Treaties Bureau in the Department of Justice, an Indian Health and Welfare agency in the Department of HEW, and an Indian Land Management Assistance agency within the Department of Interior. Whatever it may be, some sort of fundamental change at the federal level needs to be explored, developed, thoroughly debated and then implemented.

We have seen major changes occur in a peaceful manner between other nations such as the United States and Panama, regarding the Panama Canal, and Great Britain and the Peoples Republic of China over Hong Kong. Changes and agreements of this magnitude could happen here as well. It certainly would be better than the present situation where there is almost a total lack of direction with no one knowing what form Indian policy will take from one federal administraton to the next.

In any event, the future of the Montana Indian is precarious. There are great hopes and dreams, but for them to be realized, Indians themselves need to be successful in their push for self-determination. They need success in building an adequate power base. If not, cultural genocide may well prevail. At the same time, we as non-Indians need to re-order our own priorities so that we understand the American Indian's unique situation. We also need to work with Indian tribes, through our local, state and federal governments, in assisting with their search for a viable future. This will not happen by continuing to think that "the Indian problem" eventually is going to disappear, and it will not happen with the federal government's Indian policy lacking any kind of continuity and direction. Furthermore, there is no room now for soft, liberal Great Society thinking. But there is plenty of room for sensitive but tough, innovative thinking that understands the past, respects the present, and fights for the future.

BIBLIOGRAPHY

This bibliography is by no means exhaustive, but will lead the reader to additional information on Indians in general and Montana tribes in particular. A detailed resource catalog of Indian references is available from the Great Falls Public Schools at the Indian Studies Resource Library at Largent School, 915 First Avenue South, Great Falls. Extensive resource materials on Montana Indians can also be found in the libraries of the state universities and colleges and the Museum of the Rockies in Bozeman and the Montana Historical Society in Helena.

American Indian History

Andrews, Ralph W. *Curtis' Western Indians.* New York: Bonanza Books, 1962.

Berkey, Curtis. *Indian Sovereignty.* Washington, D.C.: Institute for the Development of Indian Law, 1976.

Bowden, Henry W. *American Indians and Christian Missions.* Chicago: Univ. of Chicago Press, 1981.

Canby, William C., Jr. *American Indian Law in a Nutshell.* St. Paul, Minn.: West Publishing, 1981.

Costo, Rupert. *Indian Treaties: Two Centuries of Dishonor.* San Francisco: Indian Historian Press, 1977.

Edmunds, R. David, ed. *American Indian Leaders.* Lincoln: Univ. of Nebraska Press, 1980.

Hall, Gilbert L. *The Federal-Indian Trust Relationship.* Washington, D.C.: Institute for the Development of Indian Law, 1979.

Hassrick, Royal B. *The Sioux.* Norman: Univ. of Oklahoma Press, 1964.

Highwater, Jamake. *The Sweet Grass Lives On.* New York: Lippincott & Crowell, 1980.

Hoxie, Frederick E. *A Final Promise: The Campaign to Assimilate the Indians, 1880-1920.* Lincoln: Univ. of Nebraska Press, 1984.

Institute of the American West. *Indian Self Rule: Fifty Years Under the Indian Reorganization Act.* Institute of the American West, 1983.

Jackson, Curtis E. and Marcia J. Galli. *A History of the Bureau of Indian Affairs and Its Activities Among Indians.* San Francisco: R and E Research Associates, 1977.

Jahoda, Gloria. *The Trail of Tears.* New York: Holt, Rinehart & Winston, 1975.

Josephy, Alvin M., Jr. *The Indian Heritage of America.* New York: Knopf, 1968.

Josephy, Alvin M., Jr. *The Patriot Chiefs.* New York: Viking Press, 1958, 1961.

Kelly, Lawrence C. *The Assault on Assimilation: John Collier and the Origins of Indian Policy Reform.* Albuquerque: Univ. of New Mexico Press, 1983.

Lane, Harrison. *The Long Flight: History of the Nez Perce War.* Havre, Mont.: Griggs Publishing and Printing, 1982.

McNickle, D'Arcy. *They Came Here First.* Harper & Row, 1975.

Marquis, Thomas. *Custer, Cavalry & Crows.* Ft. Collins, Colo.: Old Army Press, 1975.

Otis, D.S. *The Dawes Act and the Allotment of Indian Lands.* Norman: Univ. of Oklahoma Press, 1973.

Philp, Kenneth. *John Collier's Crusade for Indian Reform 1920 to 1954.* Tucson: Univ. of Arizona, 1977.

Prucha, Francis Paul. *American Indian Policy in Crisis.* Norman: Univ. of Oklahoma Press, 1976.

Prucha, Francis Paul. *American Indian Policy in the Formative Years.* Lincoln: Univ. of Nebraska Press, 1962.

Sandoz, Mari. *The Battle of the Little Bighorn.* Lincoln: Univ. of Nebraska Press, 1966.

Sandoz, Mari. *The Buffalo Hunters.* Lincoln: Univ. of Nebraska Press, 1954.

Saum, Lewis O. *The Fur Trader and the Indian.* Seattle: Univ. of Washington Press, 1965.

Seymour, Flora Warren. *Indian Agents.* New York: D. Appleton-Century Co., 1941.

Sunder, John E. *The Fur Trade on the Upper Missouri, 1840-1865.* Norman: Univ. of Oklahoma Press, 1965.

Taylor, Graham D. *The New Deal and American Indian Tribalism.* Lincoln: Univ. of Nebraska Press, 1980.

Tyler, S. Lyman. *Indian Affairs: A Work Paper on Termination, with an Attempt to Show Its Antecedents.* Provo, Utah: Brigham Young University, 1964.

Vestal, Stanley. *Sitting Bull: Champion of the Sioux.* New York: Houghton Mifflin Co., 1932.

Williams, Ted C. *The Reservation.* Syracuse, N.Y.: Syracuse University Press, 1976.

Wishart, David J. *The Fur Trade of the American West, 1807-1840.* Univ. of Nebraska Press, 1979.

American Indian Culture

Borton, Verena R. "Native American Church." Paper for History 301, Montana State University. December 10, 1962.

Caraway, Caren. *The Beginner's Guide to Quilting.* New York: McKay, 1980.

Culin, Stewart. *Games of the North American Indians.* New York: Dover, 1975.

Curtis, Edward S. *Indian Days of Long Ago: Indian Life and Indian Lore.* Tamarack Press, 1975.

Foster, Steven. *The Book of the Vision Quest.* Covelo, Calif.: Island Press, 1980.

Hunt, Walter B., and Burshears, J.F. Buck. *American Indian Beadwork.* New York: Collier Books, 1951.

Jorgensen, Joseph G. *The Sun Dance Religion.* Chicago: Univ. of Chicago Press, 1972.

LaBarre, Weston. *The Peyote Cult.* New York: Schocken Books, 1975.

Mooney, James. *The Ghost-Dance Religion and Wounded Knee.* New York: Dover, 1973.

Powell, Peter J. *Sweet Medicine.* Norman: Univ. of Oklahoma Press, 1969.

Wildschut, William. *Crow Indian Medicine Bundles.* New York: Museum of the American Indian, Heye Foundation, 1975.

Montana Tribes—History

Barry, Edward E. *The Fort Belknap Indian Reservation.* Prepared and published by author, March 24, 1972 - June, 1973.

Berthrong, Donald J. *The Cheyenne and Arapaho Ordeal.* Norman: Univ. of Oklahoma Press, 1976.

Denig, Edwin T. *Five Indian Tribes of the Upper Missouri.* Norman: Univ. of Oklahoma Press, 1961, 1969, 1973.

Dion, Joseph F. *My Tribe, the Crees.* Calgary: Glenbow Museum, 1979.

Ewers, John C. *The Blackfeet: Raiders on the Northwestern Plains.* Norman: Univ. of Oklahoma Press, 1958.

Fahey, John. *The Flathead Indians.* Norman: University of Oklahoma Press, 1974.

Fairbairn, Ron. *The Way It Was.* Hemet, Calif.: Hemet Printing, 120 East Florida Ave., 1977.

Farr, William E. *The Reservation Blackfeet, 1882-1945.* Seattle: Univ. of Washington Press, 1984.

Flannery, Regina. *The Gros Ventres of Montana.* Washington, D.C.: Catholic University of America Press, 1953, 1975.

Garcia, Andrew. *Tough Trip Through Paradise, 1878-1879.* Sausalito, CA: Comstock Books, 1967.

Grinnell, George Bird. *The Cheyenne Indians.* Lincoln: Univ. of Nebraska Press, 1923, 1972.

Grinnell, George Bird. *The Fighting Cheyennes.* Norman: Univ. of Oklahoma Press, 1915, 1955.

Historical Research Associates. "The Fort Belknap Timber Trust: A History of Forest Management on the Fort Belknap Indian Reservation, Montana 1898-1978." Prepared for the BIA, Billings Area Office, Billings, Montana, June 1980.

Historical Research Associates. "Rocky Boy's Timber: Evolution of a Trust, History of Forest Management on the Rocky Boy's Indian Reservation, Montana, 1916-1978." Missoula, Montana, June 15, 1980.

Historical Research Associates. "Skidways to the Past: History of Forest Management on the Blackfeet Indian Reservation, 1855-1978." Missoula, Montana, June 15, 1980.

Historical Research Associates, "Timber, Tribes, and Trust: A History of BIA Forest Management on the Flathead Indian Reservation (1855-1975)." Manuscript prepared for the Confederated Salish and Kootenai Tribes of the Flathead Indian Reservation and the BIA, Branch of Forestry, Flathead Agency, Ronan, Montana, May 1977.

Jackson, Joseph, et al., "A Forest Management Plan for the Blackfeet Indian Reservation, Montana." The Blackfeet Tribe, Browning, Montana, June 1984.

Johnson, Olga Weydemeyer. *Flathead and Kootenai.* Glendale, Calif.: Arthur H. Clark Company, 1969.

Koury, Michael J. *Military Posts of Montana.* 2202 Victoria, Bellevue, Neb.: Old Army Press, 1970.

Lang, William L., and Myers, Rex C. *Montana, Our Land and People.* Boulder, Colo.: Pruett Publishing, 1979.

Linderman, Frank B. *Plenty Coups, Chief of the Crows.* Lincoln: Univ. of Nebraska Press, 1930, 1957.

Lowie, Robert H. *The Assiniboine.* New York: AMS Press, 1975.

Lowie, Robert H. *The Crow Indians.* New York: Holt, Rinehart and Winston, 1935, 1956.

McGinnis, Dale K., and Sharrock, Floyd W. *The Crow People.* Phoenix: Indian Tribal Series, 1972.

Malone, Michael P., and Roeder, Richard B. *Montana, A History of Two Centuries.* Seattle: Univ. of Washington Press, 1976.

Marquis, Thomas B. *The Cheyennes of Montana.* Algonac, Mich.: Reference Publications, Inc., 1978.

Nault, Fred. *Fred Nault: Montana Metis.* Rocky Boy, Mont.: Rocky Boy School, 1977.

Ortiz, Roxanne Dunbar. *The Great Sioux Nation.* Berkeley, Calif.: Moon Books, 1977.

"Proceedings of Councils of the Commissioners Appointed to Negotiate with the Fort Belknap Indians." Records of the Department of Indian Affairs, 25450-1922-051.

Rocky Boy School. *Chippewa and Cree.* Rocky Boy, Mont.: Rocky Boy School, 1977.

Rodnick, David. *The Fort Belknap Assiniboine of Montana.* New York: AMS Press, 1978.

St. Martin, Joanne, ed. *Montana's Indians, Their History and Location.* Great Falls, Mont.: Great Falls Public Schools, 1981.

Sealey, D. Bruce, et al. *The Metis, Canada's Forgotten People.* D. Bruce Sealey and Antoine S. Lussier, 1973.

Weist, Tom. *A History of the Cheyenne People.* Billings, Mont.: Montana Council for Indian Education, 1977.

Montana Tribes — Culture

Dusenberry, Verne. *The Montana Cree.* Stockholm: Almquist & Wiksell, 1962.

Ewers, John C. *Blackfeet Crafts.* U.S. Dept. of the Interior, 1945.

Ewers, John C. *Indian Life on the Upper Missouri.* Norman: Univ. of Oklahoma Press, 1968.

Grinnell, George Bird. *Blackfoot Lodge Tales: The Story of a Prairie People.* Lincoln: Univ. of Nebraska Press, 1962.

Ground, Mary. *Grass Woman Stories.* Browning, Mont.: Blackfeet Heritage Program, 1978.

Hart, Jeff. *Montana: Native Plants and Early Peoples.* Helena: Montana Historical Society, 1976.

Kroeber, Alfred L. *Ethnology of the Gros Ventre.* New York AMS Press, 1978.

Lowie, Robert H. *The Material Culture of the Crow Indians.* New York AMS Press, 1975.

Lowie, Robert H. *Myths and Traditions of the Crow Indians.* New York: AMS Press, 1975.

Parsons, Jackie. *Educational Movement of the Blackfeet Indians from 1840-1979.* Browning, Mont.: Blackfeet Heritage Program.

Schultz, James Willard. *Blackfeet and Buffalo.* Norman: Univ. of Oklahoma Press, 1962.

Stands in Timber, John, et al. *Cheyenne Memories.* Lincoln Univ. of Nebraska Press, 1967.

Stewart, Omer C. "Peyotism in Montana." *Montana the Magazine of Western History* 33:2 (Spring 1983), pp. 2-15.

Wildschut, William and Ewers, John C. *Crow Indian Beadwork: A Descriptive and Historical Study.* New York: Museum of the American Indian, 1959.

Wissler, Clark, et al. *Mythology of the Blackfoot Indians.* New York: AMS Press, 1909, 1975.

Regular Tribal Publications

Char-Koosta, Confederated Salish and Kootenai Tribes, Box 278, Pablo, MT 59855.

Blackfeet Tribal News, Blackfeet Media, Box 850, Browning, MT 59417.

Wotanin Wowapi, Assiniboine and Sioux Tribes, Box 493, Poplar, MT 59255.

Fort Belknap Camp Crier, Assiniboine and Gros Ventre Tribes, Fort Belknap Agency, Harlem, MT 59526.

Northern Cheyenne Tribal News, Box 128, Lame Deer, MT 59043.

Montana Tribes — Other

Alwin, John A. *Eastern Montana: A Portrait of the Land and Its People.* Helena: Montana Magazine Inc., 1982.

Craman, Sr. Carlan. *A Portrait of St. Labre Indian Mission Through 100 Years.* Ashland, Mont.: St. Labre Mission, 1984.

Indian Studies Resource Library Catalog. Great Falls, Mont.: Great Falls Public Schools.

Fort Belknap Planning Office. "Fort Belknap Overall Economic Development Plan." 1984.

"Overall Economic Development Plan for the Assiniboine and Sioux Tribes, Fort Peck Indian Reservation, Poplar, Montana 59255, November, 1984."

The Northern Cheyenne Research Project. "The Northern Cheyenne Air Quality Redesignation Report and Request." The Northern Cheyenne Tribe, December 11, 1976.

Northern Rockies Action Group. "The Proceedings of the Native American, Environmentalists and Agriculturists Workshop, December, 1975, Helena, Montana."

Pease, Eloise, et al. *Grass, Tipis, and Black Gold.* Billings, Mont.: Artcraft Printers, 1976.

Toole, K. Ross. *The Rape of the Great Plains.* Boston: Little, Brown, 1976.

Trosper, Ronald, et al. "Overall Economic Development Plan for the Confederated Salish and Kootenai Tribes on the Flathead Indian Reservation, January, 1985."

Contemporary Indian Issues

American Indian Policy Review Commission. *Final Report.* Washington, D.C.: Government Printing Office, 1977.

Bataill, Gretchen M. and Sands, Kathleen M. *American Indian Women Telling Their Lives.* Lincoln: Univ. of Nebraska Press, 1984.

Berkhofer, Robert F., Jr. *The White Man's Indian.* New York: Alfred A. Knopf, 1978.

Brophy, William A. and Aberle, Sophie D. *The Indian, America's Unfinished Business.* Norman: Univ. of Oklahoma Press, 1966.

Brown, Dee. *Bury My Heart at Wounded Knee.* New York: Bantam Books, 1970.

Burt, Lary W. *Tribalism in Crisis: Federal Indian Policy, 1953-61.* Albuquerque: Univ. of New Mexico Press, 1982.

Deloria, Vine, Jr. *Behind the Trail of Broken Treaties: An Indian Declaration of Independence.* New York: Delacorte Press, 1974.

Deloria, Vine, Jr. *Custer Died for Your Sins.* New York: Macmillan, 1969.

Deloria, Vine, Jr. *The Indian Affair.* New York: Friendship Press, 1974.

Dippie, Brian W. *The Vanishing American: White Attitudes and U.S. Indian Policy.* Middletown, Conn.: Wesleyan Univ. Press, 1982.

Hart, K.E. Richard, ed. *Wealth and Trust: A Lesson from the American Indian.* Sun Valley, Idaho 83353: Institute of the American West, Box 656, 1982.

Josephy, Alvin M., Jr. *Now That the Buffalo's Gone.* New York: Knopf, 1982.

Josephy, Alvin M., Jr. *Red Power: The American Indian's Fight for Freedom.* New York: American Heritage Press, 1971.

Lovett, Vince, et al. *American Indians.* Washington, D.C.: Bureau of Indian Affairs, U.S. Department of the Interior, 1984.

Manuel, George, et al. *The Fourth World.* New York: Free Press, 1974.

Report on Reservation and Resource Development and Protection. Washington, D.C.: U.S. Government Printing Office, 1976.

Steiner, Stan. *The New Indian.* New York: Delta, 1968.

Ziontz, Pirtle, Morisset, Ernstoff and Chestnut Law Firm, *Environmental Law and Policy Course for Indian Tribes,* February, 1983. Course proceedings, Seattle Wash.

Next in the Montana Geographic Series

The Continental Divide in Montana

On a line it appears as a crest of perhaps 500 miles, but it would take a hike of 1,500 miles to cover this national watershed in Montana alone. This book takes us through at least six definable areas along the Divide starting at the sawtooth ridges of Glacier country, moving into the wide open parks of the Bob Marshall area, through mining country around Butte, and winding around most of southwest Montana. The Divide is a natural, historic, economic, and social feature that makes a uniquely Montana story. By Bill Cunningham.

Eastern Montana Mountain Ranges

Sentinels of the plains, the isolated mountain ranges of Eastern Montana offer magnificent vistas not found in Western Montana. The so-called mountain outliers are unique as Montana mountain ranges go — well-defined bodies visible from tens of miles on the prairie landscape. This little-known resource includes the Snowy, Judith, Moccasin, Big and Little Belt, Highwood, Crazy, Bighorn, and Pryor ranges as well as other landmarks such as the Sweetgrass Hills and Square Butte of central and northcentral Montana and the Chalk Buttes and Medicine Rocks of southeastern Montana. You'll discover how these intrusions on the vast plain came to be and how they contribute to the local history and economy. You'll visit each and learn of its recreational opportunities. This volume makes an excellent companion to Mountain Ranges of Montana, first in the Geographic Series, which concentrated on Western Montana. By Mark Meloy.

Montana's Flathead River Country

Its North Fork comes from Glacier Park Country. Its Middle and South forks emanate from the heart of the Bob Marshall Wilderness. The lake that shares its name is a national magnet. It is the Flathead River system and its significance to Montana is profound. This book tells of its natural history — the wildlands, the waters, the wildlife; and its human history —how the Flathead Valley was settled, steamboats on the lake, the cherry industry. And you'll visit the beautiful Flathead country today — see communities as diverse as Polebridge, Bigfork and Kalispell, learn about recreation on the lake and the river, and follow the little known part of the river from Kerr Dam to the Clark's Fork River. By Bert Gildart, author of *Montana's Missouri River,* and co-author of *Glacier Country* and *Montana's Wildlife* — all books in the Montana Geographic Series.

The Montana Geographic Series:

About Our Back Cover Photo

This photographic mosaic was compiled from Earth Resources Satellite Photo passes made from a height of 570 miles. It was pieced together in black and white and interpreted in color by Big Sky Magic, Larry Dodge, Owner.

Front cover photos:

Left: Dancing at Native American Indian Days, Blackfeet Reservation.
Middle top: Skeletons of sun dance lodges, Rocky Boy's Reservation.
Middle bottom: Wesley Spotted Elk monitoring air quality on Northern Cheyenne Reservation.
Upper right: Honor guard, Rocky Boy's Reservation.
Lower right: Horses atop Bighorn Canyon, Crow Reservation.
Michael Crummett photos